FAILING SIDEWAYS

FAILING SIDEWAYS

Queer Possibilities for Writing Assessment

**STEPHANIE WEST-PUCKETT,
NICOLE I. CASWELL,
AND WILLIAM P. BANKS**

Mike—
Thank you to all your
generous support of my
writing — large parts of this
book were written at your
place! Much love.
Will 5/22/23

UTAH STATE UNIVERSITY PRESS
Logan

© 2023 by University Press of Colorado

Published by Utah State University Press
An imprint of University Press of Colorado
1624 Market Street, Suite 226
PMB 39883
Denver, Colorado 80202-1559

 ASSOCIATION of UNIVERSITY PRESSES   The University Press of Colorado is a proud member of
the Association of University Presses.

The University Press of Colorado is a cooperative publishing enterprise supported,
in part, by Adams State University, Colorado State University, Fort Lewis College,
Metropolitan State University of Denver, University of Alaska Fairbanks, University
of Colorado, University of Denver, University of Northern Colorado, University of
Wyoming, Utah State University, and Western Colorado University.

∞ This paper meets the requirements of the ANSI/NISO Z39.48-1992 (Permanence of
Paper).

ISBN: 978-1-64642-447-4 (hardcover)
ISBN: 978-1-64642-369-9 (paperback)
ISBN: 978-1-64642-370-5 (ebook)
https://doi.org/10.7330/9781646423705

Library of Congress Cataloging-in-Publication Data

Names: West-Puckett, Stephanie, author. | Caswell, Nicole I., author. | Banks, William P.,
author.
Title: Failing sideways : queer possibilities for writing assessment / Stephanie West-
Puckett, Nicole I. Caswell, and William P. Banks.
Description: Logan : Utah State University Press, [2023] | Includes bibliographical refer-
ences and index.
Identifiers: LCCN 2023000151 (print) | LCCN 2023000152 (ebook) | ISBN 9781646423699
(paperback) | ISBN 9781646424474 (hardcover) | ISBN 9781646423705 (ebook)
Subjects: LCSH: English language—Rhetoric—Study and teaching (Higher)—Evaluation.
| English language—Rhetoric—Study and teaching (Higher)—Social aspects. |
Academic writing—Study and teaching (Higher)—Evaluation. | Academic writing—
Study and teaching (Higher)—Social aspects. | Academic writing—Ability testing. |
School failure. | Queer theory. | Homosexuality and education.
Classification: LCC PE1404 .W4547 2023 (print) | LCC PE1404 (ebook) | DDC
808/.0420711—dc23/eng/20230131
LC record available at https://lccn.loc.gov/2023000151
LC ebook record available at https://lccn.loc.gov/2023000152

This work was supported, in part, by East Carolina University.

Front-cover design by Rob Puckett

CONTENTS

FOREWORD

Norbert Elliot
New Jersey Institute of Technology

Writing assessment is about consequences for individuals. Writing assessment researchers must therefore gather evidence related to fairness, reliability, and validity under frameworks deeply attuned to the consequences of the assessment for individual students. Further, if the individual impact is estimated to be negative, the assessment should not proceed.

I wonder if such assessment principles could have been proposed in the early 1980s when I first began working in writing assessment—a time when Ronald Reagan was president, the US accountability movement continued to gain ground, and large-scale assessments such as the New Jersey College Basic Skills Placement Test were enacting neoliberal commodification on students, teachers, and administrators alike. I wonder if these principles can be proposed now—a time when individual differences exist in a world apart from Florida's HB 1557 (Florida 2022) and its proposition that school districts may not encourage classroom discussion about sexual orientation or gender identity in primary grades.

Whether allowed or not, many believe individual-consequence principles can and should be proposed for writing assessment. A measurement basis for such principles can be found in the most recent version of the *Standards for Educational and Psychological Testing* (American Educational Research Association 2014). There, a single fascinating statement has been given little attention: "Test developers and publishers should document steps taken during the design and development process to provide evidence of fairness, reliability, and validity to intended uses for individuals in the intended examinee population" (85). There are two historically important parts to that sentence. First, the authors of the standards

https://doi.org/10.7330/9781646423705.c000a

acknowledge that fairness is a foundational form of evidence in its own right, not a subsidiary to traditional categories of reliability and validity. Second, the authors draw attention to individuals—a unique student seated at a particular desk—a truly radical advancement in educational measurement, in which impact has often been considered in terms of groups. For those in writing assessment interested in theory building and empirical research, the link in the standards between evidence of fairness and consequences for individuals is unprecedented. Surely if test developers and publishers are to follow this overarching principle, those in writing assessment can do the same and, indeed, should take a leadership role in advancing individual-consequence principles.

In the book you are about to read, Stephanie West-Puckett, Nikki Caswell, and Will Banks offer an authentic innovation in writing assessment—queer validity inquiry (QVI)—that places individual students at the center of all we say and do. As an assessment model, QVI invites assessment stakeholders, particularly designers and instructors, to adopt lenses of failure, affect, identity, and materiality. These lenses, the authors hold, can be used to identify missing domains of writing constructs such as the affective competencies—those often-ignored, critically significant personality factors missing from traditional assessments. Absent the intrapersonal domain, the authors imply, we find ourselves with such thin slices of writing constructs that we may wonder what the pie was in the first place. Conversely, once we introduce into our assessments robust writing constructs that reflect the way people really learn, we expose what is hidden, displaced, and negated to focus on individuals and their identities. In our assessments, the authors demonstrate, QVI is a substantiative, principled lens that allows us to think about what the National Academies of Sciences, Engineering, and Medicine (2018) identify as the complex ecology of context, cultures, neurological processes, and motivation that must be present if deep learning is to occur across the individual life cycles of our students.

QVI is far more than a niche area of assessment; we see important resonances between the lens of QVI and contemporary measurement research. David H. Slomp, Julie A. Corrigan, and Tamiko Sugimoto (2014) use a consequential validity lens—emphasizing the impact of the social and ideological aspects of assessment that often remain hidden—to propose an anticipatory design framework of integrated design to categorically identify and ecologically model consequences at each stage of assessment design. To support highly mobile populations with complex linguistic identities, Mya Poe and Qianqian Zhang-Wu (2020) modify the consequential validity lens to develop a program assessment method based on multilingualism (attention to proficiency and exposure to multiple languages) and super diversity (acknowledgment of the many ways linguistic identity is deeply shaped by mobility). Continuing the work of writing assessment scholars Slomp, Poe, and their colleagues, educational measurement scholar Jennifer Randall (2021) has advanced a justice-oriented antiracist lens for assessment. Rejecting Cartesian-inspired, cognitively fetishized rhetorics that enact binaries and dualisms at every turn, Randall explicitly asks whether an assessment adequately addresses the diverse ways of knowing that Black stakeholders possess and value. Each of these ways of framing assessment design is profoundly connected to QVI in reminding us writing assessment is never only about textual artifacts. Writing assessment can only be useful to students when the material conditions of their lives—from the killing presence of language dominance to the generative force of individual difference—is acknowledged in each phase of an assessment.

While resonance is important in establishing QVI as an important part of research programs in writing assessment, it is equally important to understand that QVI charts new directions. While the QVI lens is an authentic innovation, it is equally innovative in its affordance. QVI is enacted through a killjoy stance. Informed by scholarship in queer and feminist rhetorics, notably the work of Sara Ahmed (2010a), this standpoint allows designers to recognize the many heteronormative investments within an assessment—the impulse, for example, to create success narratives when evidence reveals individual disenfranchisement—and to replace them with evidence that something went sideways. This sort of (re)visioning, central to the antinormative project of queer theory for over three decades, compels assessment designers to consider how normative rhetorics frame realities in binary ways, such as success/failure, in order to normativize one part of the binary at the expense of the other. As a systematic strategy, the killjoy stance raises the overarching question of plausibility. In the case of multilingual writers, the killjoy would ask, Is it possible to assess writing under a common construct drawn down from a normativized sender-and-receiver communication model? Himself an assessment killjoy when mechanistic models are in play, psychometrician Robert J. Mislevy (2018) simply says that "this is not how human communication works. Even the notion of a situation is deeply embedded in the activities and practices of people as they interact" (237). In place of success, the assessment killjoy calls out those sources of incomparability between the targeted construct and the unique identities of individual students.

While the QVI theoretical lens and the killjoy design strategy are important across assessment genres, West-Puckett, Caswell, and Banks wisely focus on formative assessment. While grassroots, classroom-assessment practices are the daily practice of teachers of writing, the authors attend closely to the impact that queer rhetorics can have on classroom-assessment frameworks and feedback activities. To the question of what is next for formative assessment, Heidi L. Andrade, Randy E. Bennett, and Gregory J. Cizek (2019), editors of a volume on classroom evaluation, identify discipline specificity as the next big thing. As West-Puckett, Caswell, and Banks brilliantly illustrate, attention to the ontology and axiology of QVI productively guides the epistemological design and assessment of a writing-classroom curriculum. Throughout the book, they provide case-based examples of pedagogies and assessments informed by a celebration of contingency and a love of diversity. As readers will see, a sideways vision for teaching and assessing writing helps us see ourselves, and our students, more fully than we have before.

ACKNOWLEDGMENTS

A book about failure is fundamentally ironic. To bring something to press, to see our words and ideas go through countless drafts and extensive peer review and editing and then to be out there in the world, available to others to read and engage and critique, and to also then be part of our CVs and annual reports—all these things look like success in the academic marketplaces where we labor and live. And, of course, writing and publishing are a type of success and they also bring a type of happiness to us as writers. So, while much of the text we've written here will challenge Western imperialist notions of success and happiness, we need to acknowledge our own success and happiness here, and even more important, we need to thank the people who have helped make this book on queering writing assessment a reality. In providing funding, time, and space to do the research, teaching, and writing that were needed to create this book, we thank our respective universities and departments: the Department of English, the Thomas Harriot College of Arts and Sciences, and the University Writing Program at East Carolina University (ECU) and the Harrington School of Communication and Media in the College of Arts and Sciences at the University of Rhode Island (URI). We are fortunate to work at research-intensive universities that provide us with time and resources to carry out the research that is important to us as teachers, activists, and scholars.

In acknowledging our institutional homes, then, we also feel it is important to acknowledge the Indigenous peoples on whose ancestral lands we have been allowed to do our work as part of these public institutions. To that end, we acknowledge the Narragansett Nation and the Niantic People of Rhode Island, on whose lands the University of Rhode Island engages in teaching, research, and service. We also acknowledge the Tuscarora Peoples of Eastern North Carolina, who are the traditional custodians of the lands on which East Carolina University now resides.

https://doi.org/10.7330/9781646423705.c000b

In doing so, we acknowledge eight recognized tribes who have also been part of these lands: Coharie, Eastern Band of Cherokee, Haliwa-Saponi, Lumbee, Meherrin, Occaneechi Band of Saponi, Sappony, and Waccamaw-Siouan.

We are also grateful to the scholars who reviewed our manuscript and made copious suggestions that shaped the draft you now have before you. While our reviewers were originally anonymous, during the revision process Norbert Elliot offered to engage with us based on his feedback and made himself known as an early reviewer. Norbert provided pages and pages of thoughtful, supportive critique, and he stands as a model for what peer review should look like. Likewise, Travis Webster's advice and support were instrumental in shaping this final draft of the project, and we are immensely grateful to him for the kind words that kept us motivated as we revised. Both reviewers took hours to read and reread our manuscript across multiple drafts and to provide us feedback that held us accountable to our discipline and the scholars we cited while also making sure we felt our work was seen, heard, and valued for the contributions they saw it making to the field.

We are also grateful to the supportive and dedicated staff at Utah State University Press (USUP) / University Press of Colorado (UPC). From our first informal meeting with her during the Conference on College Composition and Communication, Rachael Levay has been a steadfast supporter of this project and our work, and we are eternally grateful for her leadership in bringing this project to the USUP/UPC board for approval. To Darrin Pratt, Dan Pratt, and Laura Furney, who shepherded this manuscript through the publication process and helped us to make tough decisions about cover design, we are especially thankful, and to Kami Day, who served as the copy editor and indexer for this text, we know how much better this draft is because of her careful and attentive review. We are so happy to have this book in the USUP/UPC catalog, where so many of our discipline's most impactful books have been published.

Finally, we want to offer a special thanks to Robert Puckett, who designed the cover for this book, as well as all the figures we use in the text. Robert is a tremendous visual artist and does magical things with digital design tools. He listened to our ideas, helped us to think through possibilities, and was always eager to help when it came time to fix or adjust images we had taken while doing the assessment work of the book.

STEPHANIE

First, I would like to acknowledge my own body and say to it publicly, "Body, you were never the problem." Throughout the writing of this book, my body has done its best despite chronic illness and reexperiencing traumas associated with assessment. When I was in seventh grade, I was "identified" by the Duke University Talent Identification Program, and to qualify I had to score at or above the 95th percentile on the Scholastic Aptitude Test. On the morning of the exam, I had nerves and a churning gut. Per guidelines, I was only allowed one bathroom break, and that one bathroom break was not enough. Instead of leaving the exam, forfeiting my opportunity, and forcing my parents to pay back the exam fee, I stayed. I carefully filled in those little circles, willing my mind to focus on analogies while my body betrayed me. When time was called and the room cleared, I asked my best friend for her sweater to tie around my waist. Not only did she lend me her sweater, but she also kept my secret so I could tell it here myself. Thank you, Cheryl. And thanks to my mother, who washed my clothes without admonition that day and would do it again today.

I am also grateful to Will and Nikki for helping me to reframe assessment as cultural practices that can attend to physical bodies and to the materialities of writing; to our complex and constellated identities; to the affective currents that swirl around those bodies and identities; and to the importance of failure as a queer tactic for dismantling brutal ecologies of assessment. I've been fortunate to work with students and colleagues at both East Carolina University and the University of Rhode Island who've challenged, forwarded, and embraced this work in the classroom and on the programmatic level, particularly my department chairs, Jeremiah Dyehouse and Genoa Shepley. A Faculty Summer Research Program Award and Project Completion Award given by the URI College of Arts and Sciences, under the leadership of Dean Jeannette E. Riley, provided crucial support as well. None of this would have been possible, however, without my partner, Robert Puckett, who takes care of me and all the other human, canine, and feline bodies who inhabit our home. Last but not least, I thank the four not-so-little-anymore kiddos—Rylan, Calder, Violet, and Stosh—who force me to leave my desk and live a life beyond the screen.

NIKKI

This text was a labor of love made possible by students willing to try something new. While Will, Steph, and I always knew this book was something worth writing, we also grappled with the *hows* and *whys*. I'm thankful for their conversations that pushed the boundaries of our thinking and for the time and space we had to develop this text. I'm also thankful to Mackenzie, who timed her entry into the world right when we were finishing up the text and not any earlier; to my partner, James, who always believed in the work and took pleasure in arguing assessment with me; and to Michelle, Shane, Erin, and Sammy for keeping me grounded.

WILL

I would like to thank Stephanie and Nikki most especially for their generous collaborations over the last several years of writing this project. Without Steph's ability to challenge my assumptions or my rush to closure, I know that my own thinking would not have been nearly as expansive or exciting; and without Nikki's ability to focus Steph's and my extroverted chatter and exploration, there's no way this text would have materialized. I certainly wouldn't understand assessment scholarship nearly as well, if at all, if Nikki had not patiently sat with me as we plowed through articles and books on the subject and if she had not invited me to audit her graduate seminar on writing assessment several years ago. Beyond my coauthors and dear friends, I'm also especially thankful to my friend-family at ECU—Michelle, Shane, Erin, and James—for the ways they have shown up for me when I needed to write, needed to travel for conferences or research, or just when I needed to vent about the frustrations of work and life. Most especially, I'm grateful for my unconventional queer family—Rachel, Susan, and Jackson Spangler—and the ways they always support me as a writer, teacher, and human being. Ultimately, it's the important young people in my life—Jackson (now 15), Sammy (now 3), and Mackenzie (now 1)—who continually remind me that the choices we make about writing and assessment have very real and lasting impacts on human beings in our school systems. I hope this book can help create spaces for these and other young people to fail sideways.

ACKNOWLEDGING COLLABORATION

Finally, we want to recognize how this text came into being and acknowledge the ways that collaborative writing is often a very queer composition practice of both/and. But we also know that as academics with jobs in higher education, we are often required to name our contributions to scholarship in coauthored projects. We want to resist that sort of mindless bean-counting that works primarily to undervalue meaningful research and scholarship in the humanities by embracing colonialist rhetorics of individual ownership and some supposed superiority of genius that comes when one person has no meaningful engagement with or connection to another. This model is as absurd as it sounds, and in naming its absurdity here, we want to be sure that no one reading this book thinks that we would support a model of authorship that does not see all three authors of this book as equally invested, equally valued, and equally responsible for the contents. Simply put, this book could not exist without the three of us working together, each providing 100 percent of the effort needed.

But we also recognize that there is value in sharing our process because we need more texts in the humanities that unpack these complexities rather than assume they are merely shared or understood. So, here's some of what we did, as best we can remember it. This project started when we decided to create a reading group in queer theory around the same time that Stephanie was a doctoral student in an assessment seminar that Nikki was teaching. As the three of us met to discuss queer theories, questions about how this often-esoteric work could impact something as seemingly structured and boxed-in as writing assessment began to dominate our thinking. From there, we imagined a conference presentation, and then another, and then we began to think about how much work we all did with assessment, from the classroom to the writing center to the writing program to the work we were all involved with in terms of campus reaccreditation efforts. Assessment was everywhere and nowhere, and at some point, we had to reckon with the reality that none of those assessments felt good to us.

When we finally got to the point of writing this book, Steph had taken a tenure-track job at the University of Rhode Island, Nikki had just gotten tenure, and Will had survived a horrific promotion case that required his campus provost to step in and overturn his colleagues' negative votes. Our lives were being impacted, or soon would be, by assessments of a different kind from the ones we're used to talking about in writing studies. The book began in earnest during weekly Zoom conversations where we discussed ideas, shared examples from our teaching and administration that fit our framework, and ultimately drafted large chunks of text together. Most of the first two chapters were drafted this way as the three of us worked together to be sure we understood the larger theoretical project. Because we had all read together and written together and presented at conferences together, we then divided the four chapters related to our queer validity inquiry (QVI) Pyraminx among us based on whose classrooms or programs would be used for the examples in the chapters. Each of us then took responsibility for drafting the bulk of those chapters based on those examples, meeting regularly online to review the work we'd done, to draft and revise our work together, and then to swap the chapters with each other so that another of the three of us could revise/rewrite large chunks of that chapter or add our own examples to those chapters where there are multiple examples from different contexts. When the COVID-19 pandemic hit and teaching moved online and away from structured in-person days and times, we found that it offered us space, oddly enough, to meet in person again as a small group of carefully quarantined folks, and we spent October 2020 radically rewriting our chapter drafts while all sitting in a large room together in the University Writing Center at East Carolina University.

When peer reviewers provided extensive feedback—nearly twenty pages of single-spaced questions, suggestions, challenges, and encouragement between the two reviewers—we met again in a mountain cabin in April 2021 to draft and revise. Those wonderful, if at times overwhelming, responses led to the massive rewrite that is now this book, and at every stage, the three of us were all writing, reading, and revising chapters together. At this point, it would be hard to imagine that any one of us could look at the different chapters and figure out who wrote which sentence, even in the site-specific examples attached to a single author in chapters 3–6.

For that reason, we each claim 100 percent credit. This is our book, a queerly complex text that exists only because of the special and transitory events that brought us together with certain texts, at a certain time, having had certain experiences as teachers and scholars and administrators. In fact, because of this intertextual composition process, we even toyed with the idea of publishing this book not with our names at all but as The Queer Assessment Collective, an homage of sorts to the brilliant and groundbreaking work of the Combahee River Collective. In the end, political and rhetorical exigencies won out: we have chosen to list Stephanie's name first, Nikki's second, and Will's third, not because this order indicates anything about our effort or time spent on the project, but because the publication is most immediately meaningful to Stephanie, who will be going up for tenure, and for Nikki, who will use this book as part of her promotion to full professor. Will has had his last promotion and doesn't need the credit to satisfy any T&P committee anywhere. We hope that readers will find this book interesting and useful, and we hope they will cite all three of us when they use this book, as this work is very much ours collaboratively.

FAILING SIDEWAYS

1

RISKING FAILURE
Hope for a Queer Assessment

Is there anything we are not failing at when it comes to education in the United States?

In 2021, in the wake of an ongoing pandemic, the media is amplified something they called "learning loss," and parents were meant to be scared. What will we do if our children get "behind" on some fictionalized learning plan? For much of 2020, children were at home, experiencing school through various virtual models of instruction, which naturally failed from time to time and especially so for those families without access to reliable internet and working computers, tablets, and smartphones. In fact, a recent study from the US Department of Education's Office for Civil Rights noted multiple ways the COVID-19 pandemic had disproportionately impacted students who already occupied racial, ethnic, or economically marginalized positions (Goldberg 2021). It's hard to imagine any student who was unaffected or any K–12 classroom that did not have to veer off its carefully planned lessons and pacing guides. But all around us is a conversation not so much about what students learned about themselves, about life, about viruses and pandemics, about coping with difficult global issues, about inequities built into our various institutions and systems—nor, indeed, about just surviving at all, for those who have—but instead about how "behind" students are in their schoolwork. The teachers who in early 2020 were our "saviors" for shifting their teaching online so quickly during those first lockdowns had become the problem by the fall of 2020 when they didn't want to go back to teaching in person or when they had not found a way to engage all online students in the same ways that had seemingly worked before in traditional classrooms. And now we are facing a new threat in this thing called "learning loss," an alliterative and catchy phrase that reminds us how scary it must always be when we "fail."

But before the COVID-19 pandemic, there had been a seemingly endless series of failures and crises in education meant to keep us emotionally fraught and ready for some new plan that would fix things.

https://doi.org/10.7330/9781646423705.c001

Over just the last twenty years, US politicians have wrestled with how to fix public education through three different but ideologically linked projects—the No Child Left Behind (NCLB) Act in 2001, Race to the Top (RTT) in 2009, and the Every Student Succeeds Act (ESSA) in 2015—all intended to save public schools through increased "accountability measures" that involved privatizing as much of the work of teaching and assessment as possible. NCLB came about in large part because of fears that US students and schools were no longer globally competitive. In a post-9/11 nationalistic fervor, Congress voted overwhelmingly to enact a new plan that would secure US educational dominance on the world stage through increased testing and benchmarks related to "adequate yearly progress" (AYP), all while simultaneously providing less and less financial support for public schools. A key policy change diverted general funding into specialized Title 1 funding to support private tutoring for students who were not meeting expectations and also provided "school choice," which meant that when a particular public school did not meet its AYP two years in a row, districts had to allow parents to move their children to ostensibly better-performing schools in the district.

RTT took that model for privatizing public goods and services further by making school funding highly competitive. States could imagine innovative plans for "moving the needle" on student success and, if their plans were good enough, win one of a handful of large federal grants to enact their projects. Because the funds were not permanently part of state or federal education budgets, however, they could not really be used to hire more teachers or fix deep pay inequities among existing teachers; nor could they be used for long-term, strategic investments in change at the local level. These one-time funds had a small window and were most often used to fund a host of private and not-for-profit educational reform corporations (educorps) to build big-box curricula and implement a host of standardized testing frameworks in order to hold teachers and students "accountable" to various external stakeholders. RTT also expanded the option of school vouchers, which further diverted public funds from schools that were struggling by paying for students to attend private and charter academies; these schools were often exempt from the same federal standards for success or the same frequent testing models for accountability.

When the federal government returned significant control to states in 2015 with the eighth reauthorization of the Elementary and Secondary Education Act of 1965, known as the Every Student Succeeds Act, states could choose how they met certain goals, develop individual plans for success, and articulate how they planned to address their failures, but regular testing in core subjects is still required regardless of local choices for how schools meet their goals. It's no surprise that this plan has been met with little resistance or outrage. In a space framed consistently as failed or failing, as public schools regularly are by politicians and parents across the political spectrum, accountability is a rhetorical common-place that is hard to argue against. And, of course, there is big money and big profit in testing: Pearson, Educational Testing Service (ETS), and College Board have consistently pulled in billions of dollars each year over the last several decades, most of which has come from public funds diverted from schools into test preparation, test implementation, and curriculum materials to address the failures the tests create.

But before the neoliberal[1] shift to privatizing as many aspects of public education as we could, there were crises and failures that had politicians, parents, and pundits wringing their collective hands:

- In the 1990s, the Oakland School District in California made national news when it attempted to recognize and value the African American language variations and dialects that were common among many young people in their schools. People across the political spectrum—from Rush Limbaugh and former US Secretary of Education William Bennett to then-education secretary for President Clinton Richard Riley to noted political operative Jesse Jackson and to celebrities like Bill Cosby and Maya Angelou—fomented a national wave of fear and anxiety around the languages young people used to write and speak and engage with the world.

- In the 1980s, the anxiety had come with the publication of *A Nation at Risk* (1983), a report compiled by the National Commission on Excellence in Education, which was chaired by David P. Gardner. America's schools were in decline, the report warned, and out of its recommendations we got a longer school day, more school days per school year, and a significant increase of gifted-and-talented student programs. We did not, however, get the recommended competitive salaries for teachers.

- In the 1970s, we were anxious and fearful because *Newsweek* wondered "Why Johnny Can't Write" (Sheils 1975), which *U.S. News & World Report* followed up on a few years later with "Why Johnny Can't Write . . . and What's Being Done" (1981). As Harvey A. Daniels (1983) notes, these stories "insist on seeing imperfect student writing as something new and ominous; [they lay] the blame on irresponsible teachers and lame-brained [*sic*] theorists; [they hold] the weakest student writers up to public ridicule"; and they continue the troubling myth that writing is "basic" and simple, so failure to master it is a key indicator of a nation in decline (218).

As Robin Varnum (1986) has noted, where literacy is concerned, we seem to move from "crisis to crisis," from failure to failure, while Bronwyn T.

Williams (2007) has similarly recognized that "every generation, upon reaching middle age, finds itself compelled to look at the literacy practices of young people and lament at how poor the work produced today is compared to that of idyllic days gone by" (178). And lurking behind all these late-capitalist literacy crises is the fear of unemployment or a weak (nationalist) economy. There can be nothing fundamentally worse to us, it seems, than to imagine that school activities do not translate into direct and immediate employment and economic growth. In our national consciousness, school seems always to be about workplace training and preparedness rather than about learning, student growth, or creating spaces where human beings might become more fully alive, more meaningfully engaged, and more purposefully connected to each other. But if embracing those things is a failure of education, then we say give us excess of it.

So here we are as researchers—as teachers, as students, as parents, as administrators—rejecting the shame and blame we are meant to be embracing out of this ongoing national dialogue around the failures of US education. Because despite the emotional and physical precarity that continues to catch us in its wake, we can still imagine other possibilities, other ways of being, knowing, and doing that may serve to disrupt the educational status quo. Out of precariousness, we seek possibility; against the constraints of normativity, we imagine a queer liminality of affect that challenges hegemonic narratives of education's endless failures. Rather than run away from failure, we've chosen to orient ourselves toward it. *Failing Sideways* is our attempt to address some of the limited and limiting ways that common assessment frameworks and practices continue to keep us all spinning on an educational failure-go-round. *Failing Sideways* is about getting us off.

WHO ARE WE WITHOUT OUR FAILURES?

Of course, one could argue that the project of institutionalized education has always been a project of marking and remarking on failure. For those of us in writing studies, this connection to failure and the anxieties that emerge when failure meets American exceptionalism are certainly not new. In the literature of our field, we recognize how college writing, particularly the creation and implementation of a first-year required writing course (first-year composition/FYC), became a defining feature of higher education in the late nineteenth and early twentieth centuries. In these histories, we recognize the anxieties that circulated at Harvard when Adams Sherman Hill was Boylston professor of Rhetoric and

Oratory. Shocked by what he and his colleagues saw as the appalling state of writing and thinking among the undergraduates at Harvard, Hill worked to implement a written entrance exam for new students that would effectively place students into a specialized composition course with a curriculum designed to address their perceived shortcomings.

Outside elite Ivy League schools, we can also see several movements in our field as failure based or failure oriented. Consider the shift Robert J. Connors (1997) articulates at the heart of his important study *Composition-Rhetoric: Backgrounds, Theory, and Pedagogy*. For Connors, where much of college debating and writing had been agonistic in nature, engaged in arguments between young men about issues of the day or of the discipline they were studying, the mass influx of women into university life after 1860 precipitated a change to the genres taught in college, as well as the types of responses/assessments considered appropriate. The presence of women, Connors argues, led to a more "irenic rhetoric" that valued narrative, description, and different types of expository prose, all models predicated on the idea that female students neither needed nor could handle the rhetorical practices necessary for civic or public life (24ff). Since these students would not be entering the male-dominated professions of law, medicine, and ministry, they had no need for the skills that argument/debate provided. Instead, they were encouraged to reflect on their experiences, to tell stories that emerged from their life experiences, and to explore topics appropriate to domestic life. Such a move may not seem, on the surface, to be failure based, but part of the rationale for this curricular and pedagogical shift was the assumption that women students would fail at more traditional genres and modes of expression—and that even if they did not, to encourage them toward a life of the mind was to make them into social failures, women who would no longer be suited for domestic life (see also Johnson 1991, 2002). Additionally, should male students lose their debates with female students, such a failure might also register as a failure of the supposedly natural superiority of men to women.

Of course, each moment of significant change in higher-education demographics has necessitated similar anxieties around what students do or do not know/need to know and how colleges can either police these students *out* of the institution or redesign curriculum to better meet their needs. In her history of Theodore Baird's writing program at Amherst College after World War II, Varnum (1996) explores just such a moment, one often ignored in the more dominant histories of our field, in part because the result was markedly different from many other such moments. Amherst College offered one of the many organized first-year writing programs that "first appeared in significant numbers between 1920 and 1940" (15; see also Berlin 1987). At Amherst, as at many colleges around the United States, World War II effected significant changes, not least of these the influx of large numbers of former enlisted men through the Servicemen's Readjustment Act of 1944, a.k.a. the GI Bill. Part of what is interesting in Varnum's history is the way Baird, the program's designer, and his colleagues approached the change. In a personal communication, Baird told Varnum, "The war was the thing that shook us up" (83). While other similar shake-ups in higher education had led to extensive testing and ever-shifting standards like Hill's at Harvard, or shifts in assignments like those Connors (1997) chronicles in *Composition-Rhetoric* that worked against preparing women for public life, the Amherst faculty approached this change by making major, non-failure-oriented changes to their pedagogies. In a report in 1946, Baird noted that he and his staff "found that the students in uniform had the common knowledge of basic training, and that assignments dealing with techniques learned outside the classroom were unusually successful" (83). Through an early version of a "funds of knowledge" approach to pedagogy (Moll et al. 1992), Amherst faculty told students to "tell us what you know" (Kennedy 1955, quoted in Varnum 1996, 83) and then worked with them to connect what they knew to other contexts and other ways of communicating effectively. This was more a pedagogy of abundance than one of deficit.

While Varnum's history serves as one powerful reminder that not all responses to educational crises have focused on failure in the same ways, it is also a lesser-known and understood history. More often, we find the national conversation focused on manufactured literacy crises, like the one that emerged around the publication of the 1975 "Why Johnny Can't Write" cover story from *Newsweek* (Sheils 1975). Similar to other failure-oriented moments in literacy across the last 150 years, from Hill's underprepared Harvard student to the national problem *A Nation At Risk* (1983) created, what ultimately emerges from these events is a sense of failure for writing/literacy teachers and their inability to teach an extremely heterogeneous group of students some set of always-shifting ideas about literacy. The 1970s and 1980s also initiated substantial growth in the numbers of writing labs/centers on college campuses as spaces to inoculate "correct" writing into "diseased" (failed or failing) student bodies (Boquet 1999; Wardle 2013). The creation of writing centers as institutional fix-it shops for poor/weak writers represents another space in our disciplinary history that we recognize as problematic, if initially well intentioned. As the open-access movement spread across college campuses, it was assumed that students not prepared for college would be unsuccessful in a college writing classroom. Thus, their deficiencies would be addressed by a writing center or writing lab. Writing centers were to be the cure-all for unprepared writers and incorrect writing. As Elizabeth H. Boquet (1999) mentions, "Writing centers remain one of the most powerful mechanisms whereby institutions can mark the bodies of students as foreign, alien" (465). Boquet references the development of the University of North Carolina's Composition Condition Laboratory, where teachers who thought students needed grammar support would label student papers *CC*. The failure of students was reinscribed on their bodies as an individualistic, rather than systematic, concern (468). Students are directed to writing centers, even today, to work on and correct their writing in a context of public and performative shaming. Despite the fact that most writing and literacy teachers recognize that successful writers talk to others about their writing, in practice, squeezed for quick fixes for the slow process of learning new discourses, many continue to identify certain student writers as lacking or deficient and send them on to the center to get fixed, too often making writing centers into punitive spaces. While many writing centers actively resist this narrative, the systematic nature of ill-defined poor student writing overrides the nontraditional, social-justice-oriented work of writing centers.

Ultimately, the deficit model of education is so pervasive as to be nearly impossible to break out of, even among some of our most effective and progressive literacy projects. Consider the National Writing Project (NWP), a once federally funded network of K–college teachers, whose emergence in the 1970s (at the same time we were learning that poor Johnny couldn't write) further developed, though certainly unintentionally, this narrative of failure through its annual trips to Capitol Hill to advocate for more funding for an important, high-impact national literacy initiative. For nearly thirty years, the NWP enjoyed federal funding to support its network of engaged and effective teachers; to date, it represents one of the most successful pedagogical and educational interventions in the United States, in large part because of its success at receiving federal funding that could then be leveraged with local funding sources to provide innovative, research-based professional development for teachers in all disciplines and at all levels of education (Banks 2016; Gray 2000). But we also must recognize that success often relied on continuing a deficit narrative around students and teachers—at least for an audience of politicians who needed good reasons to divert federal funds toward public education at a time when *privatize* was the consistent buzzword in education reform. On the Hill each spring, and through letters to elected officials during the year, even as NWP teachers highlighted meaningful changes to writing and reading in their own classrooms, that narrative also required them to tell senators, representatives, and their various legislative aides about how young people in most classes and schools were struggling as writers, readers, and thinkers and how teachers were also struggling to know how to support those students who were not already strong in the English language arts. Pragmatically, Congress wasn't going to throw millions of dollars at an organization unless it was fixing something that was broken; the least effective arguments many NWP site leaders, like Will, made during their visits each spring were those that started with "the kids are all right." While part of the stories NWP teachers and site directors shared involved examples of star students who had been successful through NWP-inspired practices, those examples worked with the immediate audience in large part because they were set against a vast framework of underperforming young people and the teachers who did not know how to help them. Of course, this irony wasn't lost on many of the NWP teachers who showed up in Washington, DC, each spring; Will can remember a number of conversations he and his NWP colleagues had with each other about the problematic framing of students and schools in ways that were not really what they believed to be true, but the issues most pressing to teachers and students were simply not the ones that were going to loosen Congressional purse strings. Because it turns so easily to the advantage of whoever has power, the success/failure binary doesn't allow for the nuances we need in education, at least not at the level of actually working with and supporting students.

Obviously, these failure-oriented moments are not inherently bad or ill-intentioned. In other contexts, from the Digital Is initiative—now The Current at Educator Innovator (https://thecurrent.educatorinnovator .org/)—to *NWP Radio*, the NWP offers brilliant stories of students' and teachers' transformational experiences with literacy. The failure rhetorics themselves seem carefully selected for moments in which the group is asking for support in a context where failure/deficit sells, in large part because of the neoliberal project of defunding public education that has been central to US government policy for so many decades now. But the NWP has also seen how this framework, once partnered with neoliberal values of privatizing public services, can backfire: in 2011, Congress discontinued direct public funding to the NWP and several other literacy campaigns, as those funds were rechanneled to Educorps like Pearson and ETS, whose in-house tests were used to prove how widespread literacy deficits were and whose off-the-shelf professional development and interventions could supposedly cure those illiteracy ills. As education and professional-development projects have become increasingly reliant on competitive funding models (e.g., privatization), these narratives of success versus failure have become endemic, shaping our national conversation in troubling ways that feed back into our classrooms and assessment models as well.

What we've begun to wonder as we look back over the last century of research and practice in literacy studies and writing studies is whether or not our disciplines know how to function outside this failure-crisis narrative. If history is any indicator, there is always going to be a new failure marked on our field's narrative arc. To establish disciplinary respect, we continue to develop narrative arcs that provide us legitimacy. In terms of writing assessment, we have often turned to educational measurement and psychometrics as discourses valued both inside and outside the academy. While the wholesale adoption of measurement discourse runs counter to how we believe writing and learning to write can happen, our focus on how to establish reliability between readers or how to objectify/objectively study a highly subjective activity like writing has offered us the ability to be closer in alignment to educational assessment discourse. But this move has also created new moments of failure when writing hasn't fit neatly into the epistemological settings we've imported.

The tensions we as teachers and administrators feel about assessment broadly conceived and writing assessment more specifically are also tensions that are reflected among the assessment communities themselves. Recently, what *is* and what *counts* as assessment have been debated in articles from the *Chronicle of Higher Education* (Gilbert 2018) and *Inside Higher Ed* (McConnell 2018) and, more locally, among separate discourse communities on the ASSESS listserv and the recently defunct WPA-L listserv. Depending on our positionality, then, assessment is/isn't about bureaucracy and accreditation, is/isn't about teaching and learning, and is/isn't about success/failure. Among so many different groups, the term *assessment* becomes unbounded and misunderstood. Or perhaps, more accurately, it becomes open to multiple interpretations wherein those linked to statistical or big-data frameworks most often are taken as valid or superior. In our current contexts at colleges and universities, institutional assessment offices are often read by faculty as "the others," those subscribing to assessment as rigid documentation designed by some outside (accrediting) body, where institutional assessment personnel are hired not to challenge or critique necessarily but to address through reports and documentation a vision of success that prevents the university from facing external sanctions. Here, arguments for success function to prevent institutional failure(s). Of course, when assessment serves as a response to an external pressure, faculty somewhat naturally resist. Scholars in (institutional) assessment communities like Linda Suskie (2010) and David Eubanks (2019), however, are critical of these reductive views of their work, arguing for what we believe writing faculty want: a valuing of local and scholarly expertise in learning environments. Institutional assessment personnel tend to promote a practitioner perspective that seeks buy-in from faculty for collaboratively driven assessment design and reporting. Yet for the most part, assessment is experienced by writing program administrators (WPAs), writing center professionals (WCPs), and writing faculty as additional, top-down demands with little value to their classrooms and programs—which is, unfortunately, all too often the case. Experienced in this way, assessment work ends up becoming a reductive routine in which writing studies practitioners trudge along someone else's well-worn path of assessment design. In such a context, faculty and midlevel administrators may seek the path of least resistance, subscribing to assessment practices that are expedient and cheap but that reduce learning to the lowest common denominator in the hopes we can just get it over with and get back to teaching and other research projects.

In *Failing Sideways*, we imagine alternative paths for assessment. Rather than following those well-worn paths that lead us only where we've already been, we have begun to imagine queer methodologies for (writing) assessment that can help us answer the kinds of questions we as WPAs/WCPs, scholars, teachers, and learners ask. These questions engage queer rhetorical practices (Banks, Cox, and Dadas 2019, 12–16) in order to understand writerly intentions and processes as much as they address outcomes; they recognize failure as a meaningful end to exploration just as much as they recognize success or even moments of failure-as-success, moments of failing now to get better at something on the next try; and they understand the need to forget past successes and frameworks that prevent us from trying alternative, perhaps disruptive and unsettling, options.

What our history has demonstrated is that collecting failure moments is easy and identifying failure moments is easy, but how those moments are interpreted and communicated beyond the hyperlocal is often a real problem. In those contexts, failure moments are reappropriated as examples of successful learning. They become the metaphorical roadblocks students overcome as part of the required success narrative of contemporary education, bumps in the road, detours students always seem to find their way around in order to achieve. We think that engaging failure differently, not as a bump in the road but as *both* the end point of some types of writing, composing, and learning *and* part of the intersections among our learning highways, might open new pathways of thinking about our work and about assessment more broadly. This shift in thinking could change how we talk about the work we do, exploring failure in ways that suggest we are not only okay with it but that we embrace it.

QUEER ORIENTATIONS: BECOMING ASSESSMENT KILLJOYS

As writers, teachers, researchers, assessors—as bodies that occupy space on our campuses and in our classrooms—it is important for us here to explain how we came to disidentify with the assessment frameworks we had learned about in our own graduate training and the writing constructs that shape so much of what happens in writing classrooms across the United States. Rather than simply giving up on assessment, tempting as it may be, we have chosen instead to follow José Esteban Muñoz's (1997) disidentificatory practices in order "to discern seams and contradictions and ultimately to understand the need for a war of positions" (101). This is a story, then, about orientations, about the ways we turned from the ideas about writing and assessment we had learned throughout schooling and toward more diffractive understandings of reading, writing, response, and evaluation to develop queer orientations that have shaped the ideas in this book. In short, this is how we became what we now think of as *assessment killjoys*.

According to Muñoz (1999), there are three modes of identity entanglement that do the work of individuation: identification, counteridentification, and disidentification. Each of these modes can produce distinct personalities or personal (dis)continuities that allow individuals to be recognized by others in social groups. For Muñoz, the process of identification occurs when a " 'Good Subject' chooses the path of identification with discursive and ideological forms" (11). On the flip side, counteridentification is characterized as "bad subjects" rebelling against and resisting those dominant discursive and ideological forms. Disidentification, however, occurs when an individual "neither opts to assimilate within such [an identity] structure nor opposes it; rather, disidentification is a strategy that works on and against dominant ideology" (11). To do so, disidentification becomes a way of working from inside an identificatory site to disrupt the social norms that already exist, not by submitting to them (identification) or by completely breaking with them (counteridentification) but by acting with others, often in collaboration with those others, to consciously subvert social norms. Disidentification is a model of personal and social praxis built out of our entanglements with each other and with the materialities in which we teach and learn.

As scholar-practitioners, we have, at times, engaged dominant paradigms of assessments via each of these modes. When we began this work of queering writing assessment, of engaging failure as a sideways project, Stephanie was a non-tenure-track (NTT) faculty member at ECU. From this vantage point, Stephanie was eager to participate in new programmatic portfolio assessments in the English Department to understand whether students were proficient in the course outcomes she had been teaching toward for sixteen years. If she understood student failure as a practitioner, Stephanie thought, she could fix it by teaching more directly toward the program outcomes. Similarly, when she was a graduate student and then a pretenure faculty member, Nikki had at times gone through the motions of the dominant paradigms of assessment, particularly when the assessments were inconsequential to the stakeholders involved. Identification, then, can be motivated by a belief in the process to "close the loop" and/or a desire to take the path of least resistance, especially when there is little to be gained from resistance.

However, at times, when the stakes have mattered to the everyday lives of students and teachers (and ourselves), we have actively counteridentified with dominant assessment paradigms. When assessment practices leave indelible marks on teachers, writers, programs, institutions, and classrooms, resistance may be the most appropriate and ethical response. For example, around 2010, when the University of North Carolina System sought to implement a critical-thinking test designed to assess upper-division students' ability to analyze, evaluate, and make informed judgments, we worked hard to disrupt that work at ECU. Developed as a writing test that gauged students' mastery of critical thinking through constructed writing responses, this assessment was pitched as a measure that could independently validate the students' undergraduate diplomas. Appalled that faculty and WPAs across the university system, including our own institution, weren't consulted, we actively worked to resist this initiative and sabotage its success on campus because embracing this model of assessment would mean real harm to ECU students and faculty. From our institutional positions, there seemed no way to subvert this perverted plan from within, so we worked to refuse and resist by actively dissuading students and faculty from participating in the testing pilot. When there were not enough faculty and students to participate, administrators began asking why and eventually decided this type of assessment project wasn't going to work because it lacked buy-in.

More recently, however, we've adopted the queer tactic of disidentification by performing as assessment killjoys. To imagine what disidentification might look like, we have worked to read and reread queer theory, queer rhetorics, educational measurement studies, and writing assessment scholarship diffractively in order to perceive what becomes visible as one conversation passes through a narrow opening or across the edge of another as they become interoperably entangled.[2] We stumbled upon this diffractive method accidentally, rather than intentionally, which is also in keeping with a discovery process that fails sideways rather than simply up or down. While each of us identifies as an activist-scholar committed to making our classrooms, programs, institutions, and communities more accessible and equitable, we come to that work from different academic lineages and different embodied experiences. As compositionists and queer rhetoricians, Will and Stephanie have been engaged in a host of theoretical and practical projects to work out how *queer* refigures relationships among readers and writers, teachers and students, writers and other writers, and writers and writing tools, as well as writers and their own texts. With Will and others, the faculty in ECU's doctoral program in rhetoric, writing, and professional communication (RWPC) had existing expertise in cultural rhetorics; however, it could not boast the same for writing assessment. When Nikki joined the ECU faculty in 2012, her graduate work in educational measurement and a research agenda that examines the emotional labor of writing assessment added an important puzzle piece Will and Stephanie didn't even know they were missing. When she was a doctoral student focused on cultural/ queer rhetorics, Stephanie wasn't terribly interested in an assessment seminar Nikki offered one term. After all, what could possibly be queer about assessment? As her academic advisor, however, Will suggested the seminar could be useful, especially if Stephanie were to accept a faculty position as a WPA. Early in the seminar, Stephanie became intrigued by the course readings in educational measurement (for example, Kane 2006, 2010, 2011, 2015; Mislevy 2016; Mislevy et al. 2013; Moss 1994; Parks 2007) and the focus on conceptual and critical issues in writing assessment. Nikki taught her assessment seminar through a theoretical and critical approach to assessment practices that traces the power relationships involved in assessment scenes, as well as how hegemonic deployment of assessment regimes works to mediate access to a host of tangible and intangible resources. Stephanie raved to Will about how useful and intellectually stimulating this approach was, and Will decided to audit

Nikki's assessment seminar the next time it was offered. Once Nikki had trained Stephanie and Will to talk, think, and write about educational measurement through more recent critical validity frameworks, all three of us started to see how conversations about assessment dead-ended with objective approaches to validity. Until we could work out alternative approaches to validity, assessment as a project of social justice seemed to us an unattainable horizon. Around the same time, Nikki expressed interest in starting a queer theory reading group in order to address a gap she had felt in her own graduate training. As the three of us met each month to discuss books and articles on queer theory, we got excited about the possibilities that queer and feminist rhetorics could offer in order to reimagine the language and conceptual frameworks of writing assessment to ream validity from the inside out. Through an affective economy that traded in feelings and motivations of duty, excitement, ennui, optimism, shame, disgust, and hope, we have carved out a space to disidentify with monolithic approaches to writing assessment and take on the mantle of assessment killjoys.

Despite this disidentification as an intellectual move, we also need to acknowledge our own identifications and the privileges those afford us in this work. While she started this project as a doctoral student and a long-term NTT faculty member, Stephanie is now an assistant professor and WPA at the University of Rhode Island. Will is a tenured professor who directs the University Writing Program (writing across the curriculum) at East Carolina University, while Nikki is a tenured associate professor at ECU in charge of a robust and valued writing center that is part of that larger writing program. To be a tenured writing center director remains a place of significant privilege given national data on how often this work is performed by NTT faculty and staff (Caswell, Grutsch McKinney, and Jackson 2016). We are also all three white, cis-identified scholars who enter classrooms and various assessment scenes with different types of power and privilege because of those visible markers, many of which the readers of this book may not share. And yet one of the reasons we have found Muñoz's idea of disidentification and Sara Ahmed's idea of the feminist killjoy so powerful is that we know we must actively push back against the privileges that we embody and that are also actively given to us by those with both more and less institutional power. We also know any writing construct we imagine and any assessment framework we develop will similarly be working within this complex context of institutional power, privilege, and value. As such, any critical framework we develop must also be sensitive to those issues and must work to advocate with and for those who may have been marginalized by or excluded from more traditional scenes of writing and assessment.

To that end, we embrace the antinormative and disruptive identity of the killjoy. This move involves recognizing alternative paths and orientations toward knowledge, toward schooling, and, of course, toward each other and ourselves; it involves disidentifying with systems of power and privilege that feel to many like the natural path, the way things are. To embrace the killjoy is to resist the "but we have to be pragmatic here" apologists. As writing teachers, administrators, and assessment scholars, we have come to claim our killjoy orientations through work with feminist and queer rhetorics, particularly Ahmed's *Queer Phenomenology: Orientations, Objects, Others* (2006), *The Promise of Happiness* (2010c), *On Being Included: Racism and Diversity in Institutional Life* (2012), and *Willful Subjects* (2014), which provide writing studies a queer lens for understanding identity as a continual (re)production of orientation(s). To orient, Ahmed reminds us, is to turn toward or away from another body or object in the world; thus, identity orientations are perpetual "happenings" as we are turned around; propelled forward, backward, and sideways; knocked off course; slowed down or sped up from our embodied engagements with objects, both human and nonhuman. Similarly, in "Feminist Killjoys," Ahmed (2010a) names a particular mode of identity creation that comes from refusal and resistance, arguing that *killjoy-as-orientation* emerges through the drag we create for others, complicating their collective movement toward heteronormative investments like *happiness, success,* and *achievement.* By slowing down, by questioning, by pointing out and creating counterstories that are not happy or successful, we *drag* others down affectively; we forestall their happiness by making them think about how the same frameworks, activities, or objects—the same rubrics—do not yield happiness and success for others equitably or at the same time. For Ahmed, then, identity is not a static experience of self but a moving and malleable line of feeling and investment; it is a layering of accumulated performances that we take on and that are also put upon us when our bodies and activities complicate the happiness (success) of others. When we call out and/or put our bodies in the way of practices that are colonialist, racist, sexist, ableist, homophobic, and so forth, we enact the killjoy, the agent who blocks the unquestioned (though sometimes hard-fought-for) happiness of others (Ahmed 2012). In writing programs, when we refuse rubrics, we enact a killjoy move that denies convenience, unthinking happiness, and normative investment in the illusion of objectivity.[3] As WPAs, we have observed a number of teachers and students who become annoyed when we don't provide traditional rubrics or encourage their use in first-year or advanced writing courses. We exist in a moment in assessment history when rubrics have become so normative that to resist them is to create real drag in our local assessment systems and classrooms.

By momentarily denying this happiness, however, we enact an important space of resistance; by refusing to "just get on with it," we not only interrupt the smooth and efficient flow toward some assumed better place—being done with this year's assessment, for example, so we can all just get back to the better parts of our jobs—but we also challenge whether or not this happiness is real, whether or not this better place we think we're getting back to is really *better* or simply not the horror of the now. We call happiness itself, this better place of the profession, into question. By refusing a rhetoric of futural salvation from the oppressions of the moment, the killjoy asks us to risk happiness altogether if doing so means we can no longer ignore the problems of the present moment. Given all the affective and embodied pressures of our profession, particularly the ways our jobs/contracts and pay are often determined (or voted on) by others outside education, enacting the killjoy is risky, but it's also the space where affective frictions create the very tensions we believe are necessary to better understand our assessments and the values they often work to hide from ourselves, our students, and other stakeholders.

ANOTHER WHALE OF A WRITING CONSTRUCT

Bringing together Ahmed's feminist killjoy with Muñoz's practice of disidentification, then, allows us to frame the assessment killjoy not as the writing assessment scholar who seeks only to tear down what has come before (though there may also be time and space for that work) but as one who seeks to investigate the writing construct(s) we know and to challenge those models that do not yet reflect the nuanced and complex spaces of writing we value. With that goal in mind, we turn our attention to one of the more recent and significant versions of the writing construct in our field as developed by Edward White, Norbert Elliot, and Irvin Peckham (2015) in *Very Like a Whale: The Assessment of Writing Programs*. Building on work around constructs and domains forwarded by the National Research Council (2012), these scholars argue that any meaningful writing program assessment must be based on a full understanding of the writing construct that operates in that program. That way, whether the assessment involves only a small piece of that construct or is one built across multiple parts, that assessment is created with a

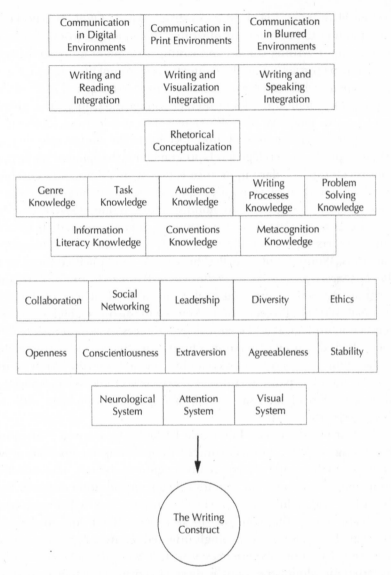

Figure 1.1. Nomothetic span of the writing construct (reprinted from Very Like a Whale*)*

recognition of how it impacts and is impacted by the larger framework in which writers and writing teachers are operating.

In figure 1.1, reprinted here from *Very Like a Whale,* we see a broad and expansive vision for how writing might operate on college campuses in the "hypothetical taxonomy of the writing construct as it might be defined across an institution's postsecondary curriculum" (White, Elliot, and Peckham 2015, 74). In this construct, White, Elliot, and Peckham pay attention to key elements of writing that emerged from decades of scholarship in writing studies and writing assessment more specifically. Level one pays attention to the contexts ("environments") in which writing happens, while level two situates reading, writing, and understanding in an ideological model of literacy (Street 1984, 1995) that shapes most English language arts (ELA) teaching and learning contexts of the last thirty years, and level three recognizes the central role rhetoric (should) play in any college-level/programmatic mapping of the writing construct. Of particular importance is that White, Elliot, and Peckham resist aligning rhetoric with only argument but situate argument as one among many "discursive and nondiscursive" modes (74). Rows four and five connect specifically to cognitive domains related to writing, while rows six and seven advance interpersonal domains; across these four rows, White, Elliot, and Peckham make an explicit connection to the *Framework for Success in Postsecondary Writing* (Council of Writing Program Administrators, National Council of Teachers of English, National Writing Project 2011). Row eight disrupts ableist linkages between neurological and cognitive experiences to pay attention to the "neurological capacity (nerve function), attention capacity (the ability of the brain to attend to a task), and vision capacity (the ability of the brain to stimulate pathways into the visual cortex) necessary to perform those acts of reading, visualization, and speaking associated with the writing construct" (76).

Of their model, White, Elliot, and Peckham (2015) note, "Mapping the writing construct in this manner through campus consensus draws attention to the core environments, cognitive abilities, and affective competencies embodied in a rhetorical conceptualization of the writing construct" (76). While this model calls our attention to "affective competencies," the writing construct in *Very Like a Whale* does so through language that to us is unsurprisingly oriented toward a normative model of success. Given our experiences as writers, writing teachers, and writing program administrators, it is these affective competencies that we want to disidentify with here in our role as assessment killjoys. *Openness, conscientiousness, extroversion, agreeableness,* and *stability*—representing, as the authors note, the Big Five personality factors from psychology (74; see also Bandura 1997; De Raad 2000; MacArthur and Philippakos 2015; Pajares and Valiante 2008)—offer one way of understanding the affective work of writing and writing assessment, but they also stand in stark contrast to affective models that work counter to a happiness-and-success framework, such as what we theorize in the next chapter as a queer model for writing assessment. When we first encountered this particular writing construct, it was this section devoted to affective competencies that stopped us in our tracks. Were these the emotioned values of writing that we as teachers and writers were aiming for? While they might be fine as a set of values or affective experiences in some contexts, did they capture the parts of the writing construct we had watched students struggle with, the parts we ourselves as writers and as teachers often found ourselves struggling with? It felt to us that some things were missing from this particular affectivity framework.

In the same way queer and feminist rhetorics shape the assessment killjoy, they also create frameworks for recognizing what may be missing from our assessment practices, or, rather, they remind us of the parts of the assessment scene forced underground or out of view so we can keep our collective eyes on the prize of successful writing (whatever that might actually be). This sort of (re)visioning has been central to the antinormative project of queer theory since the late 1980s as scholar-activists have pushed us to consider how normative rhetorics frame our realities in binary ways in order to normativize one part of the binary at the expense of the other; this practice simultaneously maintains the either/or binary itself rather than a more complex set of competing forces. We also recognize that, under the aegis of patriarchy, male bodies and male systems of knowledge accrue power and privilege at the expense of women's bodies and experiences. Whiteness studies similarly has examined the ways whiteness across a broad spectrum can come to function as superior to other racial and ethnic embodiments and become the basis of eugenicist assessment frameworks. We recognize these binaries at work in ability and disability, as well as in framing sexuality as either homosexual or heterosexual. In challenging the simplicity of these binaries, queer and trans rhetorics call into question both the identities and objects represented as in competition with each other, as well as the system of binarization itself, to ask why these binaries have risen to prominence, how these concepts have been framed and represented, and why this type of competitive framing is valued by both those who have power in such a system and those who do not. Writing assessments have also been built on and from these power systems, often designed as gatekeeping mechanisms to dissuade (and at times to actively prevent) anyone not white, male, or financially secure from crossing the academic threshold. While many writing teachers and WPAs today might be shocked to imagine such a framework or history, choosing to believe instead that their assessment practices do not mirror supposedly older, racist, sexist, ableist, and classist models, the reality is that our assessments far too often continue to support systems of inequality and oppression (Inoue 2015; Inoue and Poe 2012a; Poe and Inoue 2016; Poe, Inoue, and Elliot 2018).

For example, recent work by April Baker-Bell (2020) on Black linguistic justice has demonstrated yet again how assessments may function across affective domains in ways white English teachers are not always comfortable acknowledging. Although Baker-Bell does not center her important book *Linguistic Justice: Black Language, Literacy, Identity, and Pedagogy* in assessment discourses necessarily, the experiences she sketches out represent examples of the myriad ways linguistic justice is assessment justice, and vice versa. When Baker-Bell discusses the idea of anti-Black linguistic racism with practicing and preservice teachers, for example, she often gets pushback that centers on affective and futural fears about what other stakeholders (colleagues, administrators, parents) will think of these teachers if they do not "correct" Black language used by students in their writing and speaking. She recounts the example of one teacher, who asked during a workshop,

> I get that people from different cultures and backgrounds communicate differently with each other, but I also understand that my students will enter a land where they will be judged based on their language. Whether this is fair or not, as their teacher, isn't it my job to prepare my Black students to communicate in "standard English" so that they don't get discriminated against? (22)

Throughout her book, Baker-Bell reminds readers that communicating in so-called Standard English has done nothing to stop Black people from being discriminated against regularly in the United States, and it certainly did not stop George Floyd's killer from ignoring his Standard English pleas of "I can't breathe!" So many in education want to believe that how we respond to student language use—both in speaking and in writing—represents a reasonable attempt to teach, to "help," to make students better in some way, to make them more effective readers, writers, and communicators, but far too often, we choose to forget that the choices we're making around these assessments are neither simple nor value-free (Randall 2021; Randall et al. 2022). Instead, when scholars like Baker-Bell, Bonnie J. Williams-Farrier, Davena Jackson, Lamar Johnson, Carmen Kynard, and Teaira McMurtry (2020) collaborate to demand linguistic justice for Black students, they also begin to enact the assessment killjoy:

> Our current call for Black Linguistic Justice comes in the midst of a pandemic that is disproportionately infecting and killing Black people. We write this statement while witnessing ongoing #BlackLivesMatter

protests across the United States in response to the anti-Black racist violence and murders of Breonna Taylor, George Floyd, Ahmaud
Arbery, Tony McDade, and a growing list of Black people at the
hands of the state and vigilantes. We are observing calls for abolition
and demands to defund the police. We are witnessing institutions
and organizations craft statements condemning police brutality and
anti-Black racism while ignoring the anti-Black skeletons in their
own closets. As language and literacy researchers and educators, we
acknowledge that the same anti-Black violence toward Black people
in the streets across the United States mirrors the anti-Black violence
that is going down in these academic streets. . . . In this current socio-
political context, we ask: How has Black Lives Mattered in the context
of language education? How has Black Lives Mattered in our research,
scholarship, teaching, disciplinary discourses, graduate programs,
professional organizations, and publications? How have our commitments and activism as a discipline contributed to the political freedom
of Black peoples?

Their questions challenge us to rethink the work we do with Black language and literacy in our classrooms and in our scholarship by denying us the simple reassurance that somehow White Mainstream English
(Baker-Bell 2020, 25) will fix the complex and commonplace injustices
that attach to Black and Brown bodies in the United States.

When we think back to those Big Five personality factors, then, we
see affective competencies that are focused on whiteness and white
supremacy, not because they represent emotive experiences and values
held only by white people but because they embody affective frameworks
that would have us see writing as devoid of conflict and controversy, as
dehistoricized and disembodied. These are affectivities that center on
what Ahmed (2004b, 2010c) would call the positive or happy emotions,
frictionless engagements that do not create drag on our writing and
meaning-making systems. *Openness, conscientiousness, extroversion, agreeableness, stability*—these are the hallmarks of a white, middle-class experience that antiracist scholarship has been calling us to attend to for at
least forty years. These are "joyful" experiences with writing that have
been the near-exclusive province of a very limited number of writers in
K–college classrooms across the country. While these values continue to
shape writing assessments as they operate among writing teachers and
assessment professionals, we have begun to embrace the assessment killjoy in order to look at our work through queer lenses, to imagine what
emotions/affects the Big Five leave out or push to the side in order to
keep us all moving along a narrow but well-trodden path that's oriented
toward a narrow and exclusive vision of success. This shift in perspective has encouraged us to engage with writing assessments that resist a

neoliberal model of success and instead look for and embrace the affective elements of writing that might lead to different outcomes, values, and opportunities—or that might lead nowhere at all, that might simply stall out, drift from focus, or no longer capture our attention. Everything we do does not have to end in a successful product to be worth doing. The assessment projects and activities we explore in this book draw us toward failure, or rather what happens when failure is taken up more intentionally as a part of writing, not as the pop-psychology model of failing forward or the success-framed model of failing backward (down) but as lateral moves that create different (im)possibilities.

BEYOND A DEFICIT NARRATIVE: FAILING SIDEWAYS

So how do we break out of these flattened spaces of writing and assessment where success is continually coded as forward movement and failure is framed through return and retreat? After all, that linear/developmental model powerfully connects to embodied experiences of growing up and maturation in which school and grades (both grade level and assessments) become metonymic for our own human development. We tend to envision our grading scale as a spectrum marking higher and lower grades, and schools call us to "move up" toward graduation. In such a framework, lateral movements can come to represent stasis and stagnation rather than meaningful alternatives to ever-narrowing visions of success. But among ancient rhetoricians, stasis was not necessarily a space of stagnation; instead, rhetoricians engaged stasis as a heuristic to help them think through the complexities and nuances of a given rhetorical situation. The stasis questions were a way of engaging issues *laterally* rather than only directly or straightforwardly. So why have we come to think of lateral moves as avoidance, diversion, stepping aside, or stepping away from the thing we should be doing, rather than a way to engage it differentially or diffractively? How might we escape these seemingly commonsense frameworks for thinking about our work? Can we make sideways moves that meet our own internal validity markers, our own needs and values as writers?

In our roles as WPAs/WCPs, teachers, department chairs, deans, and other assessment stakeholders, we are constantly asked to report on the learning students have accomplished in their programs, the successes we mark in reports that can reduce learning to a set of numbers linked to outcomes like persistence and retention. We claim that learning *worked* for X number of students, but we do not always identify how or why, and certainly not what got in the way, what detours were taken along the way, what other modes of learning spiraled out of or away from the outcomes-based horizons our assessment frameworks have come to valorize. We plot our students and programs along a line we expect to move in only one direction. In this model, particularly for teachers and program administrators, the concern for one dimension of success, while often easy to get access to or report on, seems to limit the breadth, depth, and complexity of what we know as teaching professionals about the learning and writing that happens in our classrooms. While writing assessment as a field of study has wrestled with and addressed many of these complexities, in our day-to-day work, most of us still see ourselves as small players in a larger game in which decisions about assessments and success happen without our input or expertise.

As WPAs and classroom teachers ourselves—researchers and practitioners who are working at the intersections of queer rhetorics, writing studies, and assessment—we propose questions in this book that challenge norm-based writing assessments, such as acontextual rubrics and standardized cut-off scores for placement. What we bring to the table of large-scale, programmatic assessments is an alternative validity model that reframes writing assessment in our current culture of macrocredentialing and accreditation in order to provide teachers and administrators like ourselves with a way to speak back to and rewrite harmful assessment models that serve to limit student and teacher autonomy and learning. In our experiences across many years and multiple institutions, the large-scale/programmatic assessment models we have seen enacted rarely mirror the most current work in educational measurement or writing assessment. As practitioners who have felt lost in/overwhelmed by the campus assessment machine, then, we wanted to figure out how we could reclaim assessment practices in our classrooms and programs such that we could stand in front of that machine as "willful subjects" (Ahmed 2014) that resist from an affective and embodied space. That space led us to think about how critical validity models of assessment could be taken up by practitioners like ourselves who want an ethical and resistant place to stand in our local assessment scenes.

To make this shift for ourselves, we began to bring together scholarship in educational measurement and writing studies with queer rhetorics because doing so allowed us to disrupt prevailing deficit models and to rethink what failure can mean for our discipline and the students we teach. In particular, we have turned to educational measurement scholars like Michael T. Kane (2006, 2010, 2011, 2015), Robert J. Mislevy (2016, 2018), and Pamela A. Moss (1994) because assessment in this field represents a theoretical and practical activity governed by the

American Educational Research Association (AERA)/ National Council on Measurement in Education (NCME) standards, one in which (critical) validity arguments remain the gold standard of practice. Many writing assessment scholars (Huot 2002; Elliot 2005; Inoue 2015; Inoue and Poe 2012a, 2012b; Schendel and Macauley 2012) also align themselves with educational measurement researchers in seeking theoretically savvy ways to measure and understand writing and learning. However, even as these discourse communities have sought to move beyond rigid and reductive notions of top-down assessment, writing faculty more broadly often continue to experience assessment through a burdensome checklist format divorced from more local, meaningful (or meaning-rich) contexts. When we think about our graduate student and non-tenure-track faculty colleagues who teach the vast majority of first-year writing at our institutions, for example, we see teachers who rarely shape the programmatic or institutional assessments they are required to participate in; too often, assessment is something that happens to them rather than a set of inquiry practices that engages them as fellow writing and assessment professionals. And, of course, what role, if any, are student writers playing in shaping and interpreting these assessments? Most often, a very small one.

As such, this confusion around "What is assessment?" isn't surprising given the various communities researching, theorizing, and practicing assessment—and all those teaching professionals left out of the conversation to begin with—but it creates a slippery slope in cross-discourse community conversation because we each mean something different. *Failing Sideways* situates assessment among the overlaps of these discourse communities as a way to value and represent the research, theory, and practice of assessment among college personnel while simultaneously valuing the ways assessment has been experienced by different stakeholders, especially students and teachers. In this book, we approach assessment as the ways we research and represent learning, specifically learning to write. Similarly, we resist seeing assessment frameworks and the critiques writing practitioners have made of them as representing the simple binary of qualitative versus quantitative. Too often, particularly in the humanities, this binary stands in as a simplistic framework for valuing the qualitative over the quantitative, the latter being a metaphor for dehumanized, inflexible policies and practices. Instead, we advocate for both qualitative and quantitative methods and measures of learning. In a queer assessment framework, neither paradigm is necessarily privileged, as both offer unique vantage points for understanding the complexities involved in how individuals and groups

Table 1.1. QVI framework as matrix

Western industrial capitalist assessment models	Diffraction lenses of QVI	New affective writing construct values
Success	Failure	Agency
Commodification	Affect	Consent and dissensus
Reproduction	Identities	Radical justice and lived experience
Mechanization	Materiality	Embodiment

of students learn to communicate through writing. Ultimately, we seek to resist representations of writing that do not attempt to fully capture the writing construct and instead propose a new queer methodology for writing assessment through four failure-oriented principles: (1) failure to succeed, (2) failure to be commodified, (3) failure to be reproduced, and (4) failure to be mechanized. Through these practices, we enact a queer validity inquiry (QVI) model that looks through the overlapping and distinct lenses of *failure, affect, identity,* and *materiality* in order to discover what affective competencies may be missing from a writing construct that has been overly focused on a paradigm of success. As the chapters in this book demonstrate, QVI leads us to recenter affective values related to agency, consent, dissensus, radical justice, lived experience, and embodiment in our classrooms and assessment paradigms.

One way we might represent this model would be in a table format (table 1.1). In this model, which mirrors the layout of our book, our QVI framework resembles a somewhat traditional dialectic: Western industrial capitalist models of assessment (thesis) meet the diffractive lenses of QVI (antithesis), and their interactions result in a new set of affective writing construct values (synthesis). In this framework, the current model of *success* is disrupted by our attention to *failure* as a critical assessment lens; this disruption results in our need to pay closer attention to writer *agency* in our writing constructs. Likewise, our current focus on *commodification*, when diffracted through the lens of *affect*, requires us to reimagine *consent* as part of the writing construct. *Reproduction* can give way to *radical justice* when we remember the work of writer *identities* in our assessments, and our penchant for *mechanizing* writing and assessment can similarly be disrupted through the lens of *materiality* to remind us to add *embodiment* as a key affective value in writing.

Yet central to our conceptual model is that none of these QVI lenses categorically disrupts any of the long-held and deeply valued Western industrial capitalist assessment models. Breaking out of linear

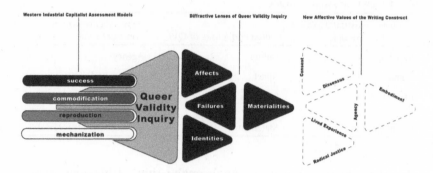

Figure 1.2. QVI framework as flattened Pyraminx

or flattened thinking models is particularly difficult, as these seemingly causal models remain central to our lives: we grow up (not down); we advance through schools in numerically ascending grades; we engage with and create dialectical models of analysis and critique throughout our disciplines. The QVI lenses we work with in this book are interactive and dynamic. As the figures that open chapters 3 through 6 demonstrate, we imagine a moving model, one that spins and rotates, one that must be looked at from multiple angles and across different vertices to be useful. When we began to unflatten this model, a tetrahedron emerged in our minds, one we explain more fully in the next chapter. To that end, while the chart in table 1.1 never felt comfortable to us, the emerging Pyraminx (tetrahedron) we've momentarily deconstructed as figure 1.2 shows how the surfaces of our diffractive lenses connect to the affective values we are working to reclaim as part of the writing construct and as more central to our writing assessment models. The remainder of this book represents our attempt to unflatten our QVI model, to quite literally take it out for a spin, and to demonstrate how our attention to the four diffractive lenses of QVI led us to want to radically rethink the ways our current writing constructs and assessment models ignore the affective dimensions of writing.

Thus, on one level, *Failing Sideways* is a book about our desire to rescue writing assessment and the profession of teaching from the flattened models currently in place for representing student success/achievement. In doing so, we explore frameworks that offer teachers and students a way out of or around overly simplistic structures currently en vogue for creating, interpreting, representing, and reporting on assessments. While many assessment professionals have argued that we can gain a lot from large-scale, outcomes-based assessment models of learning, particularly in terms of understanding the broad strokes of whether or not a program or college is meeting its teaching and learning goals, we argue that we stand to lose much more by embracing such frameworks universally and unquestioningly. While we recognize that any critique of current assessment frameworks also must acknowledge the diverse and rich types of data these models can, and at times do, provide, *Failing Sideways* foregrounds a validity framework teachers and WPAs can use to capture the complexities and nuances we know are central to the teaching of writing but that are increasingly erased by external assessment practices rooted in efficiency and commonality. Throughout this book, we suggest outcomes-based models of assessment that represent structures for capturing what we *think* we know of learning, but in many ways, such models disappoint because they focus only on what we can *see* in student writing, what we can point to in the products we collect and analyze. This book takes seriously the queer moments of teaching and learning (Waite 2017), the parts of our work that are difficult to track or are too often omitted from an orientation toward the products of student writing, particularly the affective dimensions of writing instruction that may not be easily visible but that are experienced by students, teachers, and administrators alike. These affective moments stand in significant contrast to the "affective competencies" that show up in White, Elliot, and Peckham's (2015) nomothetic span of the writing construct, so we offer in this book a look at what happens when we orient ourselves away from "successful" affects and point ourselves, instead, toward the affects, emotions, and embodied experiences that emerge when we engage failure more intentionally.

Failing Sideways is also about permissioning writing faculty to resist notions of assessment that have been foisted upon us and that we feel we must embrace in order to justify our positions, our programs, and our classroom practices. While the history of writing assessment specifically, and educational assessment more broadly, tells a story of capturing the rich and compelling work of teaching and learning, the ways these practices are often enacted now on most of our campuses make this work more about reporting on and capturing problems than about providing a space for teachers and administrators to understand teaching and learning in local contexts and to work to address local concerns. Because assessment comes *at us* more so than *from us*, faculty tend to adopt a defensive and anxious position. At times, we have done that very thing ourselves. After all, as instructors, when we turn over samples of student writing to either our WPA or our campus assessment office, how will they be read? How will the analysis of those artifacts be used when their reading and evaluation become divorced from the learning contexts that produced them? Because faculty are rarely if ever in charge of these assessments, how can we know? As teaching positions from K–12 classrooms to colleges are being tied to assessment data, it's no wonder faculty are anxious about these larger assessment practices. And, of course, as the short litany of failures and crises that open this chapter demonstrate, teachers work in a context where all our efforts seem to be understood only in terms of failure. By providing an alternative validity model for faculty and administrators to consider, we interrogate the current neoliberal paradigm in higher education from a queered assessment framework, one that focuses our attention on students and teachers as collaborative meaning makers in our varied contexts of teaching and learning. The ever-increasing mechanization of assessment is working to turn teachers into tools that can be leveraged and redirected for peak efficiency, rather than to recognize them as professionals who write and teach and learn, and who work with other writers and learners, while it turns students into numbers rather than human beings engaged in learning, in writing, and in making meaning through a host of discursive and material activities.

In framing our critique as we have done, we want to be clear that we are not suggesting writing assessment professionals, particularly those who have been working in critical validity frameworks, are the problem. In fact, this more recent work that reframes and recenters validity arguments in writing assessment has helped us see how queer theories of language, performativity, and embodiment might meaningfully engage with work in writing studies to do something quite different from what many of us were trained to do with assessment. Ultimately, *Failing Sideways* is intended to speak to our fellow writing teachers and administrators who care deeply about students as writers, thinkers, and learners and who find themselves increasingly called upon to justify the ways *writing*—the doing of it, the teaching of it, and the assessment of it—cannot be boxed in and codified through decontextualized rubrics or external frameworks. By queering both the writing construct and our assessment frameworks, we provide our colleagues in writing studies with examples of how we have used assessment to speak back to the varied external pressures that surround assessment practices and to reframe writing assessment practices in our classrooms, programs, and institutions.

As the first book-length monograph to focus on the intersections among writing assessment, student meaning making, and queer rhetorics/theories, *Failing Sideways* addresses the needs of writing teachers and those who administer different types of writing programs (first-year composition, writing centers, writing across the curriculum), as well as writing assessment researchers and queer studies scholars. In drafting this monograph, we have focused on those teacher-scholars as our primary audience, though we recognize that a much broader audience of assessment scholars and professionals may also find our theoretical framework useful. Likewise, by addressing the local needs of writing teachers—particularly the ways we can develop classroom assessment (grassroots) practices as formative assessments for those teachers while offering methods for critiquing and resisting external assessment pressures—we believe this book is particularly useful to classroom practitioners. Each chapter includes examples of classroom-based assessment projects and practices that illustrate the impact queer rhetorics can have on rethinking our assessment frameworks and activities.

By showcasing assessment practices that move out from the classroom—sometimes up, sometimes down, quite often sideways—we also believe this book will provide a sophisticated framework for various program administrators to reimagine how they engage with programmatic assessment, as well as how they operationalize assessment projects. Across several chapters, we highlight models for programmatic assessment that emerge out of queer administrative practices; these practices resist top-down hierarchies of power and instead engage administrators and teachers as collaborators in both assessment design and implementation. Through a queer validity construct, we demonstrate how program administrators can redefine their own narratives of assessment so they can resist uncritical top-down assessment models that may be imposed on them from outside.

On a more theoretical level, we see this book as opening a new space in queer rhetorical scholarship and writing assessment scholarship by initiating a space for these two paradigms to speak to each other. As we note in chapter 2, for queer rhetorics scholars who are invested in antinormative frameworks of critique, assessment scholarship can seem hypernormative (and oppressive) in its focus on measurements, norms, discrete outcomes, and quantitative data. Likewise, for assessment professionals, an engagement with queer rhetorics may uncomfortably expand a "conditional" and contextual understanding of fairness (Mislevy et al. 2013), one that lies outside the design of assessment instruments and focuses instead on the tightly integrated emergence of a more socially just curriculum and assessment design. Finally, by arguing for queer assessment as praxis—both theoretical and material practice—we provide scholars with a method for imagining and enacting more socially just writing assessments that move beyond merely naming inequities and biases that have long existed in our assessment structures. *Failing Sideways* pushes us to reimagine what matters in the teaching and learning of writing and to use assessment data to rewrite the construct of writing so it better represents what writing can be and do in a more diverse and inclusive world.

In "Queer Validity Inquiry: Toward a Queerly Affective Reading of Writing Assessment" (chapter 2), we introduce and unpack our assessment framework—the queer validity inquiry (QVI) Pyraminx—by situating it among scholarship in educational measurement, writing assessment, and queer theory and explaining why we chose a three-dimensional tetrahedron for assessment modeling. As part of that work, we offer an emotional reading of assessment to validate the felt sense of fear, shame, and uncertainty that many writing studies practitioners and administrators have experienced when engaging in writing assessment. We use affective economies that shape writing and assessment to demonstrate how writing studies has come to be so entrenched in the binary of success and failure. By embracing an assessment-killjoy orientation, we explore ways we can more effectively critique and challenge normative frameworks like failure that have bifurcated our thinking. A queer assessment framework, we argue, requires writing studies scholars to welcome the complexities inherent in our writing constructs and to design assessments that engage writing materially, spatially, and temporally.

"Failing to Be Successful" (chapter 3) explores how our current educational agenda maintains a narrow vision of success as central to the writing construct we teach and assess. We suggest that by refusing notions of best practices and success and orienting toward failure and shame, we can develop an ethic of shared agency in writing assessment. Our capacity to act together in orienting away from success turns our bodies and our pedagogical attention toward other kinds of assessment objects and stories. Such a turn allows us to glimpse different horizons of student potential and to pursue a more capacious view of writing studies practice. Including a critique of the field's uptake of portfolios, chapter 3 considers practices such as writers' memos, self-assessment, and programmatic portfolio assessment with writing-across-the-curriculum faculty as options that can lead to meaningful assessments for students, teachers, and administrators while also helping us keep our focus on student learning and engagement.

In "Failing to Be Commodified" (chapter 4), we explore possibilities for resisting neoliberal paradigms that foster standardization while unironically embracing excessive individualism and competition.

Although intended to promote fairness, standardization ignores local contexts, particularly regarding access to resources, materials, and creativity-inspiring curricula. Since learning and literacy are social practices enacted, shared, and embodied in cultural networks, we must hold on to the tensions that exist in those networks and value dissensus at least as much as we already value consensus. Through our examination of practices like rubrics and higher-order/lower-order writing heuristics, we call on writing studies practitioners to acknowledge that no, in fact, we do not all agree on what counts as good writing and that it's okay to account for and even promote divergent meanings, values, and goals. We turn to practices such as programmatic and classroom descriptive assessment and job-expectation documents for writing consultants as ways to invest in the people rather than commodified notions of writing. Valuing and enjoying diverse genres, styles, voices, and modes in our reading practices and then becoming hyperstandardized in our assessment practices creates a troubling disconnect in the writing construct itself.

Key to disrupting the "norm" of writing assessment in practice is to interrupt the "reproductive futurity" (Edelman 2004) that shapes so much of our success framework. As such, "Failing to Be Reproduced" (chapter 5) revels in the intensities and folds of new sites of assessment research by privileging what we don't expect, what we might not seek out, and what we don't know. We consider what happens in classrooms and programs when the goals and expectations of teachers and students fail to align, or even follow a line—in fact, when *lines* are not what we are after at all. In particular, this chapter disrupts sample sizes and types, as well as the contentious but persistent notion of the bell curve. By purposefully seeking out a systematically biased sample to overrepresent a population of students typically disadvantaged by assessments, we offer an example of one way we can create different statistical distribution shapes that allow us to analyze the nonnormative spaces of demographic data. Chapter 5 considers the experiences of writing and meaning making that are invisible in traditional grading schemes and turns to grading contracts and digital badging as spaces for sideways assessment practices.

"Failing to Be Mechanized" (chapter 6), however, explores some of the most visible or well-known parts of writing assessment: reading and responding. Experience and research both tell us that real readers have a diverse and complex range of evaluative responses to any given text. When institutions are interested only in numbers and agreement, it probably makes sense to allow machines to score writing instead of requiring teachers to read as though they are machines. However, when individuals are interested in meaning and communication, in the embodied experiences students and teachers have with writing and assessment—in short, when we want to know something meaningful about what writers are actually learning about language, composing, and communication—we must pay attention to the subjective, emotive components of assessment and scoring. Through a critique of criterion-referenced norming practices in programmatic assessment, chapter 6 considers the emotional labor teachers, students, and writing administrators bring to assessment and how our fear of subjectivity has driven us to adopt seemingly objective tools of assessment merely to ease our minds rather than to help us understand the complexities of learning. Chapter 6 considers practices like learning stories and assessment-as-play in order to demonstrate how we might value the subjective, emotional components of writing.

Across these chapters, *Failing Sideways* offers alternative orientations to writing assessment at the individual, classroom, programmatic, and institutional levels. These failure-oriented models move us sideways in the direction of QVI, where we can begin to value the voices of those seemingly furthest from, but also central to, the assessment scene. Paying attention to the embodied, lived experiences of students and teachers can offer us more interesting lines of inquiry around, in, and through assessment. We argue that this move is a *sideways* move, rather than a falling down or backwards or a total stopping, as failure is often constructed in our culture. In doing so, we borrow from Kathryn Bond Stockton's (2009) *The Queer Child, or Growing Sideways in the Twentieth Century* to recognize that queer growth can be a lateral practice, a movement neither backward nor forward necessarily but sideways toward other orientations, other ways of seeing and doing and being. To that end, *Failing Sideways* is about how a failure-oriented assessment model for writing studies can make available to us practices for composing and communicating that are oriented toward possibility. Such a move can help us reorient the goals and outcomes of courses in writing and rhetoric.

We end *Failing Sideways* with an examination of what happens when the assessment killjoy meets institutional barriers. In "Assessment Killjoys: In Invitation" (chapter 7), we consider the double burden of assessment that unfairly taxes faculty who are both providing accountability data for external assessors and seeking to transform the teaching of writing through QVI. We offer suggestions for turning the double burden of assessment into a double boon, focusing on ways that assessment labor can be recognized, reduced, and redistributed. Surprisingly, we've found our accrediting bodies to be helpful in this work. In familiarizing ourselves with what our accreditors actually require, we've come to see how institutions may sometimes narrowly read and interpret those criteria. The accreditation standards themselves, in addition to support from faculty labor unions, provide a useful way to push back on these narrow interpretations so our mandated assessments can use the lenses of QVI to *both* satisfy external requirements *and* provide assessment results that speak to issues of fairness, equity, and social justice. Armed with method and methodology, as well as strategies and tactics to disrupt the normative structures of assessment hegemony, our readers are ready for action. Thus, we conclude with an invitation for our readers to join our queer assessment collaborative's killjoy army.

Ultimately, this book points out a problem with success as an operational default both for writing as an activity and for writing studies as a field: quite simply, success doesn't scale up. The success frameworks we take as normative do not serve justice or equity; they reserve top spots for a limited few while keeping out the masses. We take as our theoretical frame for failure Jack Halberstam's (2011) point in *The Queer Art of Failure* that in any capitalist framework, success requires the overwhelming presence of failure in order to name and define itself. If everyone were successful in capitalism, who would do the work? If everyone is the CEO, who is working the line? If the worker at an Amazon.com distribution site is earning the same pay as Jeff Bezos, why is one working the line and the other taking joyrides into space during a global pandemic? The bosses of capitalism rely on workers who fail, every day, to become CEOs of their own companies. In the digital gig economy that has emerged in the last two decades, for every Facebook, Uber, and Instacart, there must be hundreds of bankrupt start-ups that go nowhere. If not, success has no real meaning. Under capitalism's elitist yoke, success must remain elusive for the masses, which makes failure the endless and persistent work of most of us. What scales endlessly in such a system is failure itself. After all, teachers across all levels of education worry all the time whether their grades are too high; some administrator somewhere will want to know what's going on with all this grade inflation if the scores students receive suggest success scales up and out. Sure, we say we want students to be successful, but not really too successful. If too many are successful, our current models of valuation mean something is dangerously wrong in the system.

As writers and writing teachers, we are frustrated by the capitalist and competitivist logics of success, especially by the ways they go unquestioned across educational settings and through our assessment frameworks. With this book, we want to ask why we cannot imagine a more capacious and nurturing option for writers and for writing. We want to suggest that if we suspend the neoliberal imperative for a very particular and narrow type of success that not only dominates our schools but also our culture more broadly, we might be able to imagine a host of alternative paths for writers and writing teachers that can lead us to meaningful and fulfilling work with writing and composing. And while success may not, failure scales beautifully. Not up, not down, but sideways across so many lateral spaces of opportunity and creativity. This is a world-making project, one we invite you to join us on as we imagine together new trajectories for assessment in writing studies.

HOW TO READ THIS BOOK

For several years, as we have worked on the ideas in this book, we have been engaged as writers, teachers, and researchers with the dense and intertwined theories and practices that make up *Failing Sideways*. Most of the ideas here have become somewhat second nature to us, but we recognize much of what we are exploring in the following chapters may be quite new to many of our readers who have not (yet) had occasion to connect queer and feminist theories, educational measurement, and writing assessment. In this context, we could imagine this book being a bit overwhelming to readers: How could I possibly do all these things? readers might ask. Let us reassure you, then, that you do not need to do everything we suggest in the following chapters in order to queer the writing construct or to queer writing assessment. In fact, we encourage you to fail at this process as well, over and over again, and each time to take sideways paths framed with your own intentions. While one of the limits of the book as a literacy artifact is that it seems to value a linear approach to consumption, we encourage you to read the chapters that seem most interesting to you and to do so in whatever order you'd like. Each chapter incorporates classroom and program-matic assessment models as examples of the different paths we've taken with assessment. However, if you are primarily a classroom teacher and you're looking for classroom-based practices for reimagining writing assessment—and, perhaps, for resisting the pressures of large-scale institutional assessment—then start with chapters 3 or 5, which focus on assessment practices that can be deployed in individual classrooms by individual teachers (e.g., self-assessment, digital badging). Likewise, if you are a WPA, you might find chapters 4 and 6 more immediately press-ing, as those chapters report on programmatic assessment projects and activities. Finally, if you position yourself as a writing assessment scholar or queer rhetorics scholar, then the more theoretical work of chapter 2 might provide you with an engaging entry into this work.

Finally, we acknowledge that the failure-oriented practices we share here are just as intermingled as the theories that support them. You do not need to always be engaged in all four practices to use QVI as your argumentative framework. One of the things we realized in drafting (and redrafting, and redrafting) is how interconnected these practices are. By engaging in just one failure-oriented practice, teachers and administrators pull on the threads of the other three. Some failure-oriented practices might pull readers in one direction given the assessment context that only tangentially picks up the other three practices, whereas a separate assessment context might ask readers to perform all four practices. The nature of a text-based book requires these practices to be presented linearly and temporally, which suggests that they build upon each other in a singular way—this is fake news. As you move through this book, we invite you to revel in the multilayering, upward and backward pulling, sideways growth of bodies and objects that, for us, makes queer validity inquiry both a method and a methodology for exploring and researching alternative writing assessments.

2

QUEER VALIDITY INQUIRY
Toward a Queerly Affective Reading of Writing Assessment

Across the United States, you'd be hard pressed to ride around town without eventually seeing one of those ubiquitous "My Child Is an Honors Student" bumper stickers affixed to the back of another vehicle, proudly proclaiming success for all to see. Perhaps you even have one on your own vehicle? And why wouldn't a parent be proud to show their own child and random strangers that the owners of this car have exceptional progeny. These common bumper stickers work to communicate a particular type of success outside the confines of a classroom or teacher's gradebook, to make certain types of success a public and shared project of honor—and perhaps shame as well for those who don't measure up. What may seem like an essentially silly bumper sticker also has a cumulative effect as it moves around towns and cities linking student performance in school to a communal and affective valuing of the academic one-percenters.

The sticker attaches value to the parent(s) or grandparent(s) who own the vehicle because their offspring has won victory and valor in the educational amphitheater. The idea that a relative's value increases because of a child's academic success cultivates additional pressure in education. After all, these stickers are on our cars only marginally because we want to tell our own children "we see you, we love you, you're special" (at least, as a test taker) because our children ride in those cars with us; instead, these stickers mostly communicate to our neighbors and other community members who are riding behind us and being required to recognize repeatedly that the child in the car ahead is somehow special. In such a public economy of affect, students' learning and achievement is no longer merely for their own sake; rather, they seem to be entrusted with their family's value as marked by this assessment *blazon*. Each member of the community who reads that bumper sticker becomes part of the affective economy located at the intersections of school testing, academic performance, and community values

https://doi.org/10.7330/9781646423705.c002

around success. It's no wonder students today indicate higher levels of stress and anxiety than we have seen in previous generations (Active Minds 2020; Yang 2021). From bumper stickers throughout US towns to end-of-term parties for high achievers to other public events for marking success to the very public and discussed rankings of schools, colleges, and universities in national magazines,[1] grade-based academic success is flagged as a public project of pride or shame, of individual accomplishment, and of shared failure for the schools, teachers, parents, and children who do not measure up. And as is so often the case in our current hyperprivatized models of education, success and failure are framed as individual rather than systemic issues: *my* child is an honor student; *my* child is successful—not "the systems we've built create space for some to succeed at the expense of others' failures," which is, to be fair, a bit more cumbersome for a bumper sticker.

We offer this anecdote to note some of the ways emotions circulate through and around assessment scenes—in particular, this success/failure binary—and, in doing so, we recognize that the vast majority of those emotions have become negative. When students get As (or perhaps A pluses), there is space for joy or relief, while everything else seems oriented toward failure, toward not measuring up. Whether this happens with classroom tests and essay assignments, end-of-course/year exams, college placement essays, or expensive exams like the SAT and ACT, these projects have become framed primarily through anxiety, frustration, fear, and hopelessness for far too many young people. But what if we could find a way toward more positive or affirming emotions in assessment, particularly involving those around writing assessment? What if writing assessment evoked feelings of passion, excitement, and desire for students, teachers, and parents? To help push toward passion and desire and a reframing of anxiety and shame, we offer queer validity inquiry (QVI) as an overarching framework for failure-oriented practices of writing assessment. As introduced in the last chapter, QVI pushes against normative notions of writing assessment to introduce sideways paths for learning and for engaging the connected, passionate, and communal work young people want to do with writing and learning (Ito et al. 2013; National Writing Project, n.d.).

In this chapter, we unpack our QVI framework, providing a history of how we got to this particular model and what we hope it will bring to the larger project of writing assessment as an equity-oriented project. As part of that, we examine the impact of writing studies' entrenchment in the binary of success and failure in order to unpack the affective economies that tend to shape writing and assessment in our schools and classrooms so we might more effectively critique and challenge those normative frameworks in later chapters. After we situate QVI as operating at the intersections of educational measurement, writing assessment, and queer theory, we explore how our embrace of the assessment killjoy has allowed us to operationalize QVI to develop four diffractive lenses for refocusing our assessments: failure, affect, identity, and materiality. Through these, we have discovered a set of affective (in)competencies we believe are essential to consider in our writing constructs going forward.

QUEER VALIDITY INQUIRY: ORIENTING TOWARD FAILURE

Failure, affect, identity, and materiality may seem out of place in discussions of assessment. For some readers, these at-times esoteric concepts may feel as though they have little to do with the day-to-day work of grading and responding to student writing, while other readers may wonder how these seemingly nebulous concepts relate to the shibboleths of large-scale assessments, concepts like validity, reliability, and fairness. It is precisely the normativity embedded in these too often taken-for-granted constructs that we want to pull at as we begin this chapter and establish the epistemological and methodological frameworks for the chapters that follow. By establishing our methodology early, we hope our lengthier sections on failure, affect, identity, and materiality in this chapter provide readers with various entry points into trying something different with writing assessment.

So we start with the concept of validity itself. Validity and validation are assumed normative practices in writing assessment scholarship, but we have found we must queer these concepts in order to pursue the work of social justice we need writing assessment to do. Early definitions of validity allowed us to claim validity if a test measured what it purported to measure. In this framework, validity resided in the instrument/test and its ability to correlate to a criterion score (a measurable trait). A criterion score reflected other measures of the construct; therefore, as long as a test correlated to another test that was assumed to be measuring the same construct, the test could be considered valid. No doubt, this is the model of validity in assessment many readers will be familiar with. However, more recent approaches to validity and validation have moved from a framework built around correlation to one centered on argumentation (Kane 2006, 2015). As a normative practice, *validation* is "a process of constructing and evaluating arguments for and against the intended interpretation of test scores and their relevance to the proposed use," whereas *validity* "refers to the degree to which evidence and theory support the interpretations of test scores for proposed uses of tests" (American Educational Research Association 2014, 11). While this definition of validity emerged from educational measurement, writing studies scholars across the last two decades have also taken up the validity-inquiry call (Huot 2002; Kelly-Riley and Elliot 2014; Perry 2012; White, Elliot, and Peckham 2015). In particular, writing studies scholars have emphasized the consequences Samuel Messick (1989) introduced to the validity definition, wherein score interpreters, not test designers, are required to make validation claims. In this newer understanding of validity, those who are doing the assessment and interpreting the assessment are responsible for making claims around validation. As such, validation is something WPAs and writing teachers should be doing each time assessment data is used to make decisions about students.

By framing validity as an argument-making activity, writing assessment scholars have situated validity within our rhetorical wheelhouse. Validity also aligns within our teaching pedagogies since validity is an ongoing/recursive practice, a reflective practice that assesses the assessment. For us, validity represents the argument teachers and writing program administrators make for an integrated judgment based on relevant theoretical, empirical, and consequential concerns for *how* they are going to use the assessment data. This emphasis shifts validity from the instrument (test, assignment, portfolio) to how teachers and administrators *use* assessment data to make decisions about students. In shifting validity to the uses of assessments, then, we recognize we are also locating writing assessment work squarely in the space of social justice and educational equity.

Despite these shifts in both educational measurement and writing assessment scholarship and practices, our experiences across multiple sites suggest this revised model is not yet normative across higher education assessment scenes. We recognize that, as a result, one of the reasons students, teachers, and WPAs have been so frustrated by the external assessments imposed on them is that all three of these stakeholders are far too often asked (required) to participate in assessment ecologies they themselves have no control over. Whereas validity has come to be understood in various professional assessment contexts as a rhetorical project for making our work meaningful through the ways we frame and understand our assessments, when these projects come at us from outside our classrooms/programs, from top-down institutional or accrediting imperatives, we have a felt sense that the assessments are not validated locally or contextually (Gallagher 2010, 2011). Because we see validity functioning as a reflexive method, we contend that WPAs and writing faculty generally must engage with validity and validation in order to enact the social justice work we believe is so vital to writing assessment.

Of course, we are not the first to use validity as an entry point for social justice work in writing assessment. Mya Poe and Asao B. Inoue (2016) might be credited with starting the social justice turn in writing assessment when they published a special issue on the topic in *College English*. Shortly thereafter, Poe, Inoue, and Norbert Elliot (2018) published an edited collection on the same topic. Around the same time, the *Journal of Writing Assessment* published a special issue on fairness and equity in writing assessment, and, most recently, Diane Kelly-Riley and Elliot (2020) have extended that work through the contributions to their collection *Improving Outcomes: Disciplinary Writing, Local Assessment, and the Aim of Fairness.* Throughout these collections, scholars have paid increasing attention to the ways individuals are impacted differently by writing assessments depending on various identity markers they hold in relation to racial and gender categories, as well as more intersectional framings marked by social class and global English usage. Through this work, scholars have been able to point to the ways minoritized students have been harmed and/or disadvantaged by writing assessments. Beyond calls for paying attention to nonwhite, non-middle-class bodies and to demonstrating the ways certain writing assessments harm marginalized writers, writing assessment scholars have focused on validity and validation as a way to move toward a social justice agenda. While some scholars have pointed to validity and validation as holding the answer, we haven't fully explored how validity pushes us toward socially just assessments.

As Poe and Inoue (2016) write in their introduction to their *College English* special issue, "If social justice is about creating certain kinds of relationships, distribution of resources, and decision-making along four axes, it is this last point—decision-making—where we may find a toehold for the project of writing assessment as social justice. In fact, we might say, then, that achieving justice is very much akin to the processes of validation" (121). Working within a sociocultural framework, Poe and Inoue place the onus on decision makers to shape validation efforts. For that reason, our turn toward QVI is a turn toward relationships, connectivity, and the affective flows that make such things possible. By bringing in relationships and affective connections as pieces of evidence, we can more carefully align our validation efforts with our values, recognizing that a significant part of justice-oriented work is engaging with affectivity and our embodied responses to systems not built with all students and teachers in mind.

What Poe and Inoue remind us is that as a reflexive method, validity means assessors need to know how they plan to use the scores and then argue for the relevance and appropriateness of that plan. While validity does not have a singular, clear-cut process, it does follow a logical, single loop in which assessors can, and often do, create arguments that suit their agendas—what David Slomp (2016) refers to as "confirmation bias." Validity arguments, however, should be able to withstand critical inquiry from others and should help us understand the ways our assessments impact students. Our validity arguments should assume our assessments will have consequences for students, and we should be addressing those consequences before implementing assessments. We should be asking important questions like Who is harmed, and how can we adjust our assessments to alleviate that harm? What's rendered invisible in our validity arguments? And What's being privileged through this assessment?

In "Decolonizing Validity," Ellen Cushman (2016) recognizes the pull validity has for writing assessment scholars but pushes us to be more critical of the colonialist underpinnings of validity. She argues for assessment scholars to dwell in the borders of validity and incorporate diverse ways of knowing and being rather than use validity as a tool for maintaining colonialist thoughts:

> Validity is on the one hand [an] instrumental tool, which was established to manage peoples, knowledges, lands, governments, and institutions, and on the other hand, a meta-discourse which reified the social, linguistic, and epistemological hierarchies that made it possible, hence further securing its own position of authority to identify what counts as valid.

Cushman reminds us that validity is both a rhetorical tool and a theoretical framework; consequently, writing assessment scholars must be critical of how we implement and frame our validity inquiry. Along those lines, queer theorists like Sara Ahmed (2006, 2010c, 2014), Jack Halberstam (2011), José Esteban Muñoz (1997, 1999), Lee Edelman (2004), Lauren Berlant (1997), Michael Warner (1999, 2005), and Gayle Salamon (2010) have allowed us to challenge the epistemological underpinnings of validity so that we are reimagining what counts as evidence for our queer validity arguments.

Part of that move also involves attending to the work of violence in our assessments. Josh Lederman and Nicole Warwick (2018) use violence as part of a theoretical framework for advancing a social justice agenda in writing assessment. Focusing on the ways assessment scores and decisions are representations of writers and how writing is assumed to have a normalized "end point," Lederman and Warwick sketch out the colonialist, structural, and systemic violence built into writing assessment, much as Elspeth J. Stuckey (1991) did for our understandings of literacy. To counteract this injustice, they advocate for validation research that actively concerns itself with matters of violence and injustice. To do so, they argue, we must focus on "less visible matters of power and systemic oppression—such as feminist, queer, postcolonial, anti-racist traditions which actively seek to problematize historical power-relations (including dominant or assumed/unexamined positionalities)" (Lederman and Warwick 2018, 246). QVI responds to this call for validation research that attends to injustice by advancing a framework that allows us to enact the assessment killjoy for more socially just assessments.

While writing assessment scholarship has called for critical inquiry into validity and validation, the field has not adequately engaged Jeff Perry's (2012) work on critical validity inquiry (CVI) as another way to push against normative frameworks and examine educational assessment. CVI is designed to uncover power relationships operating in and through assessment technologies by redirecting our focus to the systems (institutional, corporate, political, etc.) in which these technologies operate. CVI is a reflexive validation methodology that attends to non-normative areas typically ignored when we focus only on one kind of learner. Thus, one of CVI's main goals is to examine how assessments affect specific groups or individuals traditionally underrepresented in education, pushing us to see "assessment abuse in non-traditional sites of educational demographics that may not emerge in a focused inquiry" (199). CVI calls us to move off the path laid out by traditional validity inquiry by also looking at social, environmental, and cultural factors. Finally, CVI calls on writing assessment professionals to loop what we learn from our validation studies back into the political and legal arena of educational assessment to change the ideological climate surrounding educational assessment and reconsider the construct of writing.

Drawing from work in critical discourse analysis, CVI seeks to uncover the often invisible social/power structures governing our methods and actions and how they might direct us to consequences we otherwise would not notice. However, we find it falls short in its goal of disrupting power structures. While we can see the potential for CVI working from queer, feminist, and more intentionally intersectional lenses, in its focus primarily on how power operates, CVI ultimately has served as an extension of the formative tradition. So much of validity inquiry has historically been focused on justifying the end use of an instrument through selected data points, which are assembled along a trajectory of success, or on how data can be used to justify decisions about students (such as placement or graduation requirements). These trajectories reassure assessors that we are, in fact, orienting in the right (i.e., forward) direction, but for us, the right direction does little to move writing studies beyond restrictive notions of what counts as good writing. Our interest in queer validity inquiry (QVI), then, reflects a disinvestment in/disidentification with success and a willingness to follow the wrong paths of validity inquiry, those that promise to disrupt the demure scholarship of writing assessment. By embracing queer logics of failure, we can fail to promote some people's happiness (which was earned at the expense of others) by asking hard questions to determine how assessment instruments are impacting teaching and learning contexts. Following Ahmed (2006, 2010a, 2014), as well as Erin J. Rand (2014), we can acknowledge that our own queer agency as assessment killjoys arises out of the gaps between the known and the unknown, between what's intended by an assessment instrument and what happens when that instrument is put to use in a specific context. In terms of agency, Rand writes that queerness can involve "the lack of a necessary or predictable relation between an intending agent and the effects of an action; queerness is how agency emerges" (80). Thus, an assessment killjoy develops their agency by dwelling in those gaps and thereby using queer, intersectional approaches to determine how and to what extent assessment practices are best serving stakeholders in a particular context. The assessment killjoy keeps at the forefront questions about who benefits from the assessments we're doing, how they benefit, and why those benefits are the ethical or just results of assessment.

This unflattening of the scene of assessment allows us to approach writing assessment through a new theoretical model we are calling *queer validity inquiry (QVI)*. QVI is a methodology put into practice through four failure-oriented practices that work interactively to uncover invisible ideological structures and to interrupt the linear lines and orientations writing assessment scholarship has previously offered. These include

- failing to be successful,
- failing to be commodified,
- failing to be reproduced,
- failing to be mechanized.

We propose QVI to not only identify how power operates (CVI) but also to uncover seemingly invisible (ideological) structures and to interrupt the linear lines assumed to provide us the space to operate from the inside, to know and to work from within the discourse. By moving toward QVI, we operate both from within the structure and also from a critical stance that allows us to bring new understandings and voices to our work in meaningful ways. QVI moves us toward the messy, scattered, lateral, half-drawn lines that can redirect our attention to inequalities we (may) have yet to notice or name. To that end, Nicole I. Caswell and William P. Banks (2018) previously offered one example of what QVI might uncover when they used a set of focus-group conversations with gay male students at their university to discover the impacts local, programmatic, and large-scale writing assessments had had on the writing and composing experiences of these students. As we explore more fully in chapter 5, Caswell and Banks unflattened this particular assessment scene by over-representing the previously silenced voices of gay students, which led them to discover a new set of affective codes for understanding the particular impact writing assessments can have on LGBTQ students.

One reason we have turned to a queer validity argument is that doing so privileges the voices of those not typically engaged in assessment data: students and teachers. By disrupting notions of expertise and reorienting institutional hierarchies, QVI makes way for student voices, as well as the voices of those who often teach writing classes but who do not typically sit at the tables where programmatic decisions are made, such as contingent/NTT faculty and graduate student instructors. Second, by looking back at and involving those most impacted by assessment results, QVI aims to reexamine and rewrite what counts as success in assessment conversations. Because these conversations have traditionally happened in the absence of a diverse group of stakeholders, models of writing assessment have been developed that continue to silence and oppress the bodies and experiences that could most effectively disrupt the traditional paths and orientations that prevent a more just set of educational practices. Third, QVI disrupts the linear, reproductive traditions of writing and assessment; it acts out and acts back in order to queer the writing construct by refusing to reify a cognitivist notion of writing that may yield itself to easy and expedient assessments. Fourth, QVI embraces and enacts a methodology rooted in failure-oriented practices, which provides us with a means for reading our assessment instruments, practices, and ideologies *diffractively*. According to Donna Haraway (1997), diffractive readings, unlike reflective or refractive readings, work to map differences and are interested in the ways objects interact with other objects, paying attention to their collective emergence through relationships born of resistance, refusal, submissiveness, and compliance. Instead of reproducing sameness in a closed loop of interpretation, what Haraway calls "the same reflected —displaced—elsewhere" (268), diffractive interpretations can create multiple, often coterminous, trajectories and possibilities for knowledge making through "object horizons" (Ahmed 2006, 176). To that end, we argue that the lines of QVI can " 'point' toward different worlds" (176). As such, we envision QVI as a critical world-making project, one that can serve to reshape traditional notions of writing assessment through an investment in and commitment to social justice, and one that can hold us accountable when our senses of social justice need to be reoriented and redefined as we continually aim toward fairness and equity.

In the previous chapter, we offer two visual representations of our QVI framework to demonstrate how our four failure-oriented practices have been diffracted for us by running them through the four linked and overlapping lenses of failure, affect, identity, and materiality. Here, we unpack and define those lenses individually in order to demonstrate how each can help us imagine different affective (in)competencies that should be more central to our writing construct.

SUCCESS | FAILURE | AGENCY

As both an affective tension in assessment and a pervasive experience in our writing processes, *failure* calls out for greater understanding. Traditionally, failure-as-grade has been conceived of as a way to limit access for individuals, a well-documented gatekeeping mechanism in writing assessment (Elliot 2005; Huot, O'Neill, and Moore 2010; Inoue and Poe 2012a). In writing studies, when students fail, they have not demonstrated what has already been constructed by someone else as the ideal or appropriate text for a particular situation; normally, this someone else has both the power and privilege not only to name that distinction but also to make it have meaning. The failing student writer goes one way, while those assessing and naming the product of failure want them to go another. In these daily moments of evaluation, the teacher's job seems to shift toward aligning the student text to the ideal text rather than investigating what else may be an option, rather than discussing with the writer their choices and discovering what other possibilities this text may offer us that the original ideal cannot accomplish. However, in any number of assessment scenes, from large-scale assessment projects like higher education accreditation practices to teacher/ faculty annual self-evaluations, we are told failure must be identified in order to "close the loop" through a new/different strategy or action. A number of us have worked in contexts where, during our annual faculty reports, we are expected to name a failure or "unsuccessful moment" in our teaching that we have worked to address or fix in some way. It simply cannot be that we succeeded as teachers in the past year—not that we were perfect or that there were not a thousand other things we could have done, other paths we could have followed, but simply that we were successful. Nope, we have to find a flaw, a loose thread to pull at and perseverate over. In fact, we once had a department chair who refused to imagine new faculty could even achieve high scores in teaching in their first year; to admit they were good teachers in their first years, he noted, was to assume they already knew everything about teaching and couldn't improve. In this context, failure exists as a necessary component of improvement, growth—in both personal and professional development. Failure and success come to represent normative ends of yet another binary. The metaphor of a loop that needs closure does little to disrupt the linear logics already implied in that binary. This is the loop-as-hamster-wheel, rather than a loop that recursively explores previous data or experience in order to loop outward in multiple directions coterminously or iteratively or that spins in unexpected and uncontrolled directions.

However, some scholars in our field have begun recently to explore ideas around failure in order to pull at some of the smoother contours of our disciplinary practices. Writing studies is no stranger to failure, either as an experience or as part of an assessment framework. We know from our field's extensive histories that the formation of writing studies itself can be traced to testing and the naming of student failures, which then necessitated the creation of coursework to remediate students' past and current abilities (Berlin 1987; Brereton 1996; Connors 1997; Crowley 1998; Ritter 2009). When this history meets the neoliberal impetus for individualized success at all costs, the results can be that failure itself becomes "unspeakable" (Myers 2019) because the language we have for understanding it cannot seem to frame it in any way other than, well, *failure*. Kelly Myers (2019) has "come to understand failure experiences that do not make the imperative turn toward success as the unspeakable failures—unspeakable because we lack language or support systems for failure experiences that do not rebound quickly and consistently into forward movement" (49). Here, Myers echoes Daniel M. Gross and Jonathan Alexander's (2016) point that "success, as it trumps personal failure, can also numb us to failures that are structural" (290). Both Myers (2019) and Gross and Alexander (2016) seek to turn our attention away from individualist notions of failure as personal and toward understanding it through a more poststructuralist approach like the one Halberstam (2011) has outlined, one that moves our understanding of failure away from an individual emotional experience to one framed through affective (social/shared) economies. Building her understanding of failure in writing studies on this affective turn, for example, Allison Carr (2013) seeks "to think about failure . . . as an affect-bearing concept," one she believes helps us move beyond the "static notion of failure-as-end-point" that derives from our having only really understood failure as the polar opposite of success in traditional grading frameworks.

By moving beyond fixed (and linear) notions of failure and success, we conceive of failure in ways similar to Halberstam's conception (2011), which recognizes failure as a queer aesthetic, one "activated through the function of negation rather than in the mode of positivity" (110). Disrupting the often-unquestioned narrative of success offers an alternate frame for validation inquiry in both programmatic and classroom assessment. We contend that by looking at failure not merely as the opposite of success or as a stop on the road to success, we can construct alternative validity arguments—queer validity arguments—which highlight problems with traditional assessment trajectories. Doing so helps interrupt the ways failure has too often become embedded in student bodies as red marks they carry around in affective responses to writing and learning. In affective economies, certain bodies, before they even take a test or submit a writing assignment, are marked as bodies that won't be successful. History routinely shows us that to be successful in writing assessments, one must be (or enact) white, male, middle-to-upper-class discourse practices (Baker-Bell 2020; Inoue and Poe 2012a). While we acknowledge that white females are making significant strides, we cannot forget that writing assessments were designed with (cishet) male bodies and experiences in mind. We also acknowledge that a more intersectional look that includes race and gender reveals different patterns (López et al. 2018).

In *The Queer Art of Failure*, Halberstam (2011) offers a sharp critique of late-capitalist rhetorics of success, achievement, and accountability. With their focus on individual success in increasingly hyperprivatized and exclusive spaces, these particular neoliberal rhetorics currently shape not only our educational policies but also our broader political and cultural ideologies. As Halberstam reminds us, "Believing that success depends upon one's attitude is far preferable to Americans than recognizing that their success is the outcome of the tilted scales of race, class, and gender" (3). Echoing Barbara Ehrenreich's (2009)

Bright-Sided: How Positive Thinking Is Undermining America, Halberstam reminds us that "while capitalism produces some people's success through other people's failure, the ideology of positive thinking insists that success depends only upon working hard and failure is always of your own doing" (3). Consider, for example, the ways our field has taken up the WPA Outcomes Statement for First-Year Composition (Council of Writing Program Administrators 2014) not as ideas to be endlessly negotiated among writers and writing teachers but as a set of baseline standards students—regardless of institution, background, bodies, or abilities—should strive to meet, a document that "attempts to both represent and regularize writing programs' priorities for first-year composition" (144). While the writers of the document are explicit that these are only "'outcomes,' or types of results, and not 'standards,' or precise levels of achievement" (144), we wonder at what level that distinction is clear to student writers, contingent faculty, graduate student instructors, and the programs that operationalize the outcomes statement. Failure, we contend, particularly as a queer art, "turns on the impossible, the improbable, the unlikely, and the unremarkable" (Halberstam 2011, 88), a set of options that stands outside the outcomes—or the nomothetic span that White, Elliot, and Peckham (2015) construct for their hypothetical writing program. These options inhabit queerer spaces where intentionality may be more important than outcome, where mistakes may be more meaningful and impactful than mastery, and where forgetting may be a strategic project of undoing the master narratives of memory (and memorization/memorialization).

In their critique of both the WPA Outcomes Statement for First-Year Composition and the *Framework for Success in Postsecondary Writing*, Inoue (2014), and later Gross and Alexander (2016), highlight the ways the dispositional structures embedded in these documents serve to continually reconnect failure with individuals rather than systems/contexts. Because of the metonymic work that results from persistent racism in the United States, however, that individualist paradigm also inevitably scales up to disenfranchise nonwhite, and particularly nonwhite working-class, peoples. As "one of the most important yet undertheorized concepts in composition studies" (Inoue 2014, 330), failure in writing classrooms also impacts different bodies in rather different ways: "Writing failure stems from irreconcilable differences between expectations of White, middle-class literacies in school and the raced, cultured, classed, and gendered home literacies that learners attempt to use in school" (331; see also Baker-Bell 2020; Ladson-Billings 1995, 2021; Paris and Alim 2017). Inoue critiques two models of writing assessment common in our classrooms, both of which "produce [require?] failure as a product in the system" (334): the *slide-rule model*, in which "failure is produced by competition, in how students stack up against each other," and the *yardstick model*, in which "failure is produced by comparisons with a fixed ideal of writing, usually Standard Edited American Academic English" (333). Ultimately, Inoue ends up, like Myers (2019), Carr (2013), and Gross and Alexander (2016), connecting failure to larger systems, though he does not yet make the link to affective economies we explore throughout this book:

> Failure is not simply a product of bad or lazy students or bad or lazy teachers. Failure is not simply located in student texts, students themselves, teachers' judgments, or the processes, codes, artifacts, or products that circulate in writing assessments (e.g., rubrics, feedback, and grades). Failure is defined and produced through the interaction of all these elements in a writing assessment system. For without the assessment, there is no failure, even if there are performances. (337)

By not moving assessment failures into affective economies (Inoue 2014) or by trying to understand affective economies and failure without also engaging broader assessment frameworks (Carr 2013; Myers 2019), writing studies has lacked a coherent theory of failure and assessment we believe is needed if we are to disrupt the success-failure binary and imagine other possibilities for valuing writing, especially if we are to take the more performative approach situated in current antideficit models of education. To that end, we imagine QVI as a model that can help us reorient ourselves and the writing construct toward more meaningful understandings of failure. As we explore at length in chapter 3, through such an understanding, we might better engage *agency* as an affective (in)competency we can add to the writing construct. But failure does not work alone; it is always intraoperative with affect, identity, and materiality.

COMMODITY | AFFECT | CONSENT

Any discussion of failure is an unavoidably emotional one. We feel failure deep in our bodies; failing or being told we have failed or being called a failure are not simply dispassionate experiences in our culture. Consequently, by bringing failure out of the writing studies closet and placing it at the forefront of our QVI framework, we are also calling for the important work of emotion/affect to be more centralized in our assessments. Writing assessment is layered with emotional moments, experiences, and sensations. When we sit down to respond to student work, from early writing conferences and rough drafts to finished-for-now projects, writing teachers are fully engaged in the affective flows that swirl around writing processes and products. We ask leading questions to draw out students' ideas, we measure our spoken and written responses carefully, and we imagine how students will understand our rubric scores or holistic grades—all in the hopes that we're not shutting down students' engagement and creativity. Then again, we may decide instead to enact a tough-love pedagogy, offering direct feedback that models the type of critical discourse we think is appropriate for whipping burgeoning writers into shape. New teachers, always working to moderate their embodied performances in the classroom in order to effect a credible ethos, may likewise find themselves stuck between these differing affective poles, moving between encouragement and critique in equal measure. And whether we understand our responses as gentle or tough or honest or fair, it's hard to find a writing teacher who hasn't considered the issue of how their spoken and written comments are to be understood and interpreted by student writers. Over time, many of us are expected to develop a distanced, anti-emotioned position vis-à-vis our feedback, the same sort of expectation other professionals are supposed to have: like physicians, lawyers, even sports referees (Lewis 2019), over time, we can become numb to the ways our every move impacts the bodies and minds of those we work with. And yet, those affective moments never leave the assessment scene altogether.

Thinking of writing assessment from a queered perspective, however, requires us to acknowledge the material affects of fear and shame, pride and curiosity, anxiety and apathy, failure and disenfranchisement, which are circulating and making meaning with, through, and around the bodies, objects, and practices of writing assessment—and throughout assessment more broadly. Affect, as Mel Chen (2012) describes it, is "something not necessarily corporeal . . . it potentially engages many bodies at once, rather than (only) being contained as an emotion within a single body. Affect inheres in the capacity to affect and be affected" (11). Margaret Wetherell (2012) defines affect in relationship to emotion. Rather than positioning emotion and affect as two distinct phenomena, Wetherell draws from psychobiology, sociology, and cultural studies perspectives to advocate for emotion and affect as social components that work in tandem, neither belonging to the individual self but both working as embodied, material practices that reflect engagement with the world. Affect, in this framework, refers to the ongoing flow and movement of emotions. In particular, Wetherell turns to affective practices to capture the ways affect travels among domains, "continually dynamic with the potential to move in multiple and divergent directions" (13). Much like Chen, then, Wetherell sees these affective currents or practices as both public and distributed feelings, and for our purposes here, they can be seen as driving human and nonhuman participants caught up in networks of assessment, as our examples from chapter 1 and above all highlight. However, affective currents are also typically ignored in the same ways gatekeeping and testing frameworks have ignored the bodies and emotions of students and teachers while simultaneously policing the material and affective realities of those bodies most impacted by the discourses of national educational "risk."

Depending on our disciplinary orientation when we engage affect and emotion, we may find the distinction between the terms somewhat blurred (Jacobs and Micciche 2003). Psychology and neurobiology tend to approach emotions as individualized experiences, whereas queer and feminist approaches frame emotions as shared social and cultural experiences. This approach to emotion and affect is different from the felt sense readers might have experienced over the last few years as COVID-19 has raged around the world. In university memos and news articles, students and faculty have been encouraged to "manage their emotions" and "take care of themselves to limit burnout," as well as to participate in a host of other individualized activities as though our response to the pandemic rests solely on individual, personal responsibility. Missing from these conversations are the ways emotions have gathered and collected toward affective currents and pulses. Students and faculty might be experiencing moments of anxiety, sadness, and fear, but these moments are socially constructed through our universities' (lack of) responses. When fall 2021 became a national "return-to-normal" moment for college campuses in the United States, we could feel the affective valences when we walked onto and around campus. While it was framed across institutions as a "return," there was nothing particularly normal about trying to teach in person while also experiencing mask policing, surveillance testing, fluctuating class attendance, and vaccine hesitancy. Even after multiple assurances that classes would not pivot online, students held their breath as they waited for the email that would announce another campus closure. Collectively, students and faculty felt the lingering affective valences from the pandemic even if they couldn't quite name exactly what they were feeling or point to a single emotional trigger. We see these same lingering affective valences with writing assessment—a felt sense that something is (always already) off, but we have no language to frame the collective experience (affectivity) so much as we have language to shape individual responsibility (and blame).

We might turn to Ahmed's (2004a) notion of affective economies to think through the ways emotion moves with and sticks to bodies and objects within a writing assessment framework. Emotions are not housed only within individual bodies; instead, emotions circulate among bodies and other objects, where they pick up traces and marks along the way. Ahmed writes, "It is the failure of emotions to be located in a body, object, or figures that allows emotions to (re)produce or generate the effects that they do" (124). As bodies and objects attract emotional traces and marks, emotions become a type of capital commodified through circulation. The affective value of some bodies and objects might increase as emotion circulates, whereas other bodies and objects dissipate. Affective economies, then, are social, material, and psychic. Caswell (2022) has focused on the affective economics that shape writing center work and how affective economies perpetuate white, middle-class ideologies. Using Standardized Academic English (SAE) as an example, Caswell traces the emotional attachments on student bodies and writing as they enter a writing center: "The repetition of needing to perform SAE has placed affective value on particular bodies so that as soon as they walk into writing center spaces consultants unconsciously already read their bodies as failures, or sessions that'll take more work" (113). As we mention in the previous chapter, affective economies have thrived on the success/failure binary that has been rhetorically crafted to divide white, middle-class students from those benefiting from open-access movements. Caswell similarly reflects on writing centers' histories of being spaces where writers could acquire the Standardized Academic English to write "white enough" for the academy. Embedded within the success/failure binary are emotions of fear and shame that perpetuate an agenda of upward mobility and financial success. Affective economies continue to perpetuate patriarchal ideologies by circulating emotion in ways that have implicitly shaped writing pedagogies. The emphasis on writing in Standardized Academic English so writers sound "professional" continues to erase any notion of difference, orienting some bodies and language toward economic and social success while naming others as "unprofessional" or "inappropriate" (Hull, Shelton, and McKoy 2020; Jones 2017; Shelton 2019).

While standardized tests and end-of-course exams, the results of which mark who does and does not get those bumper stickers and other outward-facing honorifics, are framed by broader cultural and affective economies, in-course grading strategies like rubrics also carry emotional traces of power and privilege manifested under a notion of objectivity. As assessment objects, an early version of rubrics was initially developed by Paul Diederich at ETS in 1961 before the open-admissions initiative. By sorting thousands of comments made on papers, Diederich identified five factors (ideas, form, flavor [style], mechanics, and wording), which became an early holistic rubric. By 1974, the five factors had developed into a five-point rating scale with eight criteria (ideas, organization, wording, flavor [style], usage, punctuation, spelling, and handwriting). While still not called rubrics at that point, they nevertheless represented "rating slips" that helped assessors locate texts based on discrete traits or factors. *Rubrics* as a term emerged in 1977, in Charles Cooper and Richard Lloyd-Jones's NCTE book *Evaluating Writing*. What began for Diederich as a five-factor sorting mechanism eventually became the sort of rubrics writing teachers today would recognize, and, by the 1980s, this trait-based model had become the foundation for the 6+1 Trait® Writing Analysis writing rubrics that have become their own mini-assessment industry. Though this type of rubric has continued to be revised over the last several decades and is often used more contextually today, its initial emergence has been linked to its popularity with white, upper-middle-class students enrolled in universities (Haswell and Elliot 2019). In a diverse and complex world, rubrics seem to offer a corrective for the subjective and emotioned work of grading writing. Michelle Neely (2018) has even explored the impact this rejection of emotion has had on teachers and found in a pilot study that faculty valued a parallel rubric column that allowed for an "overall" or holistic score; this category "helped scorers leverage their emotional responses to facilitate the task of assessment scoring." As it turns out, rather than serving as a corrective to assessor emotions, as they are often assumed to do, rubrics actually become another object within an affective economy that circulates the power and privilege of the white, middle-class ideology in academic settings. Students become emotionally conditioned to rubrics shaping their emotional responses to writing and learning: joy and pride for an A, shame or frustration for a C, rejection and anxiety for an F. Thus, the emotions embedded in these rubrics are those framed by and around power and privilege—and the types of anxiety that emerge when those students with access and opportunity are required to remain on top at the expense of students in more precarious financial and social positions.

As more students and teachers interacted with rubrics as an assessment technology, emotional traces were then left on the bodies that were read and positioned by those rubrics. Students who didn't write to the rubric were cast as failures; bad-writer badges they often wore throughout the rest of their educational schooling were represented by the letter grades or assigned numbers on their transcripts and permanent records—or through the lore that attaches to students, bodies and moves among teachers in teachers' lounges and school hallways. The seeming objectivity of the rubrics makes these affective markers even more real, as teachers and administrators can now point students and parents alike to a clear chart of traits and values that are self-evident. For many students, the bad-writer badge would result in guilt, shame, resentment, and fear. Students who were successful with rubrics, however, continued along a path of institutionalized success, perhaps without the more negative emotional sensations attached to encountering a rubric, though we could easily argue that success creates its own affective problems as bodies struggle to stay on top. In this context, success generates its own emotionally destructive corollaries, as Halberstam (2011) clarifies in *The Queer Art of Failure* when they recognize the ways success and failure are always twinned experiences that rely on hyperindividualized and precarious notions of agency in which success is constantly threatened by the specter of failure (2–4). Our abilities to shape or to shake off these emotional traces rest on our abilities to reproduce or disengage the emotional capital embedded within the rubrics. In short, students who could read, interpret, and apply a rubric to their own writing learned to play school and were thus rewarded for playing the game by the rules teachers and schools had created. Students who struggled to play school, most likely because the rules of the game are both tacit and subject to change capriciously, were pushed into lower tracks, often labeled basic or remedial writers based on the written products they created. Students who were successful may never have had a reason to question the rubric. They saw it as a visible marker of success. We often encounter these students in our college classes now, anxious to know what's on the rubric, what traits they will be evaluated against, and suspicious of any context in which the meaning of a discourse is not simplistically reduced to a few easily named (and ranked) traits. Students who failed because of the rubric began to see this assessment object as representative of their failures. Rubrics began metonymically to represent those very failures.

Now, rubrics have become so pervasively understood as an unquestioned assessment of "good" that we find them taken up and centralized in most professional-development workshops and activities we participate in, and as such, they are a marketable and salable assessment commodity. Just recently, while going through a Quality Matters (QM) (https://www.qualitymatters.org/) training for improving his online courses, Will was frustrated when the trainer could imagine no option other than rubrics for communicating expectations and effectively assessing student work. The workshop facilitator, with extensive online teaching experience and advanced degrees in adult education, continually explained that rubrics are a key marker of "quality" in an online course and stopped just short of saying rubrics are required for any course seeking to receive Quality Matters certification, though it was clearly implied. When Will pushed back and asked if there were no other ways to be explicit about expectations for written projects or other models for grading and evaluating student work, the answer was, "No! Rubrics work, students expect them, and they are the best option available." It's no surprise QM has its own quality-based rubric that universities purchase in order to certify faculty as high-quality online instructors. Part of what is so striking here is not just that one assessment instrument is being marked as the best, regardless of context, activity, or writing construct, but that these are instruments "students expect" to see: their presence creates comfort, security, a sense of rightness, a sense that their work is being fairly read and scored; their absence suggests precarity, chaos, a sense of "anything goes" in how the teacher evaluates. These are affective experiences; these are the ways rubrics come to embody, enact, and reiterate emotional work in a classroom. Central to the research this facilitator was using in order to make such claims about rubrics in online courses was not that rubrics are necessarily better but that they are better because they are expected. They are better inasmuch as they create a seemingly frictionless experience for students in online courses where there is nothing complex or sophisticated to think through or work out or negotiate in terms of assessment.

As we continue to unpack the emotional traces embedded in writing assessment practices, we can turn to how certain teacher and student bodies are always already constructed as contagion, as both at risk and risky. If we do not critically engage this binary, we can end up seeing some students as victims of poor teaching and failing schools, where teachers become the cause of these problems, rather than bodies themselves also stuck in systems of dysfunctional assessments. If we seek to interrupt this sort of paradigm, we must recognize that assessment practices have often produced little to no joy for the vast majority of those caught in their wake. Rubrics certainly haven't created the calm sensation of grading writing many thought they would. Students and parents alike dissect those rubric scores with precision, asking why this error was worth a deduction of that many points. Parents fret over the scores their children receive on standardized testing, and by high school, they must worry about the financial burden the testing industry creates for them, both in the high costs of taking the tests and having scores sent to multiple colleges and universities and in the costs of higher education when their child's scores do not earn significant scholarships. In K–12 settings, students sit through exhaustingly long hours of test preparation and test taking, which consumes time that could be spent learning new and meaningful material. In addition to losing quality educational time to test preparation and then justifying student scores, teachers also must worry about who does and does not show up for the tests, who can and cannot take the tests, and who needs additional time or support, while school administrators must reorganize the school day to accommodate complex testing schedules, hire additional staff to proctor the tests and process the students, and write endless reports explaining the results of testing to various stakeholders. Locally, school districts also must figure out how to pay for all these constantly shifting and disruptive activities.

At colleges and universities, the assessment scene around rubrics doesn't necessarily look all that dissimilar. In programs we have directed and/or taught in, we have seen writing faculty unsettled in the absence of a standard or shared rubric, whose evaluative columns and categories represent a model against which (often tenure-track) faculty can evaluate themselves but also a standard they can point students to in order to defend/justify the grades they have placed on student papers. This may be especially true for new teachers/graduate student instructors for whom the rubric can serve as a sort of Linus blanket in a teaching context where they may lack the confidence and experience to understand the grades they assign and what those grades mean, even as they are expected to constantly place them on student work. Ultimately, it's hard to imagine anyone in this scene of assessment experiencing joy, except perhaps the testing companies and publishers who collaborate to write the tests and the test-preparation materials as part of an annual multi-billion-dollar industry—or maybe the beleaguered WPA who hopes that through a common rubric, at least one element of their writing program is under control and, perhaps, safe from attack by the different stakeholders on campuses who are also looking for someone to blame when the students' writing in their classes doesn't magically meet their expectations.

In this paradigm, when teachers, parents, and students resist rubrics, questioning investments in both ideologies and the assessment instruments that materialize those ideologies, it is they as individuals who are fingered as the problem rather than the system. Individuals who dare doubt the gold standards of assessment, whether the purchased test or the more localized writing portfolio, or even just the person who questions what we mean when we say "good writing"—these individuals become assessment killjoys. Parents who opt out of year-end K–12 tests create troubling frictions in schools as they, their children's teachers, and now school administrators must all find an alternative option for these students during testing days: Do they stay home and get counted absent? Do they sit in classrooms quietly while other students are tested? Does the school have to find space and alternative activities for them, and teachers to supervise them, while limited personnel are busy proctoring exams? Quickly, these children become the problem, the exception, that teachers, administrators, and even other students begin to frame as disruptive. The children not taking tests create problems for the smooth and frictionless use of assessment instruments and procedures designed to tell us what we already know or to construct single stories about students and their writing. According to Ahmed (2010b), "The feminist killjoy 'spoils' the happiness of others; she is a spoilsport because she refuses to convene, to assemble, or to meet up over happiness" (581), a happiness created and maintained for others. For Ahmed and other queer scholars (Edelman 2004; Palmeri 2012), happiness, like assessment, is a well-trodden path that requires investment in particular heteronormative projects that have been constructed to reproduce the status quo. When bodies fail to invest appropriately, they are marked as willful (Ahmed 2014) and credited with creating the conditions they called attention to. Ahmed's (2021) *Complaint!* examines this phenomenon in which the person issuing a complaint becomes the problem rather than the person(s) and system(s) actually causing harm. Bodies that complain or push back exert "willfulness," the act of pushing back understood in a compliance-oriented system as angry, resistant, unhappy, frustrated—all affective markers that situate individuals as joy killers in ways that render their resistance not as a meaningful critique of an unjust system but as noncompliance, as troublemaking. The marking of a "killjoy," then, has historically been a rhetorical move meant to exert pressure on willful bodies in order to bring them back in line (Ahmed 2014). In scenes of assessment, the willful bodies are diffuse and complex: they are the physical bodies of the students and teachers, of course, but also administrators and parents; they are the "bodies" of texts composed to reflect hypernormative values and genres, as well as those that resist, that make knowledge differently or in ways rubrics cannot (or refuse to) capture.

In order to engage the work of assessment in more ethical ways—through affective and embodied practices—we have begun to position ourselves as assessment killjoys, embracing the politics and praxis of Ahmed's feminist killjoy in order to enact assessment as a practice of social justice and to keep affectivity central to our work. This move resists commodified assessment practices, technologies, and objects and pushes our attention to the ways affective values around *consent* and *dissensus* can lead us to more just and equitable assessment paradigms.

REPRODUCTION | IDENTITIES | RADICAL JUSTICE

While we are, ourselves, material and matter—in fact, material that matters greatly in our own figuring of the world—we also recognize that identity functions for most of us quite differently from mere materiality. Certainly, in our understanding of assessment, whether that involves ranking, grading, or evaluating, we understand student writers as embodying selves we encounter as other people, people like ourselves with a host of identities and positionalities, even if we're often asked to separate the writer from their text. And yet, a sense of self is also wrapped up in the writing assessment labels teachers give students: I'm an A student. I'm a bad writer. I'm a C student. My English is nonstandard. I'm a basic writer. It's hard to imagine a writing assessment that does not engage students' identities in both affective and material ways when education so quickly labels and tracks students. While identity is more than a label placed on a student, these labels hold power over how students act and move through school. As we explore in chapter 6, when students see taking the SAT or ACT as a rite of passage to becoming a college student, the focus is less on how the assessment helps students achieve admission into college and more on the ways an assessment contributes to a student's sense of self. Likewise, in chapter 5, we dig deeper into the ways "average identities" are constructed through the bell curve's continued effects on school culture. Thus, our goal in placing identity in our QVI framework is to remind us of the dynamic ways identities are shaped and formed as part of various assessment processes. Part of that may involve the identities students bring with them—self-understandings linked to race, class, gender, sexuality, and so forth—but a queer orientation toward identity pushes us to resist single or essentializing markers of identity and instead to see identity as (also) performative and socially constructed (Butler 1990, 1994, 2004). To that end, identity becomes part of QVI through this recognition that student writers are both part of commonly understood identity groups *and* constantly reidentified (and disidentified) through schooling and assessment scenes that mark bodies and experiences with additional affective valences.

We see identities as fluid and contingent, as constructed and contextual, both in terms of how individuals understand their own identities as simultaneously stable and changing and in how individuals are read/understood by others. We consider the range of identities placed upon bodies willingly and unwillingly and the politics associated with claiming or being read as a particular identity. Our interest in identities is not just in the demographics of our students and how we might name those categories—though in chapter 5 we do have suggestions for how we might move beyond fixed notions of demographic categories. Rather, we are interested in how we encourage students to bring their whole multivalent and continually evolving selves to writing situations without simultaneously devaluing those identities in assessments that rank and sort.

In terms of naming and labeling identities when we engage with assessment, we might turn to James Paul Gee's (2014) work with discourse analysis. Gee considers identity as a way of being in language. Identity is socially situated and context specific. For Gee, identities can be "partial, negotiated, contested, attempted, improvised, innovated, imposed, freely chosen, hybrid, mastered, in progress, or fossilized" (23). Individuals can have multiple identities in various contexts, and we can use identity as an analytical tool to study discourse. Language allows us to enact and recognize identities and draws our attention to the ways identities are formed and sustained. For example, all three of us have engaged in alternative grading methods to devalue letter grades, and students have had significantly mixed responses. Some students welcome the change to break out of rigid rules, whereas others struggle to perform. Still others find themselves switching, thinking it sounds great to do something different with grades only to feel uncertain at some point and then crave the fixity and certainty of letters on a ten-point scale. Some students confess, "I just don't know how to operate outside the grading paradigm." As writing studies scholars are wrestling with these contradictions and concerns with nontraditional grading paradigms (Carillo 2021; Craig 2021), we recognize that students have embodied the anxiety of the situation, and without the almighty grade resting just out of reach, students can, at times, feel stuck when they try to figure out how to perform. By removing a familiar grading framework, students are left to ask "Who am I?" and "What does this mean?" This attachment students have to traditional grading and assessment frameworks fascinates and frustrates us: What is it about this particular model that keeps students (and teachers alike) trapped, especially when, as we've noted multiple times already in this book, those involved tend to feel unsatisfied and unhappy with grades/grading? How have grades taken on the power of identity categories in our lives?

We are equally curious about the ways teachers construct their identities with regard to assessment. Some teachers relish the idea that they are hard-asses, that students should rightly fear their grading pens. Relaxing standards becomes a slap in the face for teachers who identify with this assessment figure. A former chair lovingly referred to one of our colleagues as "Nails" because students often remarked in course evaluations that she was "tough as nails" in her grading. Other teachers have worked to disidentify with that moniker, choosing to see themselves as coaches or mentors in how they respond to, grade, and assess writing (Tchudi 1997). Still others, particularly when new and unfamiliar practices or values come into vogue, embrace the anxiety such assessment situations can bring by claiming, "I can't teach or assess that." In the previous chapter, we shared one of April Baker-Bell's (2020) stories of being met with just such resistance when she does workshops around Black linguistic justice.

The notion of identity we are working with here is a fundamentally performative one. In addition to the ways Gee imagines identities as multiple and contingent, queer and trans theorists like Butler (1990, 1994, 2004), Ahmed (2006, 2010a, 2014), and Gayle Salamon (2010) have provided us with ways of understanding identity linked to performativity, an antiessentializing move that keeps it from simply being understood as a consciously chosen (theatrical) performance. In the popular imagination, when we imagine identity as performance, we may frame it as purely about individual choices (how a person chooses to present themself through embodiment, clothing, etc.) and how individuals choose to embrace or connect with preexisting groups with shared traits, values, or goals (e.g., racial identity, social class identities). When queer and trans theorists argue that performativity shapes identity, they are imagining it as the ways discourses, experiences, and materialities work together to shape identities through both chosen practices and the ways culture frames those choices. In those moments of framing, identities become more than just choices; they become part of iterative (discursive) practices that settle around and on bodies to mark them in particular ways. That doesn't mean we do not *feel* those practices as real, only that parts of the work of how we come to self-mean and other-mean are not immutable or stable or even under our control. To suggest, for example, that gender is performative is not to argue there are no genetic or embodied or real elements related to gender, at least in how we perceive gender in ourselves and others. After all, a particular person may not identify as a woman or as feminine but may still be read as such by others and still feel the very real and embodied experiences of misogyny, workplace sexual harassment, or other actions that reinscribe femaleness onto their body.

We've kept *identity* central to our QVI framework because we believe our assessments must recognize these complexities, and our validity arguments, in particular, must be sensitive to the ways assessment projects mark bodies—both teacher and student—with new identities that may or may not do them justice, may or may not be welcomed or appreciated. We also recognize that part of being an assessment killjoy, of disidentifying with traditional assessment markers, might be in performatively valuing certain identity markers over others so as to understand assessment scenes and our writing constructs differently from the ways we've already done so. By embracing complex, fluid notions of identity, we can think about identity in lateral rather than purely developmental ways. We might consider what oversampling of a particular identity does to the ways we understand writing. Or we might look at the affective ways identities are shaped and formed. We might ask how passions, desires, and opportunities shape the language we use to describe ourselves and writers. Keeping identity linked to failure, affectivity, and materiality in our QVI framework reminds us of the ways our identities make up and are made through all parts of the assessment scene and our writing construct. Refusing to remove identity, to separate selves from texts, writers from (and as) their compositions, then, is also a killjoy move that reminds writing assessment professionals that our decisions about assessments always have real effects on the bodies and minds of living people.

MECHANIZATION | MATERIALITY | EMBODIMENT

While our identities can come to represent one type of materiality or matter in the ways they are operationalized in various contexts, we also know that other materials matter just as much in assessments: rubrics, technologies, books, access, and so forth are all part of the assessment scene. Of course in QVI, the arguments we make about assessment are never only about textual artifacts and/or how those artifacts are understood apart from the multiple and varied other material conditions that circulate around them. To that end, our understanding of materiality is rooted in current scholarship involving new materialisms, which offers us a method for thinking about how signs, bodies, and objects produce material and discursive meaning. New materialisms allow us to pay attention to the embodied and emotive experiences crafted within such meaning. Thus, our orientation toward new materialisms, particularly queer- and feminist-inflected materialisms, helps us approach the embodied, emotive, relational, and differential processes of composition. New materialisms shift our thinking about making and the processes of composition away from particular concerns with discrete texts and discrete composing bodies and toward ontological aspects of making and composing. This shift allows us to theorize how meaning and matter, rhetoric and objects, bodies and identities all emerge and reemerge intra-actively in and across composing networks.

New materialist thinkers like Karen Barad are interested in the concept of materialization as a process by which matter and discourse come to exist together over space and time. The term *materialization* underscores the corporeal and embodied dimension of being, and Barad (2007) often uses the phrase "matter comes to matter" (152) as a way of joining ontological concerns with epistemological and ethical concerns. This process is "entangled," meaning objects, bodies, signs, and meanings cannot be bracketed off from one another. In *Meeting the Universe Halfway*, Barad (2007) writes, "To be entangled is not simply to be intertwined with another, as in the joining of separate entities, but to lack an independent self-contained existence. Existence is not an individual affair. Individuals do not preexist their interactions; rather, individuals emerge through and as part of their entangled intra-relating" (ix).

These assertions about meaning and matter and the entanglements of bodies underpin Barad's theory of agential realism. As a rhetorical approach to becoming(s), agential realism refuses to ignore the production of difference or to devalue difference prima facie. Instead, drawing on Michel Foucault's work, Barad (2007) posits that materiality is regulated through exercises of power, and discursive practices are material structures that sanction what might be said, when, where, and by whom. Thus, meaning and matter are always already material and discursive. A material-discursive rhetoric, then, does not bracket off the things, the bodies, and the signs. It understands them to be coproductions of specific material encounters and works out their mutually constitutive effects. Through such a framework, failure is not dismissed as the devalued Other of writing/success but is understood as difference(s), as Other-but-entangled elements of meaning making. Failure is writing; writing is failure—not just some excised element in the process.

Likewise, materialization operates from the premise that matter itself is alive with an animating potentiality. All matter is lively, agentic, and performative with new materialism. According to Jane Bennett (2009), a vibrant materiality includes "the capacity of things—edibles, commodities, storms, metals—not only to impede or block the will and designs of humans but also to act as quasi-agents or forces with trajectories, propensities, and tendencies of their own" (66). Borrowing from the philosophies of Hans Driesch and Henri Bergson, Bennett reclaims the creative force of matter while also rejecting the teleology of the organism and the animating "ghost" or a disembodied "soul," as previously figured by Immanuel Kant. Instead, she argues, matter needs no soul, no animating, "free floating" force. It is matter itself that acts, and it acts in unpredictable ways. Bennett picks up on Gilles Deleuze and Félix Guattari's (1987) insistence on the aleatory or contingent nature of matter and rejects the humanist supposition that matter possesses a fixed, "stable or rock bottom reality, something adamantine" (Bennett 2009, 58). For Bennett, all matter is the result of "emergent causality" (33), meaning that the production of matter that comes to matter (*pace* Barad) has many possible shared and coresponsible causes. Becoming, existing, and mattering does not require an aggregating, active desire or intentionality. Instead, these material-discursive processes require a kind of passive receptivity—a willingness to be spun, oriented, molded, and shaped by a host of others.

In line with queer/feminist scholars like Butler, Donna Haraway, and Barad, Bennett (2009) argues for an understanding of matter and meaning as always in a state of becoming. She explains these contingent processes of becoming through what she refers to as a "vortical logic" (119), a logic not of stasis but predicated instead on endless movement. Bodies (human or not) form through material-discursive crash encounters. Matter crystallizes temporarily into things and bodies, but those bodies reform and remix (if only ever so slightly) upon contact with other matter. For Bennett and other new materialists, matter is not internally preprogrammed with a natural tendency to become a certain kind of thing with a final end state. Thus, we might think about material becoming as *enfolding* rather than unfolding. Enfolding signals an ongoing process of allowing—allowing oneself to be enveloped and swept into the fray. Inside the vortex, all matter becomes "entangled," and humanist notions of rugged individualism and singular being and agency are impossible to support.

Embracing vibrant materiality helps us better account for a multiplicity of causal explanations and implications of action in a network (e.g., a classroom, a writing program, a writing center). These theoretical approaches interrupt the blame game that can persist among writing stakeholders because we come to understand that composing capacities, tendencies, capabilities, and orientations are not innate or essential; instead, they are the results of unstable, intra-active tendencies. Composers, texts, objects, writing programs, computer software, classroom materials, social inequities are all in perpetual, intra-active motion, and each body or thing is shaped by the friction of its encounters with the others. Through this lens, we might reconceptualize how texts and their composers come to be by acknowledging that provisional, always-in-the-making reality. This reorientation toward writing as materiality calls us, then, to reconsider what it means to assess both our products and our processes, to imagine writing-as-object, writing-as-activity, and writing-as-experience in queerly performative ways in the assessments we develop and the validity arguments we use to make sense of those assessments. By working through the lens of materiality, *embodiment* and *lived experiences* come into sharper focus as aspects of the writing construct.

BUILDING THE QVI PYRAMINX

When we orient ourselves toward/in/around/through/beside failure, we realize that we must see writing assessment in significantly different ways. To capture those affective (in)competencies we noticed as missing in many of our current writing constructs—values like *agency, consent, dissensus, radical justice, lived experience,* and *embodiment,* all affective constructs that may exist outside the carefully composed student project—we must look for ways to unflatten our rubric charts and shift out of our linear Likert mindsets. When we began to think through how we might do that ourselves, we were struck by how often we've used and watched others use traditional rubrics with a sort of hyperattention to compartmentalizing traits. Whether that's the quality of the argument, the use of secondary sources, the organization of information, or the ability to copyedit text, we force ourselves to stay in a column on our charts or within a truncated set of numerical values. Somehow, the value of the total will be the sum of the parts. Ultimately, that sort of instrumental fidelity feels deceptive; as graders and assessors, we are constantly moving across the columns even when we tell ourselves we're not. We want something more playful, more multidimensional, something that moves and shifts and can represent the sorts of complexities we see happening in student writing processes and products.

So at the Queer Studies Conference at the University of North Carolina Asheville in spring 2018, as we were debating some of these very inconsistencies with our practices, Nikki made a joke about rubrics and how she'd like to put all these traits on a Rubik's Cube and give it a spin, see what emerged, what landed on top or on the sides, and in that moment we began to see the flattened, two-dimensional assessment frameworks in our minds fall apart, replaced by a Rubrics Cube. This cube excited us, in part because we knew we couldn't see all sides at once, just as there are always emotions, traits, elements affecting our assessments that are not consciously in view. But it also intrigued us because we know how hard it is for most of us to solve the puzzle, to get the Rubik's Cube back to its original, monochromatic sides, each color lined up perfectly and sequestered from the others. Most of us are no better at solving a Rubik's Cube puzzle than we are at solving the assessment puzzle. Later that fall, at the state English Teachers Association conference, Nikki facilitated a workshop on building Rubrics Cubes and using them to assess student work. She and the high-school teachers worked through traits and concepts and affects and experiences around writing and then toyed with how to represent those on the Rubrics Cubes they created. While the teachers were intrigued, they were not necessarily sold on the ideas; the lack of focus on particular elements or traits was too much for them to embrace in that moment. But the three of us—Nikki, Will, and Steph—kept coming back to this new playful metaphor for an assessment model that moved and shifted and called our attention to some things while others drifted out of sight. We continued to read work by queer theorists and writing assessment scholars, and we continued to find ourselves drawn to models for representing assessments that were precarious, slightly unstable: we wanted a model that itself represented what we were seeing as commonplace to writing, both the doing of it and the teaching of it. In the end, the Rubrics Cube still felt too stable, sitting there comfortably on one of its six sides.

And then Will remembered the other puzzle shapes that had been popular in his childhood, each one a riff on the then-ubiquitous Rubik's Cube. One of his favorites had been the Pyraminx puzzle, a four-sided pyramid (specifically, a tetrahedron) that also moved along multiple axis points like its more well-known cousin. In the Pyraminx we found a shape that mapped well to the four failure-oriented principles we had been working with since we started this project on queering assessments. The more we played with our new assessment toy, the more we liked imagining it turned in multiple ways, spinning at any point on any of its four vertices, perhaps threatening to topple over and expose a different side, angle, or edge to the viewer. There was both kinetic and potential energy in this shape that seemed to be missing with the cube. We loved the angles: to keep only one side in focus, the user really must work at narrowing their angle of vision, with three sides nearly always partially visible. In our experience, there's no way to separate discrete lenses or

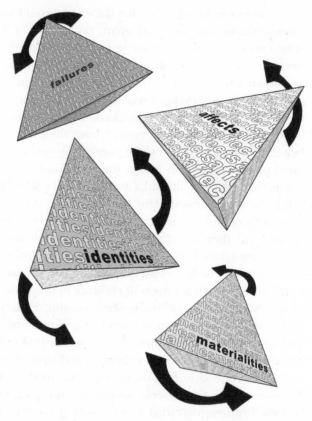

Figure 2.1. QVI
Framework as
three-dimensional
Pyraminx showing
diffractive lenses

frameworks for doing assessment; we're always working across a number
of analytical planes. But it also seemed to us that even when we were not
talking about failure as writing teachers and assessors, even when it wasn't
foremost in our minds, it was always lurking behind the scenes—and
the same was true of our other lenses (affect, identity, materiality). The
Pyraminx gave us a three-dimensional model that allowed us a visual/
metaphorical representation of the ways we were coming to engage with
assessment through QVI, and the more we've worked with it, the more
we've also realized the six edges of our assessment shape likewise map
onto the six affective additions we've made to the writing construct.

Here, we offer you our QVI Pyraminx (see figure 2.1) as an unflattened version of the QVI framework we introduced in table 1.1 and figure 1.2, and we encourage you to give it a spin in your minds as you read
through the rest of *Failing Sideways*. While we cannot provide a fully 3D
model given the particular constraints of print technology, we've created
versions to show you what it might look like if you were to approach the

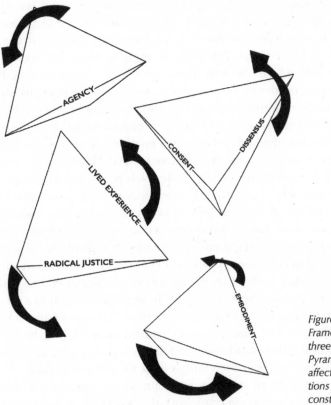

Figure 2.2. QVI Framework as three-dimensional Pyraminx showing affective value additions to the writing construct

QVI Pyraminx from different angles at different times. Each of those examples will return again at the start of chapters 3 through 6 as we demonstrate specific assessment activities and projects we developed through our work to understand the impact QVI can have on the writing construct and our writing assessments. In figure 2.2, we offer examples of the affective values the QVI Pyraminx challenges us to engage with as part of our assessment constructs. These values are examined in detail throughout this book as we look at each lens individually and the assessment projects and practices that challenged us to reimagine our writing and assessment constructs.

AIMING AT FAIRNESS AS A QUEER PRACTICE

As we work toward crafting socially just assessments through QVI, we'd be remiss if we didn't also draw out the shadow concept that permeates nearly all discussions of assessment, evaluation, and grading: fairness.

As many have noted, we tend to operate from tacit notions of fairness both in writing studies and more broadly across our culture (American Educational Research Association 2014, 49; Elliot 2016; Gere et al. 2021; Kelly-Riley and Elliot 2020). For some, a single, normed test like the SAT, ACT, or GRE is "fair" because it's the same test for every student. In this case, fairness resides in the instrument, not within the students who have different opportunities to study for the exam, hire private tutors, or attend schools that create environments conducive to the types of thinking valued on standardized tests. We might think of this as a *libertarian* notion of fairness, one that ignores societal limitations; as long as individuals are not individually or collectively prevented from taking an entrance exam by governmental intervention/legal procedures, it is up to the individual to do as well or as poorly as they can, and one individual's success or failure has no impact on another's. Similarly, an *equality* model of fairness might envision resources as distributed equally across the board so everyone gets something, even if there are some who might benefit from a little bit more and others who would do fine with less. Less, more, equal—these notions of fairness tend to fall into a zero-sum economy. As Poe (2021a) has acknowledged, "Tropes of fairness fall along a continuum from the technical (fairness as absence of bias) to the philosophical (fairness as justice). Each is deserving of our attention as our scholarship becomes increasingly alert to difference and each is needed if we are to create inclusive ways of teaching and assessing writing" (24). We need a fairness framework that works toward redistribution and equity while also engaging with a shared sense of responsibility. We hope, as you read through this book, that you begin to see the ways fairness might operate differently and differentially through a QVI framework. Because it values multiple knowledge-making practices, QVI provides openings for entertaining alternative thinking paths and for redesigning the assessments that provide for the sort of equity-focused model of fairness we should be aiming for.

To that end, Elliot (2016) has already observed that fairness involves "the identification of opportunity structures created through maximum construct representation. Constraint of the writing construct is to be tolerated only to the extent to which benefits are realized for the least advantaged." And as Kelly-Riley and Elliot (2020) also note, "Humanities scholars can continue to shape this area by imagining new ways of improving outcomes through our collective expertise about language and what it means to be human" (4). We contend that QVI can become one means for assessing maximum construct representation in a way that will cultivate more equitable learning across contexts (see also

Randall 2021; Randall et al. 2022). We can't fully attend to fairness until we engage QVI because otherwise we are merely reproducing the status quo. QVI advocates for an expanded writing construct that represents the lived, embodied experiences of writers. Our four failure-oriented practices challenge the structural thinking around fairness in writing studies and push us toward redistributed notions of fairness through an equity mindset. By interrupting the success/failure binary, we shift notions of fairness because our sense of success has shifted. Our assessments privilege the everyday, affective experiences of writing, so writers are no longer working toward a singular product. QVI encourages us to bend temporal links and redefine the multitude of paths writers can take to their products. By simply disrupting the commodity of good writing, notions of apparent fairness dissipate because there's no longer a singular gold standard to strive for. QVI calls us to work toward anticommodification by rearticulating our values and then operating more intentionally from a values-driven framework. Similarly, antireproduction and antimechanization frameworks push us toward holistic, person-centered writing instruction and writing assessments that allow for individualized notions of fairness. Such frameworks should recognize when fairness is operating primarily as a convenient myth for maintaining systems as they are. QVI permits us to challenge apparent notions of fairness by privileging alternative paths and knowledge-making opportunities.

3

FAILING TO BE SUCCESSFUL

In chapter 2, we theorize queer failure as a central tenant of queer validity inquiry and examine the four overlapping lenses through which we have come to engage writing assessment: failure, affect, identity, materiality. For our purposes here, we understand queer failure not as the kind of failure one overcomes on the pathway to success but more as a crisis moment or turning point that offers a 359-degree range of opportunities to diverge from success's narrow and well-trodden path. Because pathways to success are always already designed to facilitate the smooth progress of certain bodies (often at the expense of the laborious drag on other bodies), failure is the possession and providence of the dispossessed. Sure, dispossession is most closely associated with loss and lack, but it also has its affordances. When we are dispossessed, we are no longer held captive to/as the possession of others, whether intellectually, spiritually, physically, or emotionally. When we are dispossessed and therefore no longer captive to others' notions of success, for example, we can go in a direction that feels right to us at a particular time with particular people without a debilitating fear of failure limiting our travel.

As Halberstam (2011) reminds us, "To live is to fail, to bungle, to disappoint, and ultimately to die . . . the queer art of failure involves acceptance of the finite, the embrace of the absurd, the silly, and the hopelessly goofy" (186–87). Halberstam's words are easy to appropriate. As we have all felt, to write is to fail, to bungle, to disappoint. We get frustrated by the number of new articles and books we haven't had time to read or write. We sometimes bungle our terms and definitions and our interpretations of others' ideas and meanings as we work to figure things out. In working to meet the needs of some readers, we fail and disappoint others. The stuff that eventually makes it into a final draft is an impoverished version of the internal and external conversations that led to new ways of thinking about our topic or problem. Sometimes, we miss deadlines and disappoint ourselves, our collaborators, and our

https://doi.org/10.7330/9781646423705.c003

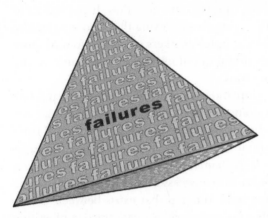

Figure 3.1. QVI Pyraminx rotated to the side labeled failures

editors. Elspeth Probyn (2005), who has explored writing as a project of abject failure, identifies shame as a natural byproduct of such repeated failure. Probyn writes, "There is a shame in being highly interested in something and unable to convey it to others, to evoke the same degree of interest in them and to convince them that it is warranted. . . . Simply put, it's the challenge of making the writing equal to the subject being written about" (72). While we might, if we're lucky, have brief moments in which we brush a gossamer thread of rhetorical success, writers are, for the most part, wrapped in the fabric of failure and shame. And writers pay differential prices for these failures.

We also argue that there is productive[1] potential in the failure-shame entanglements of writing assessment. Probyn (2005) notes that shame, particularly writing shame, can construct an ethos of responsibility: "Shame forces us to reflect continually on the implications of our writing. The insights provided by different kinds of writers will show that writing shame is a visceral reminder to be true to interest, to be honest about why or how certain things are of interest" (73). If we extend Probyn's ethics of shame through writing to the assessment of writing, we might consider shame an uneasy companion that forces us back time and again to the practice of QVI as a means of asking what we're interested in, why, and whose interests are served. It calls us to lay bare our assessment instincts, intentions, interests, and motivations and to invite others to reckon with us over our contradictions and our cognitive and social biases. It asks us to occupy the tentative, the provisional, and the precarious as we also face the absurdity of much of our common assessment practices—from translating sociocultural meaning making onto a scale to drawing broad conclusions from assessment projects limited by lack of resources such as time, funding, and attention. It permits us to redirect our assessment efforts away from proving that students, faculty, and programs have met other people's markers of success toward more profound and pedagogically useful questions about writers and writing in our classrooms and institutions.

Thus, in this chapter, we flip and spin the QVI Pyraminx to put failure on top for a while. In doing so, we invite readers to consider the possibilities that open up when writing assessment is disentangled from success. We argue that such an obsessive focus on success is driven by fear of failure and avoidance of shame, two related affective responses that limit the potential for transformative assessment practices. To demonstrate this theory, we investigate the gap that exists between theory and practice in the most ubiquitous and widespread practice of writing evaluation: portfolio assessment. Despite robust scholarship in the field of educational measurement and writing assessment that situates validity (whether it is or isn't named as such) as a central focus for justifying portfolios through both disciplinary and local arguments, uncritical uptake of these instruments persists.[2] Perfunctory use of portfolios happens, in part, because they are imbued with success as a particular gold standard of measurement. In many ways, portfolios, both traditional and electronic, have seemed to address many of the problems writing assessment researchers and teachers saw as normative in previous models. While we certainly don't blame anyone who chooses success, particularly in a larger culture that doubts and defames teachers and students, we want to illustrate in this chapter how embracing even small moments of failure and shame can open new possibilities for assessment and the expansion of our writing constructs. Through our serious play with goofy, silly, and absurdist writing assessment tools, we've discovered, often by accident, some of the ways failing sideways can foster both individual and shared agency. Thus, writing scholars and practitioners committed to assessment as social justice praxis might embrace failure as a queer tactic that can move the field away from what we already know and turn our attention to other kinds of assessment objects and stories.

WRITING PORTFOLIOS: A QUEST FOR SUCCESS

Perhaps the most familiar and widely celebrated example of success in writing assessment has been the student writing portfolio. Recently referred to as the "gold standard" of writing assessment (White, Elliott, and Peckham 2015, 104), the writing portfolio employs field-based best practices in the teaching of writing like revision over time and writer selection of assessment artifacts; similarly, it relies on instructor expertise to make value judgments about learning and achievement. As opposed to indirect writing measures or one-and-done timed writing tests, the portfolio is a cumulative representation of what student writers can produce over the course of the semester (or degree program) when they engage in a process approach to writing and use formative feedback to improve their work. Portfolio assessment values both disciplinary knowledge and local, contextual knowledge, as teachers assess students in their own writing classes. In short, portfolios work as a best practice because they serve as a material representation of broadly shared theories of writing in our field (invention, production, delivery) and the research-based practices that inform our work. Because this image of the portfolio more closely aligns with our idea of writing-construct values and practices (e.g., White, Elliot, and Peckham's [2015, 75] nomothetic construct in *Very Like a Whale*), we tend to believe portfolios can lend themselves to strong validity arguments. Likewise, at the programmatic level, assessment committees are typically composed of classroom teachers who have been tapped to review portfolio samples and make recommendations regarding any changes to current programmatic practices. To a large extent, then, writing portfolios and portfolio-based assessment paradigms often value the key stakeholders who make up this assessment scene.

There's little doubt, therefore, that the widespread use of writing portfolios in our field has represented a substantial improvement over on-demand writing samples and indirect testing of writing through multiple-choice exams. Since course-based portfolios were first adopted for large-scale use at Washington State University (Haswell and Wyche-Smith 1994), however, we may have become somewhat complacent in how we have pursued their implementation across writing programs by citing precedent as a rationale for use in other similar-but-different writing and learning contexts across institutions. In our own experiences, it seems that once teachers have decided a practice or activity works, almost regardless of context, it's difficult to dislodge that practice from the curriculum (North 1987). We too easily brush aside Kathleen Blake Yancey's (1999) assertion that what we mean by portfolio assessment is "messy" because portfolios "are composed of multiple kinds of texts, and different students compose quite different portfolios, even in the same setting and for the same purpose" (493). Ricky Lam (2020) posits that the practice of using portfolios in the classroom to teach and assess writing can be muddled because on-the-ground practitioners often lack knowledge of assessment paradigms and practices. For many teachers,

Lam argues, there are no clear distinctions between a working portfolio, a showcase portfolio, and an assessment portfolio, which leads to student confusion, general misunderstanding about the pedagogical purpose of portfolios, and teacher dissatisfaction with portfolios as integrated teaching and assessment practice (171).

This muddled and messy landscape of portfolio use, however, has provided teacher-scholars the opportunity to ask the key question of *how* portfolios should be read and scored. While the conversations about *how* were slow to get started, as Jeff Perry (2014) demonstrates, in the last decade, forums like the *International Journal of ePortfolio* have provided space for practitioners across K–higher education contexts to wrestle with the question of *how*. From articles that articulate empirical scoring frameworks to account for the needs of minoritized students (Kelly-Riley, Elliot, and Rudniy 2016) to the need for robust teacher training centered on portfolio keeping as a deep linking of pedagogy and assessment (Torre 2019) to examinations of the ethical concerns raised when taking portfolios from print to digital delivery systems (Clark 2019; Wilson et al. 2018), teacher-scholars in the field of writing studies and beyond are addressing key concerns related to portfolio use. More recently, Mary Ann Dellinger and D. Alexis Hart's (2020) collection explores the evolution of writing portfolios in theory and practice. Contributors to the collection detail experimental approaches to scoring (Carpenter and Labissiere 2020) and discuss methods to scale data comparisons across institutions (Day 2020), among other concerns. What's clear in the current body of knowledge is how much and how quickly scholarship about writing assessment has advanced; however, to us, these locally centered yet aspirationally interinstitutional practices feel quite extraordinary. Our own experiences across multiple institutions in the past two decades have tracked more closely with portfolio uptake based on lore, and we have certainly seen the sedimentation of portfolio practices at the different institutions where we've taught.

What we encounter most commonly in the field is the notion that *if it worked over there at that institution we aspire to be more like, then certainly it will work over here at our own.* In addition, we tend to operate under the unexamined assumption that portfolios naturally scale up and maintain the same level of quality we saw in classroom/individual student assessments. Even if we're working in a traditional success-focused framework, it is important to understand that success does not truly scale. Beyond the problem of success for some necessitating failure for others (Duggan 2002; Halberstam 2011), it's important to remember that the hyperlocal contexts that created success for particular portfolios do not travel across contexts easily, if at all. When we break the relational bonds that created success in those particular places with those particular people, tools, and shared experiences, we have dislodged from the portfolio itself the very things that established success in the first place. Our belief that success moves seamlessly across contexts says far more about our disciplinary needs to control our classrooms and programs in working conditions complicated by widely variant teacher preparation and student experiences than it does about whether writing portfolios are actually a best practice across all contexts. Through such critical inattention to localized validity arguments, we have perhaps created a framework for writing assessment that cloaks itself in an immutable and immovable gold standard of success.

For example, when Will and his colleagues at ECU worked on the assessments for their writing-focused Quality Enhancement Plan (QEP) as part of regional reaccreditation (Sharer et al. 2016), they often found themselves hemmed in by the notions of good writing coded in the portfolio-assessment instrument. Despite their best efforts to collaboratively create a campuswide shared rubric for faculty in upper-level writing-intensive courses, when they started doing assessments across departments and programs, they typically had to push the department assessors to reframe and rethink their intuitive responses to the traits in the rubric so as to fit them into campus outcomes. In this context, they could not really modify the rubric itself, as that instrument had been created by committee, and their accrediting body expected them to assess student work based on that established rubric. Instead, Will and his writing colleagues, along with the assessors, found themselves each summer during focused assessment meetings having to regularly reinterpret the rubric by changing how it was used across contexts, so the end result was not really normed or reliable across contexts in ways assessment experts might understand the concepts. Despite their efforts to norm in ways Will and his writing colleagues had been trained to do in graduate school, despite their sense that they needed to do this, their gut instinct was that new genres and writing contexts (disciplines), as well as the interpretive contributions of different assessors working with the instrument, meant they needed to make adjustments along the way. Chris M. Anson, Deanna P. Dannels, Pamela Flash, and Amy L. Housley Gaffney (2012) demonstrate that similar problems emerge when assessors attempt to use generic assessment tools and technologies that cannot speak directly to the key elements and contexts of a writing/ assessment scene. So, for example, during the first summer of their QEP assessment at ECU, it became clear that Outcome One ("Use writing to investigate complex, relevant topics and address significant questions through engagement with and effective use of credible sources") was really two outcomes, one that involved topic complexity and appropriateness given disciplinary standards and another that involved source use, which varies dramatically across disciplines. Will and his colleagues divided Outcome One into two parts (1.a and 1.b) because doing so met the expectation of the outcome but allowed faculty assessors to be more granular in a way they felt important if they were to value student work in the contexts in which it was created. However, in terms of what counts as a "credible source" or even as a source at all (e.g., in writing mathematical proofs, is a formula a source since the student writer did not create it?), the faculty assessment groups negotiated that on an ad hoc basis. Ultimately, the rubric remained unchanged in any substantive way, and most of the discussions were about how to bend new genres, new information, or new writing practices they saw to fit the rubric created in advance of seeing or knowing the work that would be assessed. Despite frequent disagreements and conversations, this assessment scene tended to privilege loyalty and fidelity to the assessment technologies themselves and to a retrofitted understanding of the teaching and learning environments. One result has been that programs that participated in the assessments have gone back to their units and narrowed their understanding of what counts as writing intensive/writing across the curriculum. In this context, the assessment tail has begun to wag the dog of disciplinary writing. The end result has been greater standardization of writing instruction across disparate contexts rather than a more circular and reflective engagement with assessments and student writing that feeds back into discussions with all stakeholders and impacts the daily learning and teaching experiences of students and faculty. These are the practices some of our first writing assessment scholars (White 1985) had hoped to avoid in moving away from multiple-choice testing toward the direct assessment of writing, but because assessment ecologies like these always rely on human actors and shifting contexts, it can be far too easy for us to fall back on practices that tarnish even the gold standards we've worked to create.

SUCCESS: BUT AT WHAT COST?

In Will's example, we begin to see how assessment objects are imbued with agency as they "act back" on the pedagogical practices of teachers across the disciplines. Instead of their experiences with disciplinary writing and writers across the disciplines acting on the rubric, the rubric served as an immutable incarnation of a priori values of good writing that had to be worked around or accommodated by shifting the values of assessors in different contexts. The instrument limited participants' agency and ability to articulate countervalues as part of the assessment. It also throttled sideways movement and forestalled the emergence of transdisciplinary writing constructs. This phenomenon is not new. In fact, writing portfolios as assessment technologies have, from their inception, been limited by a persistent ideological bent toward behaviorism (Lam 2020), top-down management and mandates, and values of meritocracy involving individual competition, ranking, and sorting. To further illustrate the costs of success in portfolio assessment, we recount one of the worst-case scenarios available in writing assessment portfolio literature, the Kentucky K–12 writing portfolio initiative (Callahan 1997, 1999; Scott 2005). While we are, in empirical work, often directed away from the outliers and the outdated, QVI helps us make a case for examining both past-as-present and the spectacle of a worst-case scenario. It is a provocation to break normative notions of linear time, as well as to give serious consideration to the outlier, the quirky, and the kink in the otherwise smooth flow of a larger system. Where empiricism might favor the new as progress over the old, or even just a model of development that asks us to value the most recent examples rather than past failures, we believe it important to pay attention to how things fail, when and where they break, and why they malfunction, as well as to who gets to break them and who gets broken along the way. Through such a failure-seeking lens, we can catch a sideways, diffractive glimpse of success, one that may not show its most attractive side. Thus, we draw on Callahan's and Scott's now-dated research to trace out the implications of practicing portfolio assessments inside neoliberal frameworks and to demonstrate how fear of failure and shame compromises the integrity of assessments and those who are most affected by them.[3]

As many readers may remember, in the early 1990s, the state of Kentucky adopted a statewide portfolio model to replace standardized tests in fourth, fifth, eighth, and twelfth grades. Much like other accountability assessments, the Kentucky Education Reform Act included financial benefits for teachers and schools with successful scores. The Kentucky Department of Education (KDE) had hoped portfolio assessment would reflect learning and critical thinking not captured in multiple-choice tests. Additionally, the KDE believed portfolio assessment would improve teaching through a reverse approach. Rather than provide teachers with writing theory and pedagogy, the board of education believed curriculum would shift because teachers would teach to the test, and "teaching to the test is a good thing if the test is a good one" (Callahan 1997, 300). The reverse approach worked, though not in the ways the KDE had hoped. As Callahan reflects, English teachers' jobs now rested on how well students did with writing, a subject not then taught explicitly in classrooms because it hadn't previously been assessed. With only a year to implement the new portfolio system, Kentucky teachers were left scrambling (to learn how) to teach writing. In their portfolios, twelfth-grade students were required to include a table of contents, one personal narrative, one short story, one poem or script, three pieces of writing that achieved at least one purpose from a list,[4] and a letter to the reviewer (329). Students could include writing from any subject, but the portfolio required that at least two pieces of writing had to come from subjects other than English language arts contexts. Callahan (1997) urged writing studies to avoid making portfolio assessment into another "test [not] worth taking" (295). The high-stakes nature of the portfolio assessment in Kentucky, she found, forced teachers to co-opt students' texts, conscripting their form and engaging in prolific line editing so students might produce beautiful (understood as error-free) writing in the eyes of the teachers.

Callahan (1999) later found that to promote successful scores, teachers also designed irrelevant and sometimes downright unethical writing practices in an attempt to meet the demands of success coded into the writing-portfolio assessment rubric. Students lied in their table of contents about what courses their pieces were written in, and teachers knowingly accepted the dishonesty. According to Callahan (1999), rather than being examples of students' best writing, "the portfolios often become collaboratively created pieces of fiction, a tacit agreement between teachers and students that assessment requirements take precedence over personal interests and standards" (35–36). Callahan argued that classroom teachers and program directors should pursue options for students and teachers to individualize portfolio structures and artifacts. She also advocated for teachers and program administrators to use open portfolios so students' work might be accessible to them and others beyond the course of a semester or for their enrollment at a particular institution. Her argument points to the need to consider whose interests are served by assessment. Clearly, the institution or program needs assessment data in order to argue it is fulfilling its promise to deliver effective instruction. We don't often consider, however, the value and relevance of assessment for teachers and students. Preparing a portfolio is a labor-intensive process for these stakeholders, and we should ask how this work is valued for those who invest the time, effort, and expertise in preparing these assessment artifacts. While writing portfolios in particular contexts may represent a best possible practice, when students churn out pages and pages of words for assessment projects that have not been locally validated, we run the risk of enacting yet another "canned" assessment instrument that hides a host of bogus practices or conflicting assumptions about writing.

Similarly, in his investigation of the impacts of writing portfolios on the teaching and learning contexts in secondary schools in Kentucky, Tony Scott (2005) revealed the spurious nature of students' self-assessments (i.e., reflections/self-analyses) in their portfolio cover letters. In order to understand how large-scale assessments influence pedagogy, Scott analyzed observational data, textual portfolio samples, and transcripts from interviews with eleven twelfth-grade students, three teachers, and two administrators who had participated in the Kentucky statewide portfolio assessment. Through an analysis of fifty-six students' reflective cover letters, Scott revealed how student writers tended to adopt a generic "reflective" stance geared toward earning a high portfolio score rather than an individual, self-assessment stance focused on learning. For students, the reflective letter became a bureaucratic exercise. They took their instructions from holistic rubrics and state-generated models, performing for an audience of assessors instead of using the reflective letter as an authentic moment for reflecting on their writing and learning. While practitioner wisdom has been that students use their portfolio cover letters to provide a meaningful self-analysis of their writing processes and products, Scott's investigation of the statements made in students' reflective portfolio cover letters demonstrates how students can be coerced into adopting false subject positions that reproduce the values of the institution rather than putting those values in dialogue with their own writerly aims, purposes, and goals for their work. Success, then, becomes attainable primarily through the individual's reproduction of tightly circumscribed institutional discourses, values, and ideologies.

Much like the high-school students Scott (2005) interviewed, college writers know they are engaged in a disingenuous performance, a game in which they pretend to care about the things their teachers or institutions care about in hopes of getting through the system. As teacher-scholars who have been thoroughly disciplined in/by writing studies, we have often invested in the notions of success forwarded by our field, such as the Council of Writing Program Administrators (CWPA) Outcomes Statement for First-Year Composition and the habits of mind that are part of the *Framework for Success in Postsecondary*

Writing, collaboratively written by the CWPA, the National Council of Teachers of English, and the National Writing Project (2011). Teachers and students, however, aren't necessarily invested in these same notions of success; thus, having students measure their proximity to disciplinary values and norms through self-assessment may mean little to them.[5] While teachers create detailed and nuanced prompts for self-assessment, and while students take the time to carefully answer those prompts, a good number of students don't find value in the exercise. We offer carrots and sticks to promote metacognition, but these rewards and punishments do little to overcome the affective orientations that drive writing behaviors. In this context, it is no wonder many instructors and students have deemed self-assessment a failed project. If students don't place personal value on disciplinary outcomes or even value the end products they create, a phenomenon Stephanie's dissertation explores in significant detail (West-Puckett 2017), there's no real motivation to change writing-related behaviors or to work harder to produce texts that embody other people's notions of good writing. To address some of these issues and concerns with self-assessment, Thomas L. Hilgers, Edna L. Hussey, and Monica Stitt-Bergh (2000) outline a means of assessing self-assessment in writing classrooms and programs. They argue that effective self-assessment must be systematic, frequent, and integrated into students' writing processes. They note the importance of establishing community-based norms and expectations within a classroom that align with national outcomes. They discuss the importance of breaking down the large task of self-assessment into smaller chunks and argue reflection must be paired with increased awareness of strategies available to intervene in unwanted or ineffective writing behaviors. Finally, they remind us that student writers need training and practice in developing their capacity for self-assessment as a means of modifying their writing behaviors (10).

While these approaches to assessing self-assessment may promote a slightly different kind of success than we might be used to in FYC, they also continue to construct success in narrow and normative ways. Successful self-assessors must be hyperaware of their practices and focused on writing self-regulation. They must continually work to modify their behaviors to adopt the habits of mind and body the field has identified as successful. *What strategies did you use to build* logos, ethos, pathos? *Be specific and describe their effect on your audience. How did you show flexibility, openness, and responsibility in your writing processes?* Students report that this kind of hypervigilance kills the joy of writing, as they can never express momentary satisfaction in their work when self-assessment demands they participate in the constant self-critique driven by an accountability culture that demands continual improvement. *If given more time, what would you do to improve this draft?* In this paradigm, students are burdened not only with meeting disciplinary expectations but also with arguing they have, in fact, met them, explaining when, why, and how they have excelled or fallen short. This is an issue of student-assessment labor, one that ought to be accounted for in assessment design and validity argumentation (Carillo 2021; Spidell and Thelin 2006). Students must also show how they've internalized disciplinary values and how they've managed their inappropriate or ineffective writing behaviors to better embody disciplinary values and practices. *What are the weaknesses of this draft, and how have you worked to improve them?* This kind of self-assessment is a one-way street where disciplinarity acts on individual bodies, but those bodies have no real way to act back on the discipline. Considering the homogeneous makeup of the professional organizations who define success in postsecondary contexts, we can't help but ask, *Whose habits? Whose bodies? Whose behaviors? Whose success? What does it mean to ask an ever-diversifying student body to assimilate, shape up, or straighten out their writing bodies and their written texts?*

SHAME SPIRAL? PRIDE PARADE? BOTH/AND?

These coercive approaches to assessment act on the bodies of students and teachers whose impulses, habits, and behaviors don't align with hegemonic notions of what it means to be a successful writer. Writers and writing teachers internalize repeated failure, while writing and writing assessment become shrouded in shame and stigma. In *The Trouble with Normal: Sex, Politics, and the Ethics of Queer Life*, Michael Warner (1999) argues that stigmaphobia is an enabler of the status quo. In other words, a fear of being socially stigmatized or aligned with stigmatized values/practices (stigmaphobia) perpetuates normativity. In the Kentucky portfolio case, stigmaphobia perpetuated the normative notions of successful writing that were codified in the KDE board of education's portfolio rubric, and it kept students and teachers tied to writing processes, products, and assessment technologies that served other people's interests. While failure has been part and parcel of writing studies and writing assessment since first-year composition was born of failure at Harvard 150 years ago, we continue to clamber for success. Too often such clambering results in assessment practices that are fail-proof as we focus on low-hanging fruit and scrape data to indicate we've met a particularly banal outcome.

While it's difficult to know exactly what punishments might have existed for individual teachers and students in the Kentucky public schools were they marked with the stigma of failure—or in our own programs, as writing is overwhelmingly taught by contingent faculty—we wonder what might happen if teachers and students embrace stigmaphilia instead? Building on Warner's work, Margaret Morrison (2015) argues that stigmaphiles actively acknowledge what marks them as different from and counter to subject positions tied to dominant cultural ideologies. Morrison posits that stigmaphilia can creatively expand our ways of knowing, doing, and being in the world "by making a 'space' (not a fixed one) for identity, and by motivating cognition (for creative tasks)" (18). The assessment killjoy revels in stigmaphilia. Historically, writing assessment has lacked discourses for articulating those differences and countering value hegemony in the writing construct. QVI, however, provides us with options. It permits us to use (and investigate the use/s of) other kinds of assessment objects and protocols that move us laterally, outside the hierarchical success/failure binary. Moreover, it enables us to imagine alternative assessment discourses and values. If we are to continue fleshing these out, however, writers, writing teachers, and writing program administrators must take up more space than the instruments do in writing assessment contexts. We must, as Nancy Welch (2008) argues, "make and take space" for moving sideways, building lateral relationships and discourses of resistance. In addition, there must be room to reverse course by subverting hegemonic values in service of developing more culturally relevant, emplaced, and didactic relationships with student writers. In other words, writing assessment stigmaphilia can generate an ethic of loyalty that flows sideways and downward instead of only upward toward existing loci of power.

As J. Elizabeth Clark (2019) notes, key questions about the messy practice of how to design and assess writing at the classroom, program, and institutional levels are as relevant today as they have been since the explosion of portfolio-based assessment in the 1990s. Invoking John Ittelson, Clark calls these perpetual concerns "moving targets" (62), implying we must be willing to continually move with and reorient our practices. Furthermore, the current realities of technological singularity, educational policy and practice in the "age of austerity" (Welch and Scott 2016), and fluctuating student engagement during times when attention is drained through concurrent social, biological, environmental, and political crises all call us to move *differently*. Movement, particularly transgression, is a central topos in queer theory/rhetoric. As we note in chapter 2 and again in the introduction to this chapter,

queer movements are deviant; deviation enables queer assessment subjectivities. Queer assessment killjoys stray from well-worn pathways that
iteratively move toward success; they risk the attainment of material and
social rewards in order to pursue different trajectories and horizons. As
we demonstrate in the following examples, they move across borders
and outside normative lanes in pursuit of other kinds of spaces and
relations. Shame is a faithful traveling companion to those who search
together for failure. Without it, however, we wouldn't know the flip side
of shame, which is pride. It is through the entanglements of shame and
pride that we can move under the banner of the killjoy in queer assessment parades.

QUEERING PROGRAMMATIC ASSESSMENTS: SEARCHING TOGETHER FOR FAILURE

When the campuswide SACSCOC (Southern Association of Colleges
and Schools Commission on Colleges) reaccreditation project Write
Where You Belong ended at East Carolina University in 2018, Will
had spent five summers with some smart and engaging colleagues, all
of them involved in programmatic writing assessments the university
could use to determine what impact, if any, the five-year writing-focused
Quality Enhancement Project (QEP) had had on students' writing.
Since the financial resources that would support these ongoing summer
assessments were likely to end, Will and Nikki in their roles as University
Writing Program and University Writing Center directors, respectively,
began to ask what sorts of assessment projects they might initiate.
Despite their initial desire at the start of the QEP to assess students
using a digital portfolio, troubles with technology and access had meant
they were unable to assess whole portfolios and instead had focused on
individual writing projects grouped by department/discipline. In that
assessment, faculty from a discipline were paired with faculty from an
epistemologically or methodologically adjacent discipline to read papers
from courses in those disciplines; a third reader was used when there
was significant disagreement on scores.[6] All in all, that assessment project represented a fairly traditional product-based assessment in which
individual student papers were rated on five outcomes.[7]

After 2018, when they were out from under the pressure to meet their
institutionally approved assessment goals, Will and Nikki decided ten-
tatively to explore an assessment that would involve reading individual
students' work across four or more writing-intensive courses; in short,
they wondered, What if assessors read each student's full University

Writing Portfolio and looked at what their writing did across their four (or more) years at the university? While they recognized the University Writing Portfolio was not necessarily the gold standard writing studies has prized, it still seemed to offer a more complete picture of writing development for each student than the previous product-oriented assessment. As expected, this assessment project offered new and intriguing experiences, but what really emerged in the process was an assessment of failure on the part of the faculty and the broader writing program, rather than any meaningful analysis of how student writing changes over time. Here, we want to unpack that experience and explore how Will and Nikki designed a failure-oriented assessment that still provided meaningful assessment data at the programmatic level.

In terms of design, Will and Nikki organized the summer assessment around four programs whose faculty had participated significantly in writing initiatives throughout the QEP: (1) theater and dance, (2) criminal justice, (3) music, and (4) health education and promotion. They assumed these faculty wouldn't be starting on page one, so to speak, but would know a good deal about the various changes the QEP had brought to ECU's writing culture, as they themselves had been part of creating and implementing those changes. Among the faculty from these programs were those who had served on the campus writing-across-the-curriculum committee, those who had served as writing liaisons for their departments (meeting twice per semester as a group and sharing ideas about effective writing instruction there and with their home departments), and those who had been part of the annual WAC Academy professional-development seminar. Several had also participated as assessors during the previous summer assessments. In order to create cross-level interaction, Will and Nikki also recruited four faculty who were teaching the two writing-foundations courses at the university: English 1100, which introduces students to the expectations of college writing, and English 2201, which introduces students to various discipline-specific genres of writing and research and serves as a bridge course between English 1100 and writing-intensive courses in the various disciplines.

During May and June of 2019, each faculty team was made up of two instructors from each of the disciplines included in the assessment and one writing-foundations instructor. Each team of three assessors had around ten completed portfolios to review and to assess based on the five University Writing Outcomes. Will and Nikki asked them to use the outcomes the campus had established in 2013 and, based on what they would read, to create at least one discipline-specific writing outcome that captured something about writing in the discipline that might not be easily or obviously assessed using the generic campus outcomes. In short, *Where does the common rubric fail to capture something about writing specific to your discipline, and how might we capture at least one of those specific things? Where does instrumentality break down, and what might break through when we begin with this assumption of failure as part of the assessment design?* While the initial framing of this assessment suggested the groups would be assessing student performance, what became clear to Will and Nikki from the start—and eventually became clear to the assessment teams as they worked—was that the real learning experience would be their shared exploration of all the spaces their work as teachers and our campuswide writing programs were failing to capture student learning and experiences with writing.

The major programmatic failure became obvious rather quickly. Despite some strong efforts on the part of writing studies faculty on campus, the faculty in this assessment group realized they had very little idea of what actually went on in writing courses throughout the curriculum. The faculty teaching writing-foundations courses rarely if ever had occasion to meet with and discuss writing with faculty in other departments and programs, and faculty across campus had only vague ideas about what happened in writing-foundations courses to prepare students for their upper-level writing-intensive classes—and all of this despite real effort on the part of campus WPAs to make sure faculty were aware of the vertical curricular vision we had sketched out and enacted in the QEP. Much of the time spent assessing student work was also spent discussing in small groups what they were seeing, what they didn't know was happening in writing-foundations or upper-level courses, and how surprised they were to see so many writing concepts and assignments overlapping and covering the same ground rather than building on each other to provide students with more scaffolded learning and writing experiences.

As an example, the team from the School of Theater and Dance noted again and again how many of their 3000- and 4000-level writing-intensive course assignments seemed to repeat writing activities already assigned in writing-foundations courses. When the FYC teacher assigned to their group asked why they thought that repetition was there, the theater faculty could easily name the cause: because students struggled with more advanced or discipline-specific assignments. This perceived deficit based on what faculty had seen when they assigned work led them to believe the students were missing some of those foundational writing abilities; consequently, they quite naturally felt they had to go

back and reteach those elements. In many ways, the "leveling" of institutions encourages this sort of developmental mindset. When we see
students struggling to complete assignments, it can be hard to think
beyond the idea that, well, students must not have been exposed to
this type of writing instruction before now. Realizing students in their
upper-level classes had very likely worked on these writing practices
in foundations courses led the three-person team to ask the more
pertinent question: Why might students be struggling to transfer skills
and experiences from writing foundations into upper-division theater
courses? In a space of failure, the faculty moved sideways, asking new
questions that approached the problem from different epistemological
and ontological bases. As a result, the theater professors began to make
plans for what sorts of assignments they would do differently to build on
previous writing experiences; they discussed ways to include backward-
reaching transfer discourse in their assignments (e.g., "In English 2201,
you worked on X; this project asks you to use those skills to do Y"); and
they explored options for how to respond when students did not meet
expectations on the first attempt.

Two other moments of failure centered on the assessment rubric
itself and the terms we use for talking about writing. Most of these faculty were still relatively new to the idea of large-scale writing assessment
(as opposed to only grading their own students' papers), and they were
surprised by how difficult it was to operationalize a rubric they had had
little or no input in creating. Regardless, there were clear differences
between how the writing-foundations faculty interpreted the shared
rubric and how faculty in the various programs understood the outcomes and concepts represented in the rubric. While the work of norming is meant to correct for those variations, Will and Nikki's goal was to
amplify them instead, not to step in and stop dissensus and disagreement but to let those experiences and discussions lead to alternative
understandings, more diffractive interpretations of both the outcomes
and how they were being ranked in the forced-choice 1–4 rubric we had
asked them to use for this new assessment initiative. Having disrupted
for themselves the tyranny of normativity, Will and Nikki wondered what
this sort of chaos might lead to with a diverse group of faculty trained
neither in writing assessment nor queer theory. The result was that they
were able to flip assessment on its head for a bit, and by doing so, faculty
also found space to unpack their assumptions about writing and assessment. Rather than wrap up their readings of student portfolios with neat
bows and ribbons, the faculty ended the weeklong assessment workshop
with more questions than answers. But, as we note above, they also had

some thoughtful ideas about what they might do differently when they taught their future writing-foundations/writing-intensive courses. Will and Nikki's plan to follow up on those conversations has been stalled for the moment because of the COVID-19 pandemic.

What did not happen, however, was any sort of traditional assessment report. Neither the faculty nor the program directors closed any particular loops, but they did discover some meaningful threads that needed to be pulled on and undone. Rather than imagine this scene of programmatic assessment as one that came to clear conclusions and next steps, the assessors returned to their classrooms with more information about writing, more awareness of how writing functioned around campus in different contexts, and better understanding of the complexities inherent in our often similar-and-different writing constructs. The report Will and Nikki prepared could not flatten that assessment into quickly scannable charts, tables, or metrics, but as a diffractive assessment scene, as a space that privileged failure over acceptable visions of success, what emerged was a diverse and fluid set of understandings whose trajectories will be difficult to trace. There's no doubt they will feed back into classrooms, and had ECU not shut down for the pandemic like other schools, there's no telling what opportunities for collaboration and connection might have occurred in the year following that summer assessment workshop. At the moment, those futures are utopic, filled with potential and opportunity, but because the assessment moved laterally and not only allowed for but also sought out sideways fissures and ruptures, we have a diffuse set of paths to follow up on.

Will and Nikki risked failure and shame in this assessment project, and they also asked faculty from different disciplines to take similar risks. For Will and Nikki, to suggest the University Writing Outcomes they and faculty had invested time and financial resources into operationalizing might be flawed—that was risky. Such a move turned away from success to imagine the things we get wrong, are bound to get wrong, in any human project of making knowledge. Will and Nikki also risked their credibility with the institutional assessment office, as their decision to deviate from past assessment frameworks risked demonstrating their assessments might have been bogus or unfounded. More significantly, the faculty assessors risked a lot around shame and failure themselves. We do not often talk about what it means for writing studies professionals to ask faculty from other disciplines to participate in writing assessment, for them to risk that others in the room might discover they are not doing a very good job of helping their majors learn to write effectively. Such a context asks faculty repeatedly to risk shame when they are already anxious about whether or not they know enough to teach students how to write. Or perhaps they risk shame if they discover their colleagues are doing more interesting or more impressive or more academically rigorous work in their courses than the assessors are in their own. More specifically that summer, faculty outside writing studies struggled to imagine that "new outcome" even after reading more than forty student essays. At times, they acknowledged feeling inadequate or incompetent because they couldn't think of one. The outcomes we had already framed the writing construct for them; they hadn't really seen a reason to challenge what "the writing people" said was important. Shame and a fear of failure can keep us all turned toward a premade rubric or assessment framework as a way to deal with our anxieties around writing and teaching. However, strategically forgetting the rubric, turning away from those cookie-cutter constructs, may allow for a host of sideways movements and the development of new relational responsibilities for each other, for students, and for writing, teaching, and learning. Risking shame and failure can become a way of developing shared agency, of understanding together that we can do things with writing and learning that we've not done before, and it may open us up to the frightening possibility of doing these things with students as well.

QVI can prompt self-assessments that pursue failure as a span of open-ended, lateral possibilities. In *The Queer Art of Failure*, Halberstam (2011) argues that queer lives have already been marked by failure, as they deviate from the normative lines of desire whose success is measured by hetero coupling, marriage, and reproduction. Dominant narratives of heteronormativity mark success as the attainment of these objects, and nostalgic rememberings hook past to present and future as individuals equate the acquisition of those normative objects with success. To break these futuristic lines is to create a queer disruption of time in which other possibilities—ways of knowing, being, doing, and relating—are available to us. To illustrate the affordances of strategic forgetting as an antinormative failure practice, Halberstam (2011) follows the figure of Dory in the Disney animated film *Finding Nemo*. Dory, a Pacific blue tang fish with short-term memory loss (voiced by Ellen DeGeneres), shows us how in forgetting the "quest," the object of heteronormative desire, we can make new objects or orientations possible:

> Dory, for whom the most recent experience is always a distant shadow, a name on the tip of her tongue, recalls events not as a continuous narrative learning from a past to a present; rather she experiences memory only in flashes and fragments. . . . Dory represents a queer and fluid form of knowing, that operates independently of coherence

or linear narrative progression. By some standards she might be read as stupid or unknowing, foolish or silly, but ultimately her silliness leads her to new and different forms of relation and action. . . . In each scenario a certain kind of absence—the absence of memory or the absence of wisdom—leads to a new form of knowing. (54)

Halberstam's analysis of *Finding Nemo*, along with other popular-culture texts such as the 1994 film *Dumb and Dumber*, demonstrates the subversive power of queer narratives in everyday contexts. These queer narrative lines, similar to Will and Nikki's story of failed portfolio assessment in WAC contexts, are operating in, around, behind, beneath, and on top of the dominant narratives of assessment in our field; however, we often ignore them because we become caught up in linear measurements of success and failure. What might happen if we were, like Dory, to forget the success/failure binary as a frame for assessment altogether? This is not to say we should always necessarily ignore failure's impacts on students, teachers, and programs; instead, we argue momentary, strategic forgetting can help us break the temporal links of past-present-future that keep us yoked to singular models or paths of writing assessment.

STUPID, UNKNOWING, FOOLISH: PLAYING WITH SILLY WRITER'S MEMOS

When she began as WPA at the University of Rhode Island, Stephanie entered a robust first-year writing curriculum that valued the sort of rich, discipline-framed assessment practice student portfolios provide. Not long into her first year, however, she and her colleagues began noticing something about the ways their portfolio practices were having an unexpected effect on stakeholders: both students and instructors were experiencing assessment fatigue. Not only had the program asked students to reflect on each stage of their projects through small postwrites adapted from Nedra Reynolds and Elizabeth Davis's (2013) *Portfolio Keeping: A Guide for Students*, but faculty also required project reflections and a comprehensive end-of-course reflection. Students, much like those in Scott's (2005) Kentucky portfolio survey, reported these self-assessments felt like vacuous exercises in rephrasing the question and guessing what the professor wanted to hear. *What useful feedback did you receive in your peer review? How did you integrate that feedback? My peer reviewer was really helpful and helped me write a better final draft. The helpful feedback was so helpful I integrated all of it into the final draft, and it helped me to write a more effective and helpful draft for my audience.*

While these starter questions can be helpful in engaging students in meaningful reflection if taken seriously by both faculty and students, they are also frustrating when they limit the writing construct to focus primarily on linear success narratives. As such, they ask students to engage in an endless loop of reproductive futurism, one that maintains a progressive teleology that steers ever away from failure. They assume productivity and success, and when we ask students to consider less effective parts of their writing, the clear focus of that "failure" should be on how they turned it around or could turn it around with more time, all to straighten them up and keep them focused on one primary goal. By forcing practices of metacognition into a success framework, we were asking students to envision a future writerly self that could transfer what they have done in the current learning context to some imagined future context. While we recognize the research on metacognition and transfer has shown a host of ways for learning to move across various contexts (Anson and Moore 2016; Clark and Huber 2018; Moore and Bass 2017; Nowacek 2011; Yancey, Robertson, and Taczak 2014; Wardle 2007, 2012), we also wonder why we focus so much on the future, often at the expense of the present. As writing teachers who have asked students to reflect on moments of conflict, frustration, anxiety, and failure in their writing processes over the years, we also know those moments seem to be some of the richest in terms of their development of agency as writers. These are the spaces where the students embody the bidirectional comment from the Scarecrow in *The Wizard of Oz*: some folks really do "go both ways." Rather than asking students constantly to imagine a present moment of success as evidence of future success, what if we asked them to unpack moments of failure, disruption, anxiety, confusion, frustration? What if we asked students not merely to *perform* learning, by which we mean framing current work in futural terms of how it will be successful and has become successful, but to engage with the complexities of their learning in ways that might help us get out of the bind Scott (2005) discovered in his reading of the Kentucky state portfolio reflections?

With that goal in mind, Stephanie and her colleagues at URI decided to nix the systematic postwrites and instead implement a series of low-stakes self-assessment activities meant to provide quick and dirty data that could inform instructors about students' writing experiences and orientations, as well as about ways to better meet students' needs. These non-normative assessment protocols refuse the success/failure binary and focus instead on the multitude of feelings, activities, processes, behaviors, and habits elided or erased when we ask students to assess themselves only in terms of their proximity to social and disciplinary norms and outcomes. Instead of naming and framing success (or lack thereof), these writing memos can capture something of the false starts, dead ends, motivations, and feelings that permeate our composing processes. Thus, in the next few pages, we offer five different examples of alternative self-assessment activities, four of which include visual opportunities for multimodal assessment practice, particularly the combination of text and image. We think our readers can easily grasp the first two activities, so we share those prompts briefly and without student examples, in part because Stephanie used them back in 2019 and tracking down students to secure permissions to share their work has been particularly difficult during the COVID-19 pandemic. However, we unpack at length the last three examples and include writers' self-reflections generated in response to those prompts. The self-assessment activities are (1) Writing Feelings, (2) From Individual to Systematic Critique in 10 Minutes, (3) Writing and Moving Differently, (4) Ouroboros, or a Perpetual Writing Game of Snakes and Ladders, and (5) Writing-Process Mandalas.

1. Writing Feelings

In example 1, Writing Feelings, students are asked to choose the emoji they think represents where they are now in relation to a few self-assessment sentence prompts. While inquiry into the practices of using emoticons in professional contexts is not new (Krohn 2004), more recent research has investigated the use of nonverbal and paralinguistic markers and messages in assessment contexts (Dunlap et al. 2016; West-Puckett 2016; Grieve, Moffitt, and Padgett 2019). Robyn Moffitt, Christine Padgett, and Rachel Grieve (2020) found that, with undergraduate students, the teacher's use of emojis in written feedback created more accessible and sociable assessment contexts. Furthermore, it did so without compromising teacher credibility. Maintaining a professional ethos is a valid concern for those who are new to writing classrooms and/or practicing with few institutional protections, so this finding is significant for teachers who want to queer up self-assessment. And while these emojis could absolutely be described, classified, and quantified to give the instructor a sense of the emotional range and valences circulating in the class, they could also *not* be. They might serve as ways to create affective awareness for individual students, ways to spark classroom discussions about these invisible but palpable affective currents that flow in and around the processes of composition, or a method for checking in with each other. Using self-assessment to check in—as opposed to check out or check up on—fosters relationship building in the classroom and reminds students they are not alone in experiencing both positive and negative feelings related to writing. It can also provide the instructor with an opportunity to express uncertainty and vulnerability about writing assignments and instruction in visual terms. For example, an instructor who participates with students in the writing-emoji assessment can use the blush emoji as a way of making space to talk about the gap between their intentions and the outcomes of a particular assignment.

For ease of reproduction on the gray-scale printed page of this book, we selected the bright yellow facial emojis to accompany the Writing Feelings prompt (see figure 3.2). Historically, this color has been used to represent a nonraced, all-inclusive mien; however, as scholars have noted, whiteness permeates technoculture and the emojis that are traded as currency therein (Nakamura 2002; Gay 2013). While Apple introduced a new suite of emojis to represent a diverse range of human skin tones, as categorized by the widely accepted Fitzpatrick scale used in dermatology, BIPOC users argue that digital blackface, hypervisibility, and narrow or whitewashed representations of blackness are still problematic (Sweeney and Whaley 2019). If you choose to integrate this assessment tool as a means of checking in with your students, we advocate discussing the racial and cultural politics of the emoji and letting students decide how to best self-represent in the language of unicode.

Writing Feelings prompt

Use one or more of these emojis to answer each question.
- On the first day I started this project or assignment, I felt:
- Today, when thinking about my project or assignment, I feel:
- In terms of this project or assignment, I think my classmates feel:
- In terms of this assignment or project, I think my instructor feels:
- By the end of this project, I want to feel:

Finally, use any emojis or combination of emojis to answer the following.

- To make me feel that way, I need everything shown in figure 3.2.

2. From Individual to Systematic Critique in 10 Minutes

Example 2, From Individual to Systematic Critique in 10 Minutes, also explores the affective and embodied experiences of failure in which students can both destroy their work and explore the alternative pathways their thinking and writing practices take them to. Example 2 offers a playful moment for student writers to not only articulate weaknesses/failures to themselves but to then also dispose of them, to physically tear them

Figure 3.2. Eight-six emojis reflecting different emotional states

up and be released from their grip, to not ignore them altogether but talk through them with peers. This prompt isn't about enacting a gripe session—though that's also okay—but about exploring what their struggles meant to them and then letting the experienced teacher-writer have a peek into that affective landscape of student writing. Also, as the name implies, this activity deconstructs the notion that failure is an individual burden and gives students a chance to share that burden and its shame-induced stigma with their instructors and peers. Through this exercise, student writers can begin to envision themselves as part of a writing ecology that may or may not be supporting their interests, goals, needs, and desires. Ultimately, it provides space to build shared agency and advocate for themselves in the writing classroom and a mechanism for doing so that feels less confrontational, as students are articulating the weakness of the writing assignment instead of the weaknesses of the instructor or course.

From Individual to Systematic Critique in 10 Minutes prompt
1. Spend two minutes reflecting on the weaknesses in your draft.
2. Spend two minutes reflecting on why those weaknesses exist.
3. Spend one minute tearing up what you've written into tiny pieces and sprinkling those pieces into the trash can.
4. Now, spend three minutes talking to your peers about *the weaknesses of the assignment, the project, and the instructional strategies/activities that accompanied it.*

5. Did this assignment accommodate you? Your needs, wants, desires, interests? Why or why not?

6. Spend two minutes jotting down what you talked about. Don't put your name on your notes, but submit them to your instructor at the end of the class.

3. Writing and Moving Differently

Example 3, Writing and Moving Differently, draws on the scholarship in postprocess, queer, and disability theories that foreground the role of the body in breaking normative constructions of writing, writing instruction, and writing assessment. Inspired by Hannah Rule's (2019) *Situating Writing Processes*, these self-reflection prompts turn writers' attention to the body and its affective and material relations with other objects and bodies in a writing ecology. Grounded in disability scholarship and the concept of "crip time" (Kafer 2013; Samuels 2017; Wood 2017), Rule argues that attention to real bodies, interacting in real time and space with physical objects and environments, disrupts the structuring, ordering, and punctuation of normative chronotopes. Process approaches to writing function, in part, based on these normative chronotopes. In process paradigms, we structure writing instruction, outcomes, and assessment around the expectations we have abstracted from our disciplinary and personal relationships with "normal" bodies (e.g., white, upper middle class, male, traditionally able-bodied, native speaking, etc.). This underlying bias becomes visible when we pay attention to Othered bodies, such as those that have been disabled, and to disabled people who, both intentionally and unintentionally, disrupt normative notions of pace and duration. In addition, Rule explains, composition's abstracted rhetorics attempt to explain the failures of embodied writing coordination as a cognitive problem as opposed to a mobility problem that plays out across bodies, objects, space, and time. To illustrate the problem with these cognitive rhetorics, Rule turns to the familiar example of "writer's block," or what we might also term a failure to produce:

> [We understand] this particular writing problem as a *mental* block. Just think about this writing task differently and the problem will be solved. Indeed, the picture postcard of writing seems to shape this likely well-meaning health professional's advice. Writing is a thinking problem. Writing is independent from things and places and objects. (97)

To disrupt these Cartesian-inspired, cognitively obsessed rhetorics, Rule argues we might not need to *think differently*, but, instead, we might need to *move differently*. Rule offers the example of one who avoids writing because the writing chair itself is saturated with memory—the negative affects of writing failure. Rule posits that the body/mind might just need a change of environment. To that, we add that the body might also need a change of position—what we might call, in queer parlance, *versatility*, or a willingness to move from top to bottom or from bottom to top—and/or an opportunity to write and move at different paces. To quote Alison Kafer (2013), this flexibility might mean writers and writing teachers "bend the clock" (27) instead of breaking writing bodies that don't (won't, can't) bend to the clock. Similarly, we might also encourage the transgression of boundaries, permitting student writers to miss deadlines, cross the lines of "acceptable" language and genre conventions, and use writing and assessment tools and technologies in ways they weren't intended to be used.

Writing and Moving Differently prompt
- In five minutes, draw your writing environment(s). Include the people, tools, objects, animals, plants, etc. that make up your writing space.
- What kinds of obstacles arise in this writing environment? Is your roommate loud, or is your elementary school kid in quarantine? Does your computer refuse to connect to the Internet or run like a snail when you open too many programs? Do your cats fight every hour or so? Does your iguana stare at you with a creepy look on her face? Is your chair comfortable? Do your earbuds hurt your ears? Is your phone constantly blowing up? Are your cacti too prickly?
- In five minutes, draw your writing process—not some preconceived idea of what you've been taught it should look like but what actually happened while you were actively and passively "writing."
- Did you avoid a topic, a genre, or particular kinds of research because of bad experiences or negative vibes? Did you wake up in the middle of the night with an idea? Did you go out for a run and find yourself thinking about something you had or had not written? Did you talk to other people about what you were or were not writing? Who? Did you procrastinate and write like a fiend the night before it was due? Did you blow deadlines? Intentionally? Unintentionally? Did you always feel ahead or behind? Did you feel like you were on a whole different level than the rest of the class?
- Make a plan to investigate new writing environments or, if you are mostly satisfied with your current one, make a plan to change at least one aspect of it. Then, take the same approach with your writing process. What will you change and why? How do you think these changes might affect your health, your well-being, your writing motivation, your comfort, and/or your confidence, other things that matter to you?

In response to this prompt, one student (Nia) offered the following story of her writing and moving:

> I live in a small lofted apartment with my girlfriend, a chihuahua, a cat, and 4 bunnies. My apartment has the worst Wifi as it's only extended from the main building. The power outage did not help, but we did get an extension on the deadlines. I also had an exam, a problem set, two projects, 3 quizzes, and a partridge in a pear tree due these past 3 weeks. I also went to Florida at the worst possible time (any time during the semester) and had to plan for that accordingly amidst my academic demands. I'm a little behind on deadlines, but I did have a conversation with [the professor] so I will be sure to submit quality work a couple days late rather than rushed work prior to the deadline.
>
> Even though they are important to me and my identity, I avoided writing about feminism and minorities because I didnt want to discuss anything too sensitive for my audience. I wanted to discuss an inclusive and relatable topic to ensure nobody was offended if I worded anything improperly. Most of the audience for my digital story are students. Some are art majors, some are science majors. I felt these topics were the most inclusive and relatable to my audience.
>
> I plan on spending more time writing and getting work done in the library, although I cannot speak and record my audio track there as it would disrupt other students. I can edit though. My approach would be to be overly organized in case I do slip a bit, it only lands me at the pace of the rest of the class and not behind. I did this in the beginning of the semester and I found it to be highly useful. I believe the reconstruction of my planning would improve my mental health and motivation as I will feel more confidence in myself while creating these pieces.

In Nia's story are multiple spaces where failure happens, where activities move her sideways, but we share this story because it demonstrates ways we might reflect on our entanglements with writing and failure that are not always about turning those failures into success, or at least opportunities for success. Yes, some of that language is still there, perhaps unavoidable in our culture, but Nia relates her writing processes, stops and starts, shifts and movements, in ways that help us understand the complexities around her working conditions and activities. These sorts of reflections might create space for us to honor the lateral moves writers make without our needing to rank and sort those moves as right and wrong writing practices. These are moves to embrace processes rather than The Writing Process, which must always serve at the pleasure of success.

4. Ouroboros, or a Perpetual Writing Game of Snakes and Ladders

In example 4, we have adapted the board game Snakes and Ladders into an ouroboros to demonstrate the circular nature of writing and writing assessment. In both, there is no clear beginning or end; in fact, there is no end to the work of validating assessment. The traditional game is played by rolling the dice to determine one's fate, which is either a plodding route through the spaces on the board or a sudden movement toward or away from the ending win space. Lucky rollers land on a ladder that propels them upward, while unlucky rollers slide down a snake that puts their object farther out of reach. On the original board, the ladders represent virtuous acts that help one develop good moral character, and the snakes represent wicked and immoral behaviors that lower one's social standing. In our adaptation, we use the existing symbolism to illuminate both opportunity ladders for writers and the places sideways slides can occur. Writing assessment scholars and learning theorists interested in fairness and social justice have discussed the importance of identifying opportunity structures in writing ecologies as a means of advancing equity (Gamson and Meyer 1996; Gee 2008; Moss et al. 2008; Poe, Nastal, and Elliot 2019). They argue that making these structures visible is key to understanding how an ecology both supports and/or undermines fairness.

This assessment activity can be used on either the classroom or the programmatic level to identify the snakes and ladders that impact writers' movements in the classroom or through a writing program. Bringing QVI to bear on the concept of opportunity structures, however, problematizes the fixed nature of the Snakes and Ladders game and provides an alternative way of thinking about opportunity structures within writing ecologies. Traditionally, in the game—as well as in students' movement through writing in a course, a program, or a degree—snakes must be avoided at all costs. They put us off our course, change our trajectory, and slow us down. What if, however, those slides, sideways movements, and slower, plodding paces were encouraged? Celebrated? What if our classrooms and our programs were nimble enough to accommodate circuitous routes, alternative pathways, slippages, and failures *as alternate opportunities to learn*? In other words, can we imagine the queerness of fluid signifiers and understand the snake as a ladder and a ladder as a snake? Might we see opportunity structures as ladders that take us sideways, off the board, out of the perpetuity of someone else's quest toward more meaningful and relevant writing and learning opportunities? Yes, these questions are provocative, and yes, they are meant to create queer disruptions in thinking and practice. What we've found, however, is that in these safe(r) spaces of game design and game play, we can more easily suspend dominant logics. By doing so, we might imagine other ways to write, move, and design curricular and programmatic experiences for a diversity of writers.

> *Ouroboros, or a Perpetual Writing Game of Snakes and Ladders prompt*
> Snakes and Ladders is an ancient Indian board game used to instruct children in choosing virtue and avoiding vice. This writing self-assessment adapts the traditional game as a way of visualizing your movements through our writing class. You will represent your journey starting with space 1, but space 1 does not need to correspond to the first day of class. You might start with earlier writing experiences that helped you "get ahead in the game." Use the spaces with snakes and ladders to help you identify when you felt propelled forward, backward, or sideways in your course progress. The ladders of opportunity can be thought of as assignments, activities, people, places, or tools that helped you learn and the snakes as those that brought hazard, risk, insecurity, and/or instability. Once you've identified these, ask yourself, was there a snake that was really a ladder? A ladder that was really a snake? Were there failures that might have been opportunities in disguise? Did you ever think about taking a snake or a ladder to slide out? Did you? How did you get back in? Why? What ladders do you think were missing from this writing class? What snakes were productive slides, and which ones were just random, meaningless, uncalled for, or unnecessary? Do you feel like you've accomplished something in coming to the end of the course/game, or is there a feeling of monotony, dread, or something else as you think about your next writing course or experiences that will begin after this one has come to an end?

In the following example, we see the annotated game board Rachael created and her story of her experiences with writing.

> I would describe my board as being equally filled with snakes and ladders. Completing this game board I realized how many snakes I actually encountered. You do not realize how many you actually encountered as the time period was so long. Most of my snakes were technological issues including trouble uploading the video to Brightspace, losing Wifi for the day, and figuring out how to navigate iMovie for the first time. My ladders were pretty different from one another. Some of my ladders had to do with the topics we were taught in class or consulting with a classmate who was completing the same badge. Other ladders were when ideas were flowing through my mind for creating the video and choosing my topic and sources. I guess you could say that my snake to find good sources was an opportunity in disguise as it made me search harder and be more creative in my search. A ladder that can also be a snake was choosing my topic. I remember spending over an hour in the library trying to figure out what I wanted to do for my project. I also remember asking my friends what they thought I should

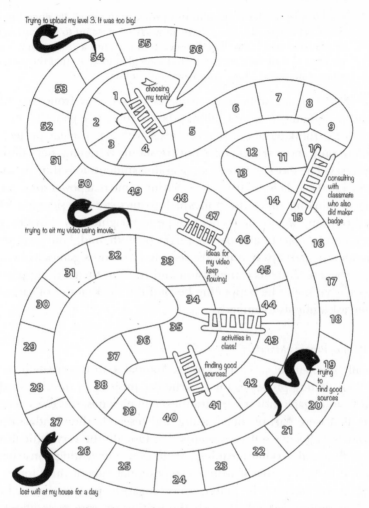

Trying to upload my level 3. It was too big!

choosing my topic!

consulting with classmate who also did maker badge

trying to edit my video using imovie.

ideas for my video keep flowing!

activities in class!

finding good sources!

trying to find good sources

lost wifi at my house for a day

Figure 3.3. Sample student ouroboros board

do. I knew I wanted to do something with cooking because it is a hobby of mine but I just couldn't figure out what exactly. At the beginning of the project I thought about changing what I was going to make when I could not find any good sources. I am glad I didn't because I really enjoyed making my soup and my friends all got to enjoy it. Ladders that could be possibly missing from class would be more time to work on the projects in class to ask questions in person. Snakes that were unnecessary were my difficulty using iMovie and trouble uploading to Brightspace. I tried uploading it three times before my roommate told me that it was too long and would never upload so I would have to create a Google drive. In the end, I feel that I have accomplished something coming to the end of this game and project. I feel proud of the hard work I have put into this project and especially since I have never been a good writer. I have always been hesitant to take any writing classes since I have literally been told I am not a great writer. I am nervous to start another badge, but I am glad to know that the project goes in steps and I have completed one before.

Like Nia, Rachael sometimes struggles to get away from the success mindset endemic to school cultures, but in this game play, she still finds spaces for thinking about her processes with a particular project that are not only about success or about constantly reframing her failures as successes. The move of inversion, of asking students to rethink what may seem a snake or ladder, strikes us as having some real power for engaging critical thinking and revision in which writers can step sideways off the path of doing what's always been done to imagine how activities, practices, events, objects, and people might be both/and, both a snake and a ladder, or perhaps neither. We see the ouroboros games as heuristic spaces where students can envision and revision their writing practices to see what might be happening beyond the stock stories of success we often ask students to embody.

5. Writing-Process Mandalas

Finally, in example 5, Writing-Process Mandalas, writers create mandalas of their writing processes for a particular project. By offering students spaces to engage with the frustrations, complexities, successes, and failures that were part of their writing and research, the mandala activity allows for affective self-assessments that validate the very difficult work of writing and making meaning. At times in our writing construct, we choose to believe that if writers are passionate about their topics, the writing will *naturally* be better, more engaged, perhaps easier, but as Probyn (2005) reminds us, it is the writing we care most about that probably creates the most anxiety for us. The desire to get it right, which comes out of our commitments and entanglements with the work, means we cannot simply write anything down and walk away. In writing studies, we've done a great job of engaging writers with meaningful projects and opportunities to write as part of the process/postprocess writing construct, but that means more than ever we must engage with "negative" affects as part of our self-assessment practices, to acknowledge the lateral spread failures lead us to, through, and perhaps away from.

Writing-Process Mandalas prompt
In Sanskrit, the word *mandala* means "circle" or "completion." In this self-assessment, you will create a mandala that focuses on your writing

journey. This mandala can be like a window for reflecting on the writing self that emerged in your last project. In assigning this project, we want to acknowledge that writing is a difficult process, one that can be marked by happiness, joy, pain, and trauma, and that creating a mandala might help you make meaning of that process and promote healing and strength. Perhaps, most importantly, through this self-assessment activity, we want you to understand that we recognize you as a whole person who brings that self and humanity to the work of writing in our classrooms.

Step 1: Decide what mattered to you most as you worked through this project. Was it making a difference in the world? Better understanding an issue or problem? Getting a good grade? Developing a relationship with your audience? Something else? Represent this central value or concern with shapes in the center of your mandala.

Step 2: How did that concern or value open out into different processes, activities, choices, and decisions? For example, if you were most interested in making a difference in the world, who did you need to write for? How did you decide on and define an audience? For your second concentric circle, choose another set of shapes.

Step 3: Repeat this process three to five more times, building your writing journey from your central value or concern out to four or five concentric layers. You can increase or decrease the frequency of shapes based on the intensity of each layer as well as turn or torque shapes to represent ways your thinking or writing changed over the course of your journey.

Step 4: Color the shapes in each layer to reflect your feelings about each of these concerns, processes, or choices. Consider using cool colors to reflect layers of calm, clarity, or ease and warm colors to reflect moments of excitement, passion, anger, or frustration.

Step 5: Create a simple key that explains what each shape and color represents.

The following example of this mandala activity represents Stephanie's own attempt to engage the writing processes that built her dissertation, the "happiness, joy, pain, and trauma" that were part of such a large and important writing project to her. She built her mandala and reflection along with students in her writing courses at URI:

The first thing that spoke to me was the hedgehog that I chose for the innermost layer of my mandala. Hedgehogs are solitary animals who curl up into tight balls when they feel threatened. In 2017, while teaching a 4/4 load, writing my dissertation, preparing campus job talks, and dealing with debilitating physical/mental illness, I became such a different person. Or maybe not a person at all—a hedgehog, perhaps. I dropped off social media and out of social circles. I don't even remember what my children looked, sounded, or felt like that year. I convinced myself that everything I could muster had to be invested in a done dissertation and a tenure line position. In record

Figure 3.4. Sample writing-process mandala

time, I succeeded. I got the position I wanted as a WPA, and my dissertation won a prestigious award.

Still now, over four years and many therapists later, it's hard to understand why success doesn't feel like what I thought it would. It didn't bring confidence, a sense of accomplishment, an air of expertise, or even a momentary feeling of relief. It feels like I just moved on to the next trial at a new place with new people and procedures. As an assistant professor, I understand failure is very much still an option, and I often wonder if/when/how it might present itself again. Moreover, I wonder if I might have the courage to uncurl and open with it. What paths would I scurry down? Another non-tenure track teaching position with a 4/4 or 5/5 load? An alternative academic or (alt ac) career path? Perhaps non-profit work in equity and human rights? Would I feel the sting of shame as I scurried away? Would my parents? (I am a first-generation college student, and my dad likes to refer to me as "the professor" when he talks to his friends.) My kids? My alma mater? My mentors who invested so much time and energy in my success? My colleagues who didn't get an assistant professor tenure-track job? That's the thing about shame; it is never only personal. It circulates and encircles us and those we feel responsible to and for. Like the mandala, it is both binding and layered.

Stephanie's mandala was created using the Staedtler Mandala Creator available at https://www.staedtler.com/intl/en/mandala-creator/.

AFTER THE GOLD RUSH

As assessment killjoys, we can draw on queer validity inquiry to bend those temporal links, paying attention to the real-time everyday experiences of writing. QVI encourages us to pay attention to students' and teachers' affective experiences that are "stupid or unknowing, foolish or silly" (Halberstam 2011, 54). QVI doesn't construct success in tandem with disciplinary norms and histories; instead, it examines the deviance of failure. It invites dissensus by creating queer assessment practices and artifacts whose meanings are not easily measured and/or reduced to a letter grade or score. The technologies we share in this chapter and those we share in later chapters—self- and collaborative assessment, narrative assessment, contract grading and digital badging—are practices and objects meant to disrupt the false clarity of success and the reduction of assessment to an efficient means for ranking and sorting bodies/texts. Ultimately, it pivots on failure as a space for effecting agency in student writers, writing teachers, and writing programs, and it calls us to make sure *agency* is part of the affective (in)competencies of our writing construct.

But what if you find yourself in a program, department, school, or state like some of those we've described in this chapter where you are required to participate in normative assessment practices that produce normative, totally expected, successful results? Are you wondering what room there may be to move if the game has been fixed and someone else has rolled the dice? Even though you may be participating in an assessment ecology geared toward achieving success despite collateral costs, we think there is almost always some wiggle room for you to exert individual and shared agency. For example, if you've had to march students through the creation of a showcase portfolio, where and how can you point out what's missing from the artifacts that have been used to judge failure or success? How much of the cognitive, affective, material, embodied, and relational work of writing and learning is missing from the artifacts that have been evaluated? Is there space in the portfolio debrief, program review, or departmental meeting to bring this up? Can you bring other artifacts to the table? What about data from some of the alternative self-assessment activities we've suggested or some you and your colleagues have created on your own? How and where can you make sure failure doesn't get lost in the conversation? Even though the program, department, or institution must pursue success, that doesn't mean you and your colleagues can't be the assessment killjoys who call these institutions to be responsive to their constituents. Organizations must be reminded whom they serve and that an ethos of loyalty and accountability should flow in multidirectional paths, not just up the chain of command. In holding those in positions of authority accountable, we suggest using a simple yet powerful question we borrow from Siva Vaidhyanathan, the Robertson Professor of Media Studies and director of the Center for Media and Citizenship at the University of Virginia. In response to *U.S. News & World Report*'s announcement that it would be enlarging its sphere of influence by evaluating and publishing rankings of middle and elementary schools, Vaidhyanathan tweeted, "Have you no shame? Seriously. What is wrong with you people?" (quoted in Jaschik 2021). The simple question "Have you no shame?" can be a powerful reminder to call those in our assessment communities to reflect on the implications of assessment and to be forthright about whose interests are being served by particular assessment technologies, practices, and protocols. Sometimes, just by asking that question—So, whose interests are being served by this assessment?—the assessment killjoy puts assessment ethics back on the table it has been so easily knocked off of by our cultural investments in expediency.

Whether you are in a position to make strategic change or use queer tactics to disrupt the assessment strategies of others, queer assessment protocols help us turn away from success as the right object and instead point us toward the shadowy, messy, complicated, contradictory, fluid, and foundering practices of writing and the teaching of writing. We share these because our experiences with them have helped us understand that success is never quite as concrete and knowable as we think, and these technologies, when applied as part of an ideology of queer validity, have allowed us to acquaint ourselves with the province of failure that seems, quite frankly, more familiar and much richer than success. They work to disrupt success/failure binaries and queer the dominant ideologies that create/require winners and losers in traditional assessment paradigms. Instead of asking what institutions want writers and teachers to (re)produce in their assessments, queer orientations toward assessment can reorient individual and disciplinary desires by asking what we want of writing and what writing wants from us.

Queer self-assessment practices can untether students and teachers not only from temporal trajectories but also from dominant linguistic modes. They can activate other multimodal, multidimensional ways of communicating and making meaning. Instead of requiring ongoing, systematic, kairotic, and laborious self-assessment practices, queer self-assessments might

- be deployed infrequently, thereby reducing assessment fatigue;
- happen unexpectedly, perhaps at the outset of a writing project or assignment;
- take very little time to complete, perhaps fewer than five minutes;
- be undertaken as a collaborative project as students consider the affective currents and strains circulating in the classroom or their groups;
- use visual, spatial, gestural, or aural modes of communication to disrupt linguistic hegemony.

Finally, and perhaps most important, queer self-assessments can revel in both shame and pride. They can function as meaningful, perhaps pleasurable, life-sustaining social activities for students and teachers alike. It is plausible to imagine writing assessment as a creative endeavor, and it is similarly plausible that certain kinds of self-assessment might reveal tremendous untapped capacity—if, and only if, we stop trying to measure performance in relation to a priori norms and move with writers, writing, and writing assessment scholarship to other places with other kinds of commitments and relationalities.

In failing to be successful with our own troubled portfolios, we found the writing and assessment constructs that had once enlivened process approaches to writing and assessment portfolios were not so much gone or lost as hidden from view by our hypercommodified and hypermechanized assessment schemas and the neoliberal frameworks that keep us all—student writers, faculty, and administrators alike—on an assessment hamster wheel: constant circular motion, constant busyness, constant revving up to go nowhere we really want to be. We decided it was time to fail, to engage with failure as a way out of that never-closing assessment loop. Across the next three chapters, we similarly find pleasure in our writing and assessment failures as we resist the commodification, reproduction, and mechanization of writing studies. We hope you'll continue to fail along with us.

4

FAILING TO BE COMMODIFIED

While the success/failure binary dominates our assessment frames of thought, throughout this book we advocate for a queer approach to writing assessment that moves beyond and beside binary frameworks. To help push us toward lateral learning and thinking, in this chapter we move *affectivity* to the top of our QVI Pyraminx as a primary lens through which to engage writing assessment. In previous chapters, we share the ways emotions permeate the assessment scene for both teachers and writers: it's hard to find an assessment scene that doesn't elicit emotions from its participants. By highlighting affectivity here, we work to unpack those emotions, demonstrating the ways we use emotions to orient ourselves (as teachers, scholars, WPAs, etc.) and others. Through affective intensities and flows, we realize (and learn) the ways bodies, contexts, and experiences shape our writing and our assessments. In particular, affectivity elicits values like *vulnerability* and *consent* that we advocate for as part of queering the writing construct.

To foreground affectivity, then, in this chapter we unpack the ways commodification continually shapes and reshapes education. We address the ways writing has been discussed as a skill to learn—not as a complex meaning-making process but as a discrete set of activities that can be named and measured. We don't have to look far to think of the ways writing has been scaled back to grammar tests, paragraph sandwiches, or five-paragraph essays. All these components of writing serve a particular purpose in a particular context but rarely transfer beyond those particular contexts. A glimpse into a first-year writing classroom where teachers are pushing students outside a five-paragraph-essay framework and students are blaming high-school teachers for not preparing them for college writing highlights how commodification limits our abilities to engage more dynamic rhetorical situations. While commodified features/traits of writing may have value in limited contexts, by working against affectivity, particularly vulnerability and consent, these limited frames for writing end up constraining writing as a human (and

https://doi.org/10.7330/9781646423705.c004

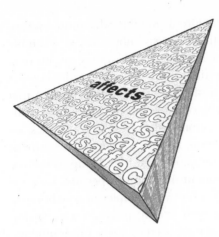

Figure 4.1. QVI Pyraminx rotated to the side labeled affects

humane) project for meaning making, self/other discovery, and change. We end up sacrificing value in writing in order to serve the engine of assessments so often outside teacher and student control. Instead, we are sold commodified features of writing because they'll help make our teaching "easier" or make grading more "efficient"; we are sold commodified features of writing to erase the human engagement in writing. Commodification erases affectivity.

In what follows, we argue that QVI can open up opportunities at the programmatic level while also invoking critical conversations in the hyperlocal space of the classroom by resisting the normative moves we have made to commodify writing and learning in both K–12 and college contexts. By engaging the most transient stakeholders in the system—the students in our classrooms—we can resist easy commodification and work to make learning to write a process of learning to assess (Huot 2002) through collaboratively negotiating the parameters of what matters in our writing communities and cultures. In this framework, assessment is about understanding, about recognizing both why and how we do things as writers and then how those choices impact others who make up our audiences/readers. Practices like dynamic criteria mapping (Broad 2003) and classroom-based assessment (Inoue 2005) have demonstrated the potential of these methods, but few have taken up validity as a critical concern at the hyperlocal or even the programmatic level.

We begin by exploring a short history of literacy and Progressive Era politics that worked to commodify writing in the twentieth century; progressivism, while at the time a major innovation in public education, ultimately led us to embrace knowledge-as-commodity across different educational levels. We explore a popular educational assessment project—the 6+1 Trait® Writing Analysis rubric—as an example of how easily high-impact practices like assessment rubrics can become commoditized in educational settings and how premade/big-box rubrics work to erase vulnerability and consent. The result is often that alternative practices that are equally or more successful can be easily edged out in the educational gig economy. After examining rubrics, we turn our attention to sites of classroom and programmatic assessment that we believe fail to be easily commodified and that disrupt simplistic reproduction into large-scale assessment mechanisms because they are situated in the value of consent. We offer two examples of collaborative descriptive assessment practices in both writing program and writing center spaces as examples of how we have tried to queer programmatic assessment practices in order to orient away from administrative progressivism and toward more constellated and relational writing assessment projects. While the processes we describe are themselves certainly replicable in different ways, the individual acts of assessment we explore must be reinvented and reimagined in each particular context. Our goal is not to replace one prefab framework with another but to offer examples that can demonstrate both why and how queerer assessment models can empower students, faculty, and programs. We believe there are ways to rescue writing studies and writing assessment from our institutional obsession with commodity capitalism and success for the very few.

LIKES, STARS, AND RANKINGS—OH MY!

At the beginning of 2020, before the world had been fully gripped by the COVID-19 pandemic, an episode of National Public Radio (NPR)'s *This American Life* explored the topic "Everyone's a Critic." In the episode, we meet Michael Schulman, a writer whose book on actor Meryl Streep had done fairly well with sales, even spending a few weeks on a best-seller list. Despite such broader and more established measures of success, Schulman couldn't stop himself from checking out his Amazon.com reviews. While two-thirds of his reviews were four- or five-star assessments, Schulman found himself obsessing over the one- and two-star reviews, not merely because they were low ratings but because he couldn't understand what led the reviewers to dismiss his book:

> If an average customer goes on Amazon and says, this book is boring, boring, boring, one star, I think it's worse than a smart book critic explaining why something did or didn't work. Boring, bland, hated it, no. There's one that just said no. And it just makes you feel terrible. So

> I would check my Amazon score an unhealthy number of times. And
> sometimes before I went to bed, which is a really bad idea, because
> then you would just drift off to sleep arguing with these people in
> your head.

Eventually, Schulman began to wonder what these folks actually valued, so he clicked on their usernames to see what other items they had reviewed. The items they gave high marks to had nothing to do with other biographies or other authors, or even other nonfiction books. They reviewed cupcake stands and light bulbs and mops—all important things but not remotely connected to a biography of a Hollywood star.

Later in the episode, B.A. Parker expresses frustration because the church she has begun to attend in Brooklyn, First Corinthians Baptist Church, has ended up on Yelp and TripAdvisor as a tourist spot where mostly European travelers can come to see what a "real" Black evangelical church is like. However, the church isn't traditional: the pastor wears blue jeans, the music mixes '70s R&B with traditional gospel, and the congregation is filled with young people. While Parker feels welcomed and at home in this space, she was surprised by the online reviews: "Quote, 'The music was loud, repetitive, and vacuous. Church is to elevate us to God, not bring him to human level.' Two stars." "From France, 'This is a scam. The children singing are circus animals.' One star." "From Italy, 'Don't choose this place if you are expecting the gospel style of Sister Act.' One star." While there is much to be critical of in terms of cultural tourism, particularly in these racist comments, what strikes us as relevant to our book on assessment is how the assessors in both these cases are not experts on the things they are reviewing. Instead, they are mostly providing knee-jerk reactions and frustrations when assumptions, stereotypes, or other expectations are not met.

We seem to be living now in a hyperconnected virtual world where assessment is its own commodity, where stars, likes, and other microassessments often work to reduce complex, sophisticated, nuanced things into overly simplistic caricatures of those once full and robust things.[1] But is that really what's happening, or is it that we understand the project of assessment itself—the activity of evaluating and understanding value and the ideologies that support such ranking practices—in fundamentally flawed ways? And is this framework we seem to share ultimately about positivist notions of fairness (objectivity, distance, commonality) and unfairness (subjectivity, interestedness, difference)?

When Schulman was reading those one- and two-star Amazon reviews, initially he was understanding them as being situated in a shared assessment ecology, one that should be fair or normed for expectations, values, goals, and so forth. And then he began to wonder what these assessors were viewing as five-star products, at which point he began to understand that despite the fact that they were all operating in the same star-rating system, there was nothing remotely normative about what they valued and why. A similar problem arose for Parker when she was frustrated that white European tourists in her church's balcony were leaving one- and two-star reviews online for her church. In addition to the unsettling optics of white people engaged in cultural tourism in a predominantly Black space, Parker wonders if there are no boundaries around what should and shouldn't be reviewed by inexperienced users, as well as those who come to the assessment scene with radically different values, motivations, desires, and expectations.

Across that episode of *This American Life*, what's at play is really a construct of fairness and assessment about who gets to assess an artifact or experience and in what context, as well as what impact their assessments have on the artifacts, experiences, or creators. In both Schulman's and Parker's experiences, the evaluations of readers or visitors become part of a larger assessment ecology with real-world implications. For Schulman, the reviews might affect his book sales as well as his reputation, which might have a long-term impact on whether his publisher will offer him a future contract for his writing; for Parker, the online reviews of her church service turn a spiritual place into something less so, a place competing for likes and stars in ways that might make the members of the church adjust their behaviors for tourists rather than for worship.

We open this chapter with these stories to remind readers, at least in part, that there are very few spaces in our lives where we are not actively reviewing/assessing others and basing our own purchases, decisions, choices, and so forth on the reviews and assessments of other people. Before we even get to a website to purchase something or show up in a store, we've likely researched the product online through *Consumer Reports* or a similarly trusted source; we've queried Google about the "best X" to see what sort of ranked list experts might have created. Then we likely compare those expert opinions against the opinions of other users on various websites to see what folks like us think about them. We regularly participate in a commodity marketplace where routine assessments become yet another commodity to be bought and sold, to be sought out and deployed. We understand commodities and commodification through a late-capitalist framework that recognizes objects, people, and ideas are not inherently commodities but become such when market capitalism can make use of them for profit. As the title of Italian economist Piero Sraffa's (1960) foundational text on late capitalism notes, capitalism has become "the production of commodities by means of commodities," which also underscores the autoreproductive functions of capitalism. As we move away from seeing goods and services as directed by human beings and controlled by craftspeople/ makers, the items and ideas we have bought and sold begin to buy and sell other commodities. This has never been more obvious than it is now as we experience the impacts of global capitalism's merging with an information economy (Huws 2014). What matters to us in the context of this book and our critique of capitalist-inflected assessment paradigms are the ways so much about writing and the valuation of writing has been commodified. Process compositionists in the 1970s and 1980s, for example, articulated a different way of understanding the ongoing and recursive work of writing and making meaning, but no sooner had they named steps, practices, or activities than textbook writers turned those often nebulous and complex processes into The Process, which moved step by step across textbook chapters in a developmental and linear framework that led novice composers from the blank page to the successful final draft. In K–12 classrooms around the United States, you can still easily spot large posters that name The Writing Process as linear and visually lockstep. The richly nuanced work of composing, particularly in classrooms where beginning/early-career teachers may lack experience with nonschool writing practices, dwindled to something formulaic and commodified, a set process that could be sold in textbooks, wall posters, teacher-training seminars, and ultimately through packaged assessments. In the context of education, assessment also becomes part of this commodity framework; the more easily commoditized the practice, the more likely it will gain traction and be bought and sold in the educational marketplace.

COMMODITIZING EDUCATION

In the introduction, we point to "Why Johnny Can't Write" as one of several failure moments that worked to maintain a literacy crisis as an affective touchstone for the United States. Here, we turn further back to the Progressive Era to consider how commodification was framed as a solution to the failures of public schooling in a time of mass immigration, industrialization, and urban migration. Our retelling of this early twentieth-century failure moment focuses on the ways relational acts of literacy and learning became increasingly conceptualized as transactional—the trading of discrete skills (products) that could be packaged and delivered at key points in students' experiences of schooling. Those same Progressive Era reform initiatives that were instituted to stem social and economic crises were also put to work in schools. These efforts were characterized by bureaucratic approaches to learning management and a growing reliance on administrative oversight to ensure a particular white, middle-class literacy was effectively packaged for mass consumption. Here, we trace the ways this "administrative progressivism" (Tyack 1974) has haunted literacy learning more broadly, particularly in the ways it has shaped both classroom and programmatic writing assessment across K–12 and higher education contexts, in order to provide a context against which to understand some of our QVI interventions.

Recent histories have pointed out that education was a central pillar of progressivist platforms (Mastrangelo 2012). To cultivate the ideal US citizen who could participate in the United States' political and economic spheres, progressivists championed a broad education in both the liberal arts and in practical subjects like science, math, and engineering.[2] While this strand of progressivism resulted from the same impetus to create educational environments that could prepare students for participation in US life, democratic aims often took a back seat to economic aspirations and the expansion of capitalism. According to David Tyack (1974), this strand of progressivism, dubbed "administrative progressivism," constructed an ideal citizen as one who could participate in an increasingly technological economy. Through rapid industrialization, the United States was poised to become an economic world power, but the US workforce, many believed, was ill prepared to make that vision a reality.

In response to the perceived technological literacy crisis of the late nineteenth and early twentieth centuries, school reform was seen as a necessary innovation. In 1917, E. F. Shapleigh, education research secretary for the Public School League, published an article in *American School Board Journal* in order to decry inefficiency and wasteful practices in US public schools. Rigorous scientific management, he argued, was necessary to reform schools and school systems. Borrowing from Frederick Winslow Taylor's (1911) *The Principles of Scientific Management*, Shapleigh and his contemporaries sought to break down the mammoth task of educating the masses into smaller actions that could be performed by a differentiated school workforce. Each task or action could be measured, analyzed, and studied to find the most productive means to reach a desired end. In his article, Shapleigh writes,

> School is a factory. The child is the raw material. The finished product is the child who graduates. We have not yet learned how to

manufacture this product economically. No industrial corporation could succeed if managed according to the wasteful methods which prevail in the ordinary school system. (quoted in Callahan 1962, 176)

While this direct framing of schools-as-factories may seem hyperbolic today, many WPAs would have much in common with their administrative progressivist forebears. Certainly, like those progressivists of old, WPAs often align themselves with the idea that better management—explicit outcomes statements, quantitative rubrics, packaged curricular interventions—can both better prepare students and better control a tenuous workforce of graduate student instructors, non-tenure-track faculty, and faculty across the curriculum who often teach writing without adequate preparation in writing studies research and pedagogy. Most of us find ourselves convinced that we live or die by the numbers, whether real or imagined: placement cut scores, scale scores, DFW rates, bell curves, interrater reliability, and so forth. In this paradigm, the qualitative experiences of education—relationship building, emotional engagement, practice in democratic living, the restructuring of experience—fail to resonate because they can't be quantified, commodified, and circled on the bottom line. When challenged, contemporary WPAs and other midlevel administrators may shrug their shoulders: "That's the reality of higher ed today. What can I do to stop it?" It's easy to imagine some large, external assessment machine breathing down our necks and stopping even our most progressive or exciting pedagogical explorations. The work of administration keeps many of us busy as those kitchen chefs, plate twirlers, and troubadours in charge of writing programs (George 1999), too busy, it seems, to have time to imagine or enact assessment models that break from such commodified programs.

Writing assessment work is certainly not immune from the commodifications that follow on progressivist models of organization and management. As Brian Huot and Michael Neal (2006) remind us, writing assessment is both political and technical. The push for new technologies of assessment in higher education grows out of neoliberal social and economic ideologies, and perpetual educational assessment in higher education contexts is directly tied to the growing commodification of education, a trend solidified in K–12 public schools with the instantiation of the No Child Left Behind policy (Moore, O'Neill, and Crow 2016). Inside this framework, assessments often work as technocratic instruments that aid in promoting individualism and competition while justifying the privatization of public enterprises. Political ideologies fueled by neoliberal economic values tend to reject commitments to the public good and promote meritocratic systems wherein success is configured as achievement gained through individual talent and ability, a frame that ignores imbalances of power, social privilege, and the cumulative effects of oppression, particularly intersectional oppression. According to Lil Brannon, Cynthia Urbanski, Lacy Manship, Lucy Arnold, and Tony Iannone (2010), in our prevailing "consumerocracy," literacy is commodified as a "thing" to be "gotten" through the course of one's education and tested to see if its various " 'components' . . . have been accrued" (16):

> Those who "have" the components (the set of skills) are named high-achieving and those who do not are low-achieving. The tests are considered "objective"—so the fault of not having the skills rests with the individual who did not work hard enough to get them. Individual children are sorted, schools are sorted, and teachers are held account-able for either giving or not giving students what they need to be suc-cessful. The sorting/accountability function helps to construct a cul-ture of competition, the hallmark of a capitalist free market economy. Capitalism depends on competition for consumers' funds. (16)

Here, Brannon et al. (2010) point to the ways assessments commodify social practices like literacy and writing, rearticulating them as "skills"; skills come to represent modular components of literacy individuals may own more or less of in relation to the construct of white, middle-class lit-eracy taught and assessed in educational institutions. Because these are discrete units assumed to move across contexts, it's no wonder so many faculty in disciplines across our campuses assume students did not re-ceive instruction in their writing-foundations courses rather than that, as we know, literacy practices are constantly shifting and changing, adapt-ing to various new contexts and tension points with varying degrees of sophistication and correctness.

We trace this history briefly in order to note how *failing sideways* might push against such commodification—of learning, of writing, of assessment, of success. We contend that part of a failure-oriented prac-tice of assessment would involve processes and activities that fail to be commodified easily; it would refuse to participate in these ideological frames that position success as a singular, linear, always-already vertical project. Thus, it would take a critical stance toward using assessment instruments to build collective capacity in our student populations and in our programs, foregrounding an understanding that writing, learn-ing, and literacy are social practices enacted, shared, and embodied in/ across cultural networks. Embedded within these cultural networks are the affective flows that orient bodies and spaces. This sort of queer, dif-fractive approach allows us to hold on to the tensions that exist in those networks and to value dissensus, acknowledging that no, in fact, we do not all agree on what counts as good writing; this shift in our framework also allows us to design our own assessment instruments in participatory (and diffractive) ways that can account for and even promote difference. Similarly, QVI pushes us to embrace the values of vulnerability and consent for all assessment users so we might more fully open ourselves up to the affective flows that surround various assessment scenes.

6+1 DOESN'T EQUAL SEVEN HABITS OF HIGHLY EFFECTIVE WRITING

One of the most familiar writing assessment practices commonly instituted in K–12 and higher education contexts is trait analysis, whether it's explicitly called by that name or not. In service for at least sixty years in US educational contexts, trait analysis is a method of assessing writing that seeks to identify and evaluate discrete components of effective writing. Typically couched in binary opposition to holistic essay scoring, which provides a score based on integrated evaluation, trait analysis privileges a core set of characteristics such as organization or editing and proofreading that are individually assessed and then added up to achieve a score on a written product. According to George Hillocks (2003), both trait analysis and holistic scoring are sociotechnical paradigms yoked to normative notions of good writing. These norms, he argues, whether applied as intimately interconnected or as modular components, are grounded in features typical of writing in a belles lettres tradition with an obsessive focus on aesthetics as achieved through diction, style, and tone. Our telling of the story in what follows might be read as a counterstory (Adler-Kassner 2008; Bell 2010; Martinez 2016, 2020). Our focus here is on what we've seen as the uptake of the trait-analysis rubrics, specifically the 6+1 Trait® Writing Analysis (Arter et al. 1994; Culham 2003b), rather than the intention of this particular technology. From our vantage point, when well-intended inventions become co-opted, reduced, and commodified into a product that's sold for big dollars as a silver-bullet solution to a problem in education, we must rethink those projects through a queered historical lens, one that selectively forgets intentionality in order to grapple with the ways the technology has come to function in support of problematic ideological systems (Halberstam 2011; Love 2009).

Trait analysis is most often articulated through the technology of a rubric, which can vary in format. However, the two most common instantiations are analytical rubrics and single-point rubrics. The analytical rubric outlines traits and provides assessors a range of options for evaluating that trait. Each trait is described on a linear continuum across four or five gradients of effectiveness. For example, if a reader were assessing organization, they could locate the text's organizational features on a continuum ranging from disorganized (no apparent structure, inattention to reader navigation, little or no connection from main ideas to a thesis, ineffective introduction/conclusion) to well organized (an effective introduction and conclusion, connections throughout the text that tie into a thesis, signposting and transitions that help the reader navigate across the composition). In contrast, the single-point rubric provides only three choices for communicating about each trait; these choices typically provide an evaluative commentary on each trait as below standard, at standard, or above standard. Criteria for each trait are placed in the center of a three-column table, and assessors can underline, circle, or highlight parts of the description to indicate standard performance or provide commentary below or above columns to describe a text's weaknesses and strengths. While the single-point rubric has often been framed as a writing assessment technology that can mediate between administrative desires for clarity and objectivity and practitioner desires for individualized student feedback (Wilson 2018), we are still left with the normative practice of taking a communicative object of meaning and reducing it to a set of finite, discrete parts that can be ranked separately from each other with no respect for how they are fundamentally interoperable. This kind of parsing lends itself well to the commodification of writing in which traits become disconnected products traded on the assessment mass market.[3] Here, we examine the Regional Educational Laboratory Northwest's 6+1 Trait® Writing Analysis product as an example of a writing assessment technology that frames writing in terms of objects of/for trade.

The 6+1 Trait® Writing Assessment is used widely in US K–12 writing contexts and even shows up periodically in two- and four-year colleges under the broader name of *trait analysis* (Bean 2011). In contrast to writing-workshop pedagogies that have been used in elementary, middle, and high-school contexts (Atwell 1987; Calkins 1994; Calkins and Harwayne 1987), 6+1 Trait® Writing Analysis is often promoted as a more refined and systematic method for teaching and assessing writing. With nationwide distribution of the product, extensive teacher training on how to use the product, and, more recently, articulation with the Common Core State Standards for English Language Arts, 6+1 Trait® Writing Analysis has come to define writing pedagogy and assessment for a large number of students and teachers across the country (Coe et al. 2011). In this model, writing is taught and assessed according to the following six (plus one) characteristics, which are consistently presented in this order: ideas, organization, voice, word choice, sentence fluency, conventions, and presentation (Culham 2003a, 2003b). The additional trait (presentation), reserved for texts that will be shared publicly, accommodates design features such as page layout and formatting. Advocates for the 6+1 Trait® Writing Analysis model note the framework develops a "common vocabulary" for teaching writing and contend that from a half century of research, it is clear "all 'good' writing has [these] six key ingredients" (Smekens 2020).

The 6+1 Trait® Writing Analysis was developed in the 1990s through work in the Beaverton School District in Oregon, with the team that created it presenting their project and findings at important conferences like the American Educational Research Association (Arter et al. 1994). By 2003, with the Scholastic publication of *6+1 Traits of Writing: The Complete Guide Grades 3 and Up* (Culham 2003a), the model had quickly spread among K–12 administrators and practitioners alike as a one-size-fits-all approach to writing assessment in schools. As Sherry Swain and Paul G. LeMahieu (2012) note, uptake of the 6+1 Trait® Writing Analysis was so ubiquitous by the early 2000s that when the National Writing Project was looking for an assessment framework for a national initiative, it was the obvious choice. However, despite its popularity, there were no large-scale studies of its effectiveness or fairness until 2011, when researchers found that students who participated in the 6+1 Trait® Writing Analysis experimental study showed statistically significant gains in holistic scoring, as well as in three individual traits: organization, voice, and word choice (Coe et al. 2011, 57). Notwithstanding that the study was funded by its developers, Education Northwest, the study ostensibly lends credibility to the claim that student writing improves when teachers use the framework to teach and assess student writing. In addition, analysis of subgroups to determine whether success was mediated according to race/ethnicity, gender, or socioeconomic status revealed no statistical differences among groups.

On the surface, these results seem promising, a hoped-for "big fix" for students, teachers, and administrators who could, from these findings, expect standardized assessment scores to increase by four percentile points (Coe et al. 2011). A closer look, however, reveals the distorted mechanisms by which success has been achieved in the 6+1 Trait® Writing Analysis model. It begins with a narrow construct of good writing that is removed from the messy rhetorical work of understanding audience, context, and genre as socially mediated (and complex) components of effective writing. It also erases affectivity. Instead, the framework privileges Romantic notions of invention as individual flashes of brilliance; couches organization as Aristotelian "containers" writers select to hold ideas; lauds belletristic notions of voice, word choice, and sentence fluency; and frames conventions outside genre to account for grammar, punctuation, and mechanics. Once these "ingredients" of good writing have been isolated and inculcated through fidelity to the model, the rubric is deployed to measure success in these same categories. For similar reasons, when they looked to adopt 6+1 Trait® Writing Analysis for the National Writing Project's large-scale study of student writing, Swain and LeMahieu (2012) quickly realized they would need to tweak the rubric significantly, as well as develop more robust models for actually performing the assessment, if they hoped to develop an assessment model that met Huot's (2002) criteria for a valid assessment. While this rubric was quickly commoditized in the assessment marketplace, those who adopted it still had to make changes because the contexts of writing assessment cannot be reduced to prefabricated models.

Likewise, the rubric, in tandem with the pedagogy it justifies, consists primarily of obvious or easy textual features that can be summarily addressed to achieve success. Imperceptive of the intersectional nature of writing that tethers organization, word choice, fluency, and conventions to audience, purpose, and context, the 6+1 Trait® Writing Analysis model misses the purpose of writing as situated cultural production. Instead, it constructs writing as a set of attainable skills that will produce good writing across all imaginable situations. Virginia Crank (2010) phrases her critique aptly: "Basically, what their research shows is that when students are trained in the traits, their writing improves when assessed according to the traits. If they are taught to the traits, they get better at meeting the assessor's expectations of the traits" (51). What Crank describes here is a closed assessment loop, one in which the end justifies the means but success is rendered meaningless beyond the hermetically sealed system of the 6+1 Trait® Writing Assessment. We describe the concept of the closed loop in more detail in chapter 5, but it's important here to recognize how these arbitrary traits can begin to function as modular commodities. They are controlled by Education Northwest; they are bought, sold, and traded while the burden of labor is foisted on the shoulders of students and teachers, many of whom have neither the power nor the space to modify or change the rubric. More important, rather than being any indication that student writers improve in terms of their ability to engage with writing in messy, complex, and sometimes contradictory contexts in the world outside school, the 6+1 Trait® Writing Analysis more accurately demonstrates that if we treat young writers as computers, we will receive mechanized responses. "Garbage in, garbage out," as computer coders might tell us.

In the context of increased accountability from federal and state education authorities, it's not difficult to see how a program like 6+1 Trait® Writing Analysis would become so dominant across institutions and systems. Designed with the dual purpose of serving as both a classroom and a programmatic assessment technology, this labor-saving instrument prompts teachers to turn the activity of writing into a product that can be more efficiently and effectively assessed. Because teachers are systematically trained to use the instrument, with hyperattention to instrumental fidelity, institutions can take student scores produced in the context of the classroom and attempt to scale those as programmatic assessment metrics. As writing studies scholars have noted, however, such classroom and programmatic assessments shouldn't be conflated, as different contexts and actors effect the need for new arguments about validity at each level (Gallagher 2010; Huot, O'Neill, and Moore 2010).

In such a reproductive assessment loop, we get what we ask for; in fact, we may even see improvement in scores. Where scores are what matter, a program like 6+1 Trait® Writing Analysis makes perfect sense. Teachers can shape their instruction and assignments based on what genres and styles will score best on a common rubric; when those texts are then scored, they will reflect the values and needs of the rubric. Yet again, the assessment tail wags the writing-construct dog. In an educational framework that ties test scores to a particular model of success to continued funding and support, 6+1 Trait® Writing Analysis offers a way for teachers and administrators to make a flawed system work for them, or at least not work against them quite so much. However, the improvement is in scores, not necessarily in learning or writing ability. Likewise, as we demonstrate here and throughout this book, this move to mechanize and commodify assessments works to remake the writing construct into one that is arhetorical, one that runs counter to much of what we know in writing studies about the socially and emotionally situated nature of writing and meaning making. What's worse, unlike the material commodities investors trade on in economic markets, the writing and assessment commodities we see replicated in K–12 spaces end up having value only in those contexts: outside the testing environment itself, student writers' arhetorical projects have little sustainable or transferable value. If we only want young people to play at school, to gesture toward learning, to perform school to an audience of one (or none, in the context of machine-based scoring), then commoditized assessment frameworks like the 6+1 Trait® Writing Analysis are certainly where we should be looking; but if we think student writers should be engaging with language in ways that will be meaningful to them outside school contexts, we must support more open assessment frameworks that recognize the messy and complicated contexts of writing.

LOOKING CLOSELY: NOTICING (AS) COLLABORATIVE ASSESSMENT

While most assessment at the programmatic level is somewhat collaborative in nature, assessment work often gives short shrift to thick description in order to get to the ranking and evaluating of student texts. The goal of traditional norming is not to continuously revel in the complexities of the texts but to efficiently get all readers reading the same way, to eschew dissensus in favor of consensus, and to then maintain a rigorously narrow understanding of the texts being assessed. Student texts, like artifacts in museums, are extracted from the fields of production and used to make arguments about their authors' capacity as composers, as well as the capacities of their teachers to ensure they meet particular outcomes. As we discussed in chapter 3, gold-standard writing portfolios were designed as a way to contextualize those fields of production and resist commodification; however, in practice, program administrators often feel they lack systematic alternatives to consider the inherent value of texts beyond a set of objective criteria. One practice we find promising for breaking these dominant logics of commodification is the practice of collaborative descriptive assessment.

Collaborative descriptive assessment involves convening different stakeholders to work together in recognizing and appreciating the intrinsic value of texts. Additionally, collaborative descriptive assessments privilege the queer writing construct values of *consent* and *vulnerability*. Through frameworks such as the Collaborative Assessment Conference (CAC) protocol, this approach to assessment dispenses with trait analysis and fidelity to rubrics, working instead to unearth and make visible the myriad ways texts work and different reviewers read and make meaning of those working texts (Blythe, Allen, and Powell 1999). In this paradigm, norming is not an assessment prerequisite. Readers aren't asked to smooth over or iron out their wrinkled textual experiences; instead, disagreement and dissensus enable multifaceted, multilayered interpretations that expand how we assess texts and, on a larger scale, how we approach the writing context. This queer approach to validity builds on the throuple we discuss in chapter 1: failure to adhere to clear measures of success, attention to the fluid and trans materiality of texts, and diverse orientations toward textual objects.

In 2015, Stephanie and a group of colleagues from the National Writing Project undertook a collaborative descriptive assessment project designed to promote more expansive and inclusive approaches to teaching digital writing. Published in the collection *Assessing Students' Digital Writing: Protocols for Looking Closely*, their experiences showcase how seven NWP teachers working in different geographic locations and institutional contexts, kindergarten through college, came together for synchronous digital meetings to collaboratively assess a textual artifact from each teacher's classroom (Hicks 2015). Each teacher agreed to select a piece of writing that kept them up at night because it was particularly confusing, exciting, challenging, confounding, powerful, distasteful, delightful, desirable, disappointing, humiliating, shocking, or unexpected. In this way, affective engagement with student writing dictated the sample data for the assessment project. Teachers also had to lean into their vulnerabilities to identify what piece of writing they'd share. Over the course of six months, each teacher took a turn sharing their selected artifact with each other prior to the group meeting, with no explanation or context regarding the artifact or the assignment for which it was produced, leveraging a strategic forgetting or deferred consideration of the text's fields of production. According to Elyse Eidman-Aadahl, Kristine Blair, Dànielle Nicole DeVoss, Will Hochman, Lanette Jimerson, Chuck Jurich, Sandy Murphy, Becky Rupert, Carl Whithaus, and Joe Wood (2013), such momentary lapses can enable artifacts to be considered from different, multidimensional perspectives: in their analysis of the Multimodal Assessment Project, for example, they acknowledge that each artifact is part and parcel of its context. However, taking the artifact out of its context helped Stephanie and her collaborators to look at it from new angles, to consider the substance of the piece and its "message in relationship to the contextual elements of purpose, genre, and audiences" (Eidman-Aadahl et al. 2013).[4]

During these two-hour meetings, all teachers, with the exception of the presenting teachers, engaged in structured conversations about the text by addressing these questions:

1. What do you notice about this text?
2. What's working in this text?
3. What questions do you have about the text and the context in which it was produced?

Each question was discussed for approximately thirty minutes, and during that time, each teacher listed something they noticed in the text, taking sequential turns until they had nothing left to notice. Once their noticing was exhausted, they could pass on to subsequent rounds, which continued until no one had anything left to contribute. During these rounds, they focused on looking closely at the selected text to notice both macro- and microlevel features. In other words, nothing was too big or too small to notice, and each teacher's noticings were indicative of the ways their attention was structured. For example, as a digital writing and rhetoric scholar, Stephanie tended to notice the ways students remixed and remediated existing texts, altering the original to forge new meaning. The most difficult part of following the protocol for question 1 was suppressing the tendency to evaluate while noticing. Statements like "I like that . . ." had to be rephrased as "I noticed that . . ." to avoid the quick rush to judgment so often practiced in assessment contexts.

Similarly, in the next phase of the assessment, teachers were not permitted to explicitly rank or privilege textual features that impressed them. Instead, they were prompted to make declarative statements such as, "This rhetorical move is effective because . . ." In this round, teachers focused on appreciative inquiry of students' digital texts, honoring the ways these writers had worked to make meaning across modes and media. Finally, teachers used their textual noticings to ask questions about the fields of production, including wonderings about the classroom context, assignment design and scaffolding, students' literacy and language backgrounds, intertextual connections among students' projects over the course of the year or semester, and ways the teacher had assessed the work inside the hyperlocal space of the classroom. During these discussions, the presenting teacher was silent, taking notes on the conversation. Once the rounds were completed for the third question, teachers were given thirty minutes to synthesize what they had heard through dialogue, as well as to address any, all, or none of the questions the group had posed. While the group limited itself to two-hour blocks, it was clear during each meeting that these conversations could have continued indefinitely, as presenting and reviewing teachers were collaboratively proliferating new orientations and approaches to students' digital composing. This collaborative descriptive assessment project reframed the ways teachers approached the materiality of their students' writing. Instead of norming and flattening their responses, the conversations allowed layered and spiraling conversations about the teaching and assessing of digital writing. These conversations fed back into their classrooms, not as an attempt to close a loop but as a means to transform what counts as good writing in a multimediated writing landscape, as well as to determine how to support students in their own approaches to producing in those complex landscapes.

While rife with potential for upending normative logics of assessment, this project is not without its limitations. One point of critique in this particular instantiation is the absence of multiple groups of stakeholders. To make this process more democratic, assessment coordinators should make space at the assessment table for students, parents and families, informal educators in after-school/community literacy programs, school-board members, and others directly and indirectly implicated and entangled in students' fields of production, which extend far beyond the writing classroom and writing program. Designing for inclusive assessment not only involves finding creative ways to engage different kinds of stakeholders but also considers representation in the assessment committee itself. While the protocol used in this example did work to disrupt dominant approaches to evaluating textual effectiveness, it would be naïve to deny that white, middle-class constructs of good writing also surfaced in these conversations. While several of the texts under review were produced by BIPOC writers, the group of teachers that convened to review those texts lacked racial diversity. All identified as white, and as we are painfully aware, white bodies and whiteness are already centered in classrooms, our profession, and our professional organizations like the National Writing Project and the National Council of Teachers of English. Inclusive collaborative descriptive assessment on the programmatic level, then, should also work to move beyond teacher and administrator representation in order to involve racially and culturally diverse bodies in uncovering the cultural and community rhetorics at work in students' texts.

After her experiences with collaborative descriptive assessment with other NWP teachers, Stephanie ported the methodology into her first-year writing classes while still a doctoral student/NTT at ECU as a way to disrupt and restructure peer review. The CAC protocol slowed down mass assessment practices and produced a divergent record of students noticing, naming, and inquiring into their classmates' writing. Because students were not bound to notice features of the texts their teacher prioritized, their responses spoke to the ways the text structured their unique readerly attention. Interestingly, students' noticings ran the gamut of what practitioners consider higher- to lower-order concerns, creating an archive of observations writers themselves could consider and approach in nonhierarchical ways. Like the teacher group, students also struggled to notice without judgment; thus, the class brainstormed phrases to leave out of the first round, such as "I like . . . ," "You did a good job of . . . ," or "The first sentence is really powerful . . ." Those phrases were again picked up in the second round as students discussed what worked for them in the text. They discussed organization, particular sentences, word choice, use of images, sound, videos, paragraph length, and other aspects they, as readers, found effective. During this part of the protocol, readers' emotional reactions were given space as students expressed their feelings, saying "I loved this part . . . ," "This right here made me happy . . . ," "I got angry here, and I think that's what you wanted . . ."

In terms of a queer writing construct, asking students to engage in a CAC protocol invites students to be vulnerable, to be open as writers and thinkers and communicators. Much like teachers are used to employing efficiency models of education, so too are students used to being assessed in often narrow and particular ways. By asking students to engage in a different assessment model, we are asking students to enter into an unknown. We are asking students to lean into that vulnerability because we know what emerges are deeper understandings of the social implications of writing. We know students experience a range of emotions when asked to produce writing—anxiety, excitement, fear—depending on how their previous experiences with writing have gone and on how they connect (or do not) to the current project and context for composing. A CAC protocol asks writers to sit with that vulnerability as students share their noticing, naming, and inquiring moments, unsure of where any comments might lead since we all bring our different experiences to the reading. Such a move also makes visible the often-tacit constructs around writing that student writers bring to the task; such a move can serve to demystify writing processes and practices, which can serve as a welcoming move for writers who have not grown up in and been nurtured by languages of power and privilege (Baker-Bell 2020; Evans-Winters 2019).

Finally, when students questioned their peers, the questions were not criticisms-couched-as-questions, a practice academics know far too well. Instead, they posed pointed questions about how and why the writers made particular choices in their texts. Students wanted to know things like

- "How did you make that photo move in your digital story?"
- "Why did you choose those songs for your soundtrack?"
- "Did you get mad trying to cite all those sources?"
- "Did you work on this in the computer lab or on your laptop?"

This kind of questioning demonstrates readerly desire to peek behind the packaging in order to glimpse the affective and material labor of composing. Once the response rounds were completed, presenting writers often expressed something along the lines of "That was a lot," indicating the need to process the glut of feedback they had given and received. Students both acknowledged the emotional labor of listening to their peers' feedback and were eager to answer questions and tell the story of their composing processes, animating and calling in other "characters" like roommates, pets, and parents who had participated or intervened in their writing processes.[5] Despite the time commitment, Stephanie found these were some of the most instructive moments in the writing classroom, calling to mind Huot's (2002) claim that learning to assess is learning to write.

It is important to note, of course, that the CAC protocol is an artifact-dependent assessment. Artifact-dependent assessments always run the risk of commodifying writing when the artifact and its market come to stand in for the labor that produced it and its intrinsic value and when the facilitator of the conversation does not take the time needed to disrupt their own disciplinary biases. In the case of collaborative descriptive assessment, however, judgments about the artifact and its market value are suspended, which enables the conversation to shift away from charting a linear path to success. Instead, assessment conversations are allowed to move laterally and engage the domains of craft, culture, community, and composition writ large. Such a model also disrupts a commodified notion of audience that far too often comes to exist in our classrooms; in this model, multiple real readers are offering multiple and often conflicting real responses to real texts. A collaborative descriptive assessment protocol pushes us to remember the rich and nuanced writing construct we tend to say we want in our classrooms but that traditional assessment models convince us is not possible or practical. Such a model asks writers to be vulnerable as part of their growth as writers, and the reward is seeing writing as a deeply humane and communicative act that connects individuals through the complex project of making meaning.

HIGHER-ORDER CONCERNS IN WRITING

While collaborative descriptive assessment protocols can help us disrupt traditional assessment frameworks and reinvigorate the writing constructs operating in our courses, these sorts of collaborative assessment models can also work at the broader programmatic level as a way to reshape and resee writing across a more complex and/or diffuse ecology. In writing centers, for example, where undergraduate and graduate students typically serve as consultants on writing projects for their peers, center directors have the opportunity to shape the broader understanding of good writing at their institutions through interventions they make with their staff, interventions that then have the potential to ripple outward through the diverse students who use the center for feedback and then further to their instructors across campus. In this section, we critique how higher-order and lower-order concerns have become commodified in writing center work and highlight one example: how Nikki worked collaboratively with the staff at ECU's University Writing Center (UWC) to revise and update their shared commitments to writing, to each other, and to the various and diverse students who seek support with their writing by reexamining the job-expectations documents that had been in place in the center for some time.

In paracurricular spaces like writing centers, we tend to promote relational approaches to writing. Writing centers are built on conversation and touted as spaces for writers to discuss their writing with experienced readers. While every writing center is configured differently to respond to local needs and opportunities, ECU's UWC is staffed by consultants from across the disciplines and works with all writers and fields on campus. To help prepare consultants to work with such diverse writers, one starting point in tutor professional development includes defining good writing. Nikki regularly facilitates writing center meetings where the consultants work to define that construct by contextualizing good writing. She grounds it in disciplinary practices, and she defines what terms carry from one major to another; for example, is concise writing in nursing the same as concise writing in chemistry? But, even with all that contextualization, Nikki and the consultants still end up with a fairly stable definition of good writing: purpose, audience, context, development, organization, style, conventions. A trait might shift here or there depending on the context of the conversation, but commodities of higher education (writing skills that lead to As) have become so ingrained that it's no surprise the writing center operates from commodified notions of good writing. Similarly, the structures Nikki has used to help professionalize and onboard consultants has further commodified notions of good writing and reinforced a trait mentality (much like the 6+1 Trait® Writing Analysis rubric discussed above). The heuristics of higher-order and lower-order concerns, often crafted to help guide writing center consultants' work, are likewise grounded in predetermined notions of good writing. As a professional-development tool, higher-order concerns are translated into questions consultants can ask writers. These questions then are used to guide writing center sessions. Though those heuristics

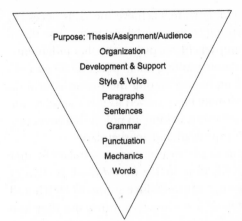

Purpose: Thesis/Assignment/Audience
Organization
Development & Support
Style & Voice
Paragraphs
Sentences
Grammar
Punctuation
Mechanics
Words

Figure 4.2. HOC/LOC inverted triangle (recreated from a University of Missouri-Kansas City Writing Studio handout)

of higher-order concerns allow for contextualized notions of writing that are discipline-specific, the heuristic still assumes particular features are what make up good writing and that those features should be worked on first. And these heuristics don't end after onboarding or at a staff meeting; they become part of the embodied work of writing centers, filtering into training texts/materials that become part of cross-campus shared writing center practice. You'd be hard-pressed to find a writing center consultant who isn't familiar with higher- and lower-order concerns as a framework or heuristic.

In fact, higher-order and lower-order concerns have become so commodified in writing center practice that they are part of the everyday lore and practice of consultants. Such a hierarchical, binary approach to tutoring writing has crafted a definition of good writing that has continued to shape students' experiences with writing and the ways consultants engage writers. Since higher-order concerns (HOCs) and lower-order concerns (LOCs) entered writing center discourse through the publication of Thomas J. Reigstad and Donald A. McAndrew's (1984) *Training Tutors for Writing Conferences* (see also Fitzgerald and Ianetta 2015, 74), writing center scholars have adopted the framework as part of the everyday work of writing centers. Within the last twenty years, writing center scholars have begun to push at the HOC/LOC framework, however, arguing that for multilingual speakers specifically, an LOC can easily become an HOC in a writing center session (Rafoth 2015; Williams and Severino 2004). Paula Gillespie and Neal Lerner's (2008) shift to "later-order concerns" helps complicate sentence-level concerns slightly, but with tutor-training guides foregrounding a need to focus on HOCs in sessions, consultants become reluctant to break "the rules." Consultants have latched onto the HOC/

LOC framework as a tool for helping writers achieve the skills necessary for that A grade. Even though writing centers work hard to distance themselves from classroom grades (only teachers can provide that judgment), it's not surprising to see consultants wanting their peers to be successful writers. And for them, working in and among the higher education system, where writing has increasingly been viewed as a commodity, the writing center is where you go to fix your writing, to polish that particular commodity to make it valuable in the academic marketplace.

More recently, we have begun to see writing center scholars further complicating the HOC/LOC distinction. In *The Oxford Guide for Writing Tutors*, Fitzgerald and Ianetta (2015, 73) introduce tutors to HOCs and LOCs as an entry point to negotiate a session's priorities, but they also remind tutors such a binary can become a rigid structure that doesn't allow tutors to use their best judgment. Elsewhere, Laura Greenfield (2019) advocates for consultants to abandon the hierarchy of concerns altogether and engage a radical politics and praxis that "supports teaching and tutoring methods in which educators work with students to develop a critical awareness that oppression is not natural, that oppressive systems can be changed, and that students themselves can be change agents" (163).

As with most examples in this chapter, we are not suggesting it is inherently wrong that writing center consultants consider HOCs before LOCs or that consultant education includes HOCs/LOCs as a framework. What's at issue here for us are the ways this binary has become so entrenched in writing center practice that consultants are beholden to it as the paradigmatic way to engage writing consultations. It represents yet another assessment framework that, once commodified, becomes hard to disrupt or reimagine. Higher-order and lower-order concerns have become the external thing we can name in writing center sessions and session reports. We can point to what traits consultants worked on during sessions to justify how the writing center is supporting writing skills. By rethinking the work of consulting and moving away from commodification, however, we can turn toward the affectivities and orientations of our work. Writing center professionals must trust their staff and their writers to make writing decisions that align with writer needs, not the needs embedded into a commodified version of good writing, such as the hierarchy of concerns. We must more actively decommodify our practices.

While it might seem simple to expand the definition of good writing or shift HOCs/LOCs onto a continuum in order to encourage consultants to move beyond such a commodified version of writing, we turn to scholars working in the intersections of race, writing, and teaching in order to help draw our attention to the fact that any expansion of the definition may merely expand a white, Eurocentric perspective of writing. To really expand what we mean by "good writing," we must be willing to make space for other ways of knowing and being. Part of QVI's work on queering the writing construct is just that: expanding the construct to capture the knowledge-making moments that exist beyond/around/beside/in place of whiteness.

Let's consider Cecilia Shelton's (2019) challenge to writing instructors in "Shifting Out of Neutral: Centering Difference, Bias, and Social Justice in a Business Writing Course." Typically, writing teachers can argue that notions of good writing must be centered on the audience, that what counts as good is fundamentally rhetorical, so audience shapes value. This particular rhetorical-pedagogical stance, however, ignores the roles whiteness can play in shaping our rhetorical knowledge, in particular how it figures into our already contrived and commodified notion of writing. Instead, Shelton advocates for marginalized bodies as the core component of writing practices. While we are focusing on the commodification of good writing, and of writing in general in this chapter, Shelton reminds us students learning to communicate, especially within technical discourses, "often operat[e] under a disciplinary logic that suggests to them that difference—including differences among bodies—should either be neutralized or commodified" (18). For Shelton, any definition of good writing must include difference, particularly bodies marked as different. Drawing from Black feminist pedagogical approaches, then, we bring up Shelton's work here as an example of how disrupting the definition of good writing is more than merely bringing in new features of writing; it's expanding our white, heteronormative, and patriarchal perspectives of what writing looks like and how writing performs. Yet, we'd be remiss if we did not also acknowledge that by truly expanding the notion of good writing, we may also be placing our colleagues in risky positions (Agboka and Dorpenyo 2022; Kynard 2018); Shelton traces one such moment in her own classroom in which centering difference promoted racist responses directly at her Black feminist body. By adopting a Black feminist pedagogy, Shelton pushes "students to reject myths of objectivity and neutrality in technical writing and identify their writing tasks as opportunities to intervene for justice—a position which is decidedly subjective in support of its cause" (21). Pushing against/devaluing those very commodities that are marketable can thus be risky, differentially so for different students, teachers, writing consultants, and administrators. QVI encourages us to focus on those risks as well when we're thinking through these processes.

Our point here is that our notions of good writing continue to be further commodified, defined in large part by white logics and white practices. Writing centers are routinely asked to do workshops for classes and campus organizations on college-level writing as though one forty-five-minute workshop will provide students with all the rhetorical tools they need. Or, too often teachers envision writing centers as quick-fix spaces for transforming papers within one thirty- to forty-five-minute session. As long as the academy is predominantly white, we will continue to operate from white-commodified views. Some writing centers have begun to make an intentional turn toward social justice work, but until we imagine frameworks for breaking out of (or at least disrupting) commodified thinking, the work of writing centers at the level of the individual session will continue to operate under the auspices of white logics. We need radical rethinking (Greenfield 2019) of our practices and centering of difference (Shelton 2019) to propel writing centers into the role of active accomplices in the work of social justice (Green 2018). We must move beyond institutional stakeholders and look toward community stakeholders as one avenue for approaching good writing as an intersectional project. Disrupting notions of good writing must be a relational and collaborative project with BIPOC colleagues, students, and community members. To that end, we explore one project of collaborative assessment and system analysis Nikki has used in ECU's UWC to create a more relational understanding among students and professional staff as they work together to disrupt some of those white-supremacist notions of good writing. Like the previous example involving descriptive assessment, Nikki and the UWC consultants' collaborative creation of a new values statement they have called "UWC (W)rites" offers an inductive model of assessment that leads to meaningful writing-construct understandings and changes.

UWC (W)RITES

Where do writing consultants come from? How do they get to our centers? What baggage about/experiences with good writing do they bring? These are questions we can forget to ask as we work to keep underresourced centers up and running. While writing centers have traditionally asked teachers to send their successful writers to apply for writing center positions, as a recruitment strategy, this does little beyond reproducing in the center those hypernormative notions of good writers and good writing we're critical of throughout this chapter. At ECU, Nikki had already pushed against traditional hiring practices by hiring consultants who enjoyed talking about writing rather than those who had been identified simply as "good at it" through grades and other affective markers of achievement. And she attributes that, in part, to her own work as an undergraduate tutor when she was hired because of her willingness to have conversations, not necessarily because of her own writing skills or performances. Similar to the ways writing centers have commodified HOCs and LOCs, however, writing centers have also commodified consultants. Conversations that begin with "What makes a good consultant?" end very similarly to conversations that begin with "What makes good writing?" Asking that question on writing center listservs or at writing center conferences results in a set of consultant "soft skills": consultants should be friendly, knowledgeable, flexible, professional, and so forth. Faculty across campus expect consultants to reinforce their expectations and help writers achieve the A grade. However, the work of the writing center is so much more than these easily traded commodities. In fact, as a paracurricular space, the writing center is one arena where directors and consultants could abandon all notions of commodification and work toward holistic, relational, affective frameworks.

Ostensibly, job-expectation documents dictate the job-related behaviors and norms for employees based on their positions and the culture of a particular workplace. At the UWC, the initial job-expectation documents followed closely what the Student Employment Office and Human Resources have suggested as best practices: a list of explicit responsibilities and duties and a list of behavioral dos and do nots in the position. Originally, our two-page job-expectation document felt like a checklist of tasks: show up on time, clock in, stay for your whole shift, check the writing center email, focus on higher-order concerns, don't wear headphones, greet each person, answer the phone, attend staff meetings, complete professional development, limit shift changes, and so on. While nothing was wrong with those particular expectations, in an effort to be continually transparent, as campus offices suggested, the list of tasks and behaviors grew unwieldy. Campus leadership had commodified what being a writing consultant means in large part by framing it by what, generally, being a good worker in a capitalist market means: a writing center consultant became defined by discrete skills and activities rather than by their orientations toward the work and the people they shared space and time with. After she attended an Employee Engagement Institute at Walt Disney World ("Disney's Approach, n.d."), Nikki realized that nowhere in this job-expectation document were the values of the UWC or a rationale for why these behaviors and activities were expected. They simply existed as self-evident traits.

In summer 2019, Nikki pulled the writing center consultants together to intentionally initiate a values-driven revision of the job-expectation document. While the previous job-expectation document had been designed in a top-down fashion by the director, Nikki wanted to dispel authority and work collaboratively and laterally with the staff. However, before the staff could begin to identify values and behaviors, they needed to articulate their shared vision for the writing center. Their first activity focused on questions like the following:

- Who are we as a space?
- Where do we want to see the writing center moving toward?
- What is a goal we could continue to strive for each semester?

After reflecting on their answers to those questions, they landed on the following statement: "to create individualized learning experiences for each writer and to cultivate an inclusive writer community across all of our campuses." This vision would become the signpost for all writing center-related activities moving forward. They wanted to ensure class visits, class workshops, orientation sessions, individual sessions, social media posts, and any related writing center task or activity would promote and reflect this shared vision. The vision represented their collective goal and what they would return to before committing to anything.

Once they knew their vision, they moved on to identify their core values as a space. Consultants were given a handout of around sixty values and asked to identify four to five values that reflected how writing center consultants should act, how writing center consultants should treat others, and how writing center consultants should expect to be treated in return. To help consultants understand how core values shape organizational practices, they used the *6Q* blog's post "190 Brilliant Examples" to explore some of their favorite companies and learned more about their values. Through this initial values exploration, consultants began to see how values-driven spaces resisted commodification. By positioning each consultant and writer to embody the values as they see fit, a values-driven space allows for multiple ways of knowing and being.

After consultants individually explored what they thought the writing center's values were/should be, they teamed up to do an organizational culture value analysis that followed Function Point's (n.d.) five steps:

1. List three to five examples of what the writing center is all about. Identify the values embedded in those examples.

2. Identify three to five people you classify as writing center ambassadors. Identify the values each person represents.

3. Draft three rules everyone should follow all the time. Identify the values those rules represent.

4. List three times students (and then faculty) were upset with the writing center. What caused it? Identify the values violated in the examples.

5. List out all the values from the first four questions.

The goal of this activity was to see how groups of consultants described the writing center and what values were embedded in those descriptions. Through shared conversation, they wanted to ensure they were reflecting the authenticity of their space and not creating a list of values too far removed from real everyday practice. Through constant conversation and reflection, they resisted commodifying this activity. Instead, they were intentionally crafting a local framework for their particular writing center work that would allow for individuality and flexibility. By resisting commodification, they were also actively resisting the reproduction of a certain kind/type of writing center tutor.

Once the working group merged individual and group value lists, they ended up with a list of ten desired values: accessibility, alacrity, passion, integrity, outreach, transparency, consent, empowerment, renewal, and active engagement. They knew they wanted to narrow down to a manageable set of core values they could both focus on and be accountable for, so they chose five as a workable number. But they also weren't sure which five best suited the writing center, so they initially began working with all ten values. They took their list of desired values and used that as an analytical tool to review the previous job-expectation document. They created a table on their central whiteboard in the writing center and worked through the job-expectation document in order to identify what values represented behavior statements in the document, what values were missing from the document, and what behaviors would reflect the desired values.

Through this collaborative descriptive noticing protocol and analysis, the consultants were able to narrow the UWC's core values from ten to the following five: empowerment, active engagement, integrity, accessibility, and consent. With this focused vision articulated and their values defined, the next step was to list the expected behaviors so as to recreate the UWC job-expectation document. The consultants broke off into groups with each group taking two values. Their charge was to list all the possible behaviors that would fall under their values. Once there was alignment between behaviors and values, the consultants returned to the new vision they had drafted at the beginning of the summer and worked

Table 4.1. UWC values heuristic

Identified values	Missing values	Desired behaviors
The values you feel are represented from the behaviors stated in the job expectations document.	The values you feel are missing from the current job expectations document.	If any of the values from the Desired List are not represented in the current job expectations document, what behaviors do you think would best reflect them? Write these behaviors in this column, stating which value the behavior coincides with.

to make sure each value-laden behavior also furthered their shared vision for the UWC. Taking one value per week for five weeks in order to conduct a collective, iterative vision-value-behavior revision cycle, the consultants spent around ten weeks building a new job-expectations document. While the center leadership did some wordsmithing of the value-behavior statements, the consultants were the primary visionaries and writers. The key to the success of this revision process was that the directors and the consultants shared power to craft the documents. Similarly, it was a community-building activity that allowed consultants to imagine a legacy of values within a space they had come to love and embrace. Because of the shared power and community emphasis, the job-expectations document—now titled *UWC (W)rites*—was no longer a list of things to do or not do. Instead, it was a list of values individuals could embody as writing center professionals.

UWC (W)rites

CONSENT BASICS

I ask if it's okay before I act.
  Understand the importance of getting consent from others.
  Show awareness that consent is not freely or automatically given or
    earned.

I listen for a yes before I proceed.
  Educate myself about what consent means.
  Ask questions to foster consent.

I speak up to make sure others have the option to consent too.
  Mutually establish boundaries with others.
  Demonstrate concern for the words and actions of others.

I am present and involved in sessions or writing center work.
  Provide undivided attention to writers.
  Be aware of body language (listen and look).

I reserve the right to say no.
  Understand the importance of boundaries for myself.

Keep academic and personal information confidential.

Accessibility Basics

I am aware of my surroundings and available to help those in the space.

Use personal devices when appropriate and in appropriate locations.

Position myself to focus on writing center projects, tasks, and work.

Ensure my conversations in the space are appropriate in topic and volume.

Check in on other coworkers to see if they need any support.

I assist writers to make appointments, understand the appointment process, and navigate appointment misunderstandings.

Contact writers who have not uploaded drafts to E-tutoring appointments in order to receive their drafts.

Answer the phone, respond to emails, greet writers, and invite writers to take the UWC survey.

I genuinely approach each person in the space.

Ensure each writer understands our vision.

Listen to understand others' perspectives.

Speak with an understanding of writers' value and acceptance.

I am reliable and punctual.

Arrive and punch in at the time of my scheduled shift.

Check in with myself before clocking in, addressing any personal needs in order to prepare myself for my upcoming shift.

Seek and try to be available for shift coverage.

Review appointment forms before each appointment.

Active Engagement Basics

I will be a good representative of the UWC.

Promote the UWC during class visits, orientations, and recruitment tables.

Share the UWC vision with my classmates and friends.

I offer reliable, unconditional support for my coworkers.

Step into sessions when asked or when appropriate.

Collaborate on writing center projects, tasks, and work.

I complete professional development on time.

Apply professional development in sessions.

Discuss application strategies with coworkers and the admin team.

Complete daily shift journals to focus on my individual growth.

I communicate with the admin team and coworkers.

Inform the admin team of any schedule changes as soon as I know.

Share relevant information and goings-on in the space with coworkers and the admin team.

Voice ideas and opinions to help the writing center grow.

Integrity Basics

I am honest and transparent with writers and coworkers.
  Admit when I am wrong or do not know something.
  Provide writers honest feedback on their work.
  Share writing center work and space tasks with other coworkers.

I respect others and treat others how I would like to be treated.
  Approach situations with patience and openness.
  Refer to everyone using their preferred names and pronouns.
  Practice active listening in every situation.
  Respect writer's knowledge base and time.
  Embrace differences in writing styles.

I practice interdependence.
  Seek and accept assistance when in need.
  Be available for questions and collaboration with coworkers.
  Utilize outside resources during sessions.
  Encourage dialogue between writers and their professors.

I practice professionalism.
  Refrain from homework and personal activities during UWC time.
  Hold myself to a professional standard by the way I engage with the
    UWC, writers, coworkers, staff, etc.
  Carry out the *UWC (W)rites* during appointments and "off-time" to
    provide a productive and well-rounded workplace.

Empowerment Basics

I provide meaningful help to writers.
  Ask questions concerning their needs and let writers decide how to
    answer/what is an appropriate answer.
  Guide the writers toward higher-order concerns to further their
    overall learning.
  Build writers' confidence to approach all elements of writing.

I acknowledge the writer's input as we determine the focus of the
  session.
  Actively listen to writer's concerns.
  Provide specialized guidance knowing that not every writer's
    concern can be solved in the way that another's was.

I empower writers during sessions.
  Convey genuine interest in the writer's work by asking questions
    about the material.
  Ask the writer about their satisfaction with any revisions suggested
    and/or made during sessions.

I support and encourage writers and my coworkers.
  Highlight the strengths and ideas of writers and coworkers.
  Validate the writer and assure them there are no errors or items to
    fix but simply things to adjust or improve.

At the time of drafting and revising *UWC (W)rites*, Nikki was not necessarily thinking about how these values might map onto a queer writing construct, though she was active in our queer theory reading group. However, as we all reflect now on that process, we see the ways affectivity filters through each value and how the *UWC (W)rites* document positions consultants to engage consent and vulnerability as everyday components of writing. In our workday discourses, consent is typically equated with sexual encounters, while in academic spaces, consent tends to be connected primarily to research ethics and inquiry practices. Rarely do we see conversations around consent as part of negotiating and understanding the more mundane elements of everyday life. And yet, we know we build our relationships, friendships, and behaviors around notions of boundaries and consent, sometimes effectively and sometimes dysfunctionally. However, we see in higher education how seeking consent is increasingly removed from students. For example, buried in the middle of their welcome-to-the-university packet, ECU students consent to their images being taken and used on marketing materials while on campus property that's considered public. Students also consent to having their every academic move coded, tracked, and shared with other academic professions through data-management systems like Banner and Starfish.[6] While not all these systems harm students, and many in fact are created expressly to support student retention and persistence, they are also part of larger moments in which students sign over their consent without fully understanding what they've signed over.[7] In an attempt to empower students, we wanted consent to be a core writing center value. We knew teachers would require students to come, which would revoke their consent to attend in the first place, but by asking if it's okay to read their paper or offer feedback, the consultants sought to re-empower writers to take control and create a learning environment that worked for them. Additionally, consent works at all levels in the UWC. Consultants know they must ask for consent before providing feedback, but equally important is that just because a writer wants a particular type of help, the consultant is not obligated to provide it. For example, if a student asks for help to make a stronger argument for racist or homophobic projects, the consultants know they can refuse that support. Consultants also know they have the power to consent or not to the professional-development activities in the writing center space. By situating consent as a core writing center value, the UWC has attempted to construct a space that encourages individuals to take ownership and control over their learning, which is particularly important given the systemic limits we all experience when we work within larger institutions.

While not explicitly named in the *UWC (W)rites* document, contextualizing our job duties in a values-driven manner requires consultants to engage in vulnerability. There is never a right or wrong answer or decision. Consultants must make the most educated choice based on the situation at hand. Handing over such decision-making power can paralyze consultants who are used to being in educational spaces that demand particular behaviors, but as we know with writing, there are no absolutes. By expecting consultants (and writers) to engage vulnerability in a writing space, the UWC is expecting that we pay attention to the features that make us human. We want consultants to feel empowered to ignore a draft and focus on building the confidence of a writer and to consider that activity just as effective as a session focused on a piece of writing. We want consultants to feel empowered to say no to helping with a specific writing skill, not because it isn't important but because it won't help the writer at the moment. Foregrounding vulnerability requires us to teach consultants the history of writing development and education and what privileging a queer writing construct does for writers.

As we review the *UWC (W)rites* document now in relation to the commodification of writing center consultants, what stands out to us is that throughout this revision process and even in the most recent finished draft, there is no singular definition of writing or expectation of a certain kind of writing promoted in the writing center. Instead, the emphasis is on trusting consultants to know what to offer each writer at that moment. The closest *UWC (W)rites* gets to commodifying writing may be under the first behavior of empowerment: "I provide meaningful help to writers." Consultants are expected generally to "guide the writers toward higher-order concerns to further their overall learning." Otherwise, what is key to writing as part of empowerment is the relationships that develop between the consultant and the writer. The job-expectation document no longer points to skills consultants have; instead, it is oriented toward working with others. By moving our thinking from commodification toward orientations and affective frameworks, UWC consultants have moved closer to decommodifying the writing center.

ASSESSOR NORMING AND COLLABORATIVE
DESCRIPTIVE ASSESSMENT PRACTICES IN QVI

If we imagine writing assessment in very narrow terms, the creation of the *UWC (W)rites* document and the research project around multimodal composing described earlier in this chapter may not feel like traditional models of assessment. However, a key component to building an effective assessment ecology involves norming assessors around key values, goals, outcomes, and so forth. In more positivist assessment frameworks, the norming activity is focused on aligning human readers to predetermined outcomes, making sure readers understand the outcomes and what those outcomes look like in action so they can assign preset values to samples they read against the outcomes and the rubric. As an assessment framework, traditional norming embodies the faux objective and disinterested values of a positivist epistemology; such a framework offers one story of what writing is doing, but far too often, this story becomes *the story*. That model becomes essentially commodified in the assessment marketplace, and alternative models struggle for consideration. Among the 6+1 Trait® Writing Analysis and HOCs/LOCs, we see examples of writing becoming packaged and taken up as the only/right way to do something. Both are examples of big-box solutions even though both began in more organic, from-the-ground-up projects. But in the collaborative descriptive assessment models we highlight here, norming is a very different activity with very different goals. In these examples, relationships and collaborations are privileged. While both examples involve noticing protocols that, we suppose, could become commodified—after all, the values-driven framework from Disney is very much a framework that costs a lot of money to get access to—because these noticing protocols are open-ended and focus on letting groups work together to navigate various paths, to move sideways as well as forward and backward, we believe these slow and inefficient models offer tremendous promise for helping us rethink the concept of norming as part of assessment. Where marketplace economies value products and services that can be replicated, bought, and sold almost regardless of local context, our models for slow assessments work to engage the often-invisible labor, practices, and processes that commodity frameworks serve to hide from the system or ignore altogether.

Our queering of writing assessment in these examples has focused on affectivity. Our goals in the collaborative descriptive assessment and *UWC (W)rites* are centered on bringing the unique features of each writer and consultant to the forefront by paying attention to the varied and complex affective (in)competencies involved in writing and responding to writing. We value the differences each being brings to the assessment scene, and we emphasize the relational components of writing. Throughout writing assessment scholarship, scholars like Asao Inoue (2005, 2015, 2019), Mya Poe and Inoue (2016), Huot (2002), and Anthony Edgington (2005) have all emphasized the conversations teachers have about students. Those conversations, in many ways, are more valuable than the scores or assessment projects. We anecdotally share these professional-development moments as persuasive reasons for why teachers should participate in assessment readings. However, we also note that we do not yet know how the community building and the relationship making have impacted or influenced teachers' assessment practices; that work comes next as we begin to trace the ripple effects that move outward from projects we've reported on in this chapter. QVI advocates for anti-commodity frameworks by valuing relationships and crafting assessment practices that work to understand the folds, intensities, and flows that occur throughout writing. We want to create spaces where teachers (and writers) are able to be more vulnerable in their learning journeys, as we believe vulnerability lends itself to lateral learning paths rather than the types of upward success paths discussed in the previous chapter.

To align with QVI, we argue that part of our alternative validity argument must privilege our values in writing—especially values like *consent* and *vulnerability*. While commodification functions to erase labor, relationships, emotions, and histories, QVI privileges those things, calling them back into our shared work around writing and assessment. In traditional validity and assessment models, as long as an individual demonstrates the skill, how the individual got to that point and what the individual interacted with to reach that skill is erased in the process. As a field, writing studies should be more concerned with labor, relationships, emotions, and histories than we have been, particularly given the central space writing process has occupied in our disciplinary literature and lore; we should pay greater attention to how an individual reaches a marker and make that process a more central part of our assessments. Writers should be able to opt in and opt out of writing processes with a full understanding of what they are consenting to in doing so. Such a shift, however, requires that we craft spaces where writers understand the ways relationships, emotions, and histories shape our individual processes and practices. Similarly, we must recognize the inherent value of people, not as a homogeneous group of students or as members only of individual demographic groupings (see chapter 5) but as unique individuals bringing their own ways of being and knowing into the scene of writing. As each new cohort of consultants is hired into the writing center, for example, the conversation isn't "This is how you act and do your job" but rather "These are the values of our space, and how you embody these values is up to you." Ongoing self-assessment focuses on the consultants in the center and the students who use the space, which makes assessment and revision ongoing practices of self-awareness and relationship building. *UWC (W)rites* advocates for each consultant to resist commodification and strengthen their own individual ways of being. Similarly, the noticing practices Stephanie and her NWP colleagues used focused their attention on how they understood themselves and their relationships to emerging literacies and technologies as much as it was also about creating any finished list that named discrete digital composing practices or skills.

As we reimagine a queer writing construct, we envision the ways consent and vulnerability would direct our attention in more equitable ways. Consent would create pathways for writers to establish their own boundaries. In an educational system where students are herded along with very little say in their own learning goals, valuing consent would create unique spaces where students get a choice to engage or disengage based on their identities/positionalities/emotions at that moment. Rather than require the same system and process for each student, valuing consent allows students to create a system and process that works for them. Teachers, too, can benefit from values of consent. Collaborative descriptive assessments can empower teachers to break from traditional, commodified notions of assessment in order to allow them space to engage what they see in student writing at a particular moment. While our values of consent and vulnerability create new assessment pathways for teachers to engage, they also create new affective environments for teachers to work within. Vulnerability positions writers to break out of commodified thinking and craft their own decisions based on a reading of the rhetorical expectations of the space or assignment. Valuing vulnerability removes the emotional safety blanket of rubrics, checklists, or step-by-step processes and instead asks writers to figure out the best answer to the rhetorical puzzle in this context at this moment. Critics will no doubt express concern that this work is risky: it's risky to ask students and teachers to be vulnerable in precarious spaces and times. And that's true, of course—but it is no riskier than erasing all the elements of writing and learning we value or ignoring those things that allow some students to move through writing systems built on unearned privileges for some while booby traps are hiding around every turn for others. We currently operate in systems where risk is not remotely shared equitably across all persons; we believe attending to affectivity in the ways we do in this chapter can help us to get closer to a model of shared risk and reward.

5

FAILING TO BE REPRODUCED

In previous chapters, we work to unpack the success/failure binary that permeates much of Western thought, particularly the ways this binary is framed in hyperindividualistic terms in the United States and other aggressively late-capitalist contexts. As part of that, we also note the ways greater attention to affectivity in our assessment models can serve to disrupt traditional notions of success and failure in order to advocate for more sideways approaches to learning, writing, and shared growth. In this chapter, we examine various writing assessment scenes through a lens rooted in *identities*, in the ways embodiment and self-understandings, while always changing, shifting, and fluid, remain a key vector for understanding both where traditional notions of writing assessment might be problematic and how we might reimagine the writing construct to include *dissensus* and *radical justice* as central to our understanding of learning to write and writing to learn.

To do that work, we challenge some of the ways traditional writing assessment models/frameworks serve to *reproduce* our always-already hetero/sexist, racist, and classist writing constructs by turning again to queer theorists whose work has problematized "reproductive futurity" (Edelman 2004) as a teleological imperative in Western cultures. Throughout this book, we lean on various queer theories to critique success frameworks that come to feel extremely linear and forward moving; these liberal models tend to assume that what is yet to come will be inherently better—more enlightened, more advanced, more sophisticated, more free—than the assumed darkness, backwardness, and constraints of what came before. Such a framework is central to how we articulate, teach, and assess writing in both process and postprocess models. Drafts are assumed to come first; we treat them as incomplete and unfinished, as building blocks that will, in the future, turn into something meaningful, something better, something more polished, something more professional. Even when the steps are different for each writer, less linear, as is the case in much postprocess thinking (Breuch 2002; Kent 1993, 1999;

https://doi.org/10.7330/9781646423705.c005

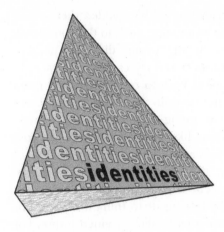

Figure 5.1. QVI Pyraminx rotated to the side labeled identities

Lotier 2021), the end result is still assumed to be a good final piece of writing. Peer review, instructor review, revision, and editing are all steps along this journey toward producing a successful final draft. And, of course, we sometimes talk to students about how even the "final" draft is only really "final for now," that all writing can be revised, that there's always another way to draft and revise. This caveat seems important for at least two reasons: (1) after postmodern theory and a revaluing of sophistic rhetorics, we remain anxious about the idea that any writing is ever really done, that ideas and words stop, that there's not more that can be done given audience, context, purpose, and so forth; and (2) it seems as though we are also trying to reassure students that perfectibility is not the end result of a writing class, which simultaneously offers us a back door for justifying why their grade may not be what they expect (you can do more) or may not indicate the end of learning (this is A work now but might not be in other contexts).

Deeply rooted in our shared pedagogical and theoretical understandings of writing is that sense of endlessly forward momentum: something better is on the horizon, even if better is highly contextual. We see this just as clearly in the writing center as in the writing classroom. Students visit the writing center under the premise that their drafts will be one step closer to that final copy, or that a single writing center visit will put them on the path to classroom success. But one of the dark secrets of writing center work, of course, is that there is no direct one-to-one exchange happening. We say that if students use the writing center, their writing will improve, possibly their grade will improve, but frequently, the opposite happens: perhaps their revisions are more scattered/disorganized than previous drafts because they like all these new ideas they had while chatting with a consultant and have added them all in; perhaps they miscommunicated the assignment goals to the consultant, who then helped the writer move in a totally "wrong" direction; perhaps they found the consultant's ideas suspect and rejected good advice. In all these scenarios, writer agency exists both to revise effectively given the context and to not do so, and not do so in any number of different but perhaps equally interesting or intriguing—and meaningful—ways.

Through the work of queer writers like Lee Edelman (2004), José Esteban Muñoz (2009), Jack Halberstam (2011), and Lauren Berlant (2011), we have come to challenge the easy utopia of futural success, in particular the ways the future seems always to hinge on reproducing the past or limiting the past by forcing us to think and limit our choices in the now so we might have a particular imagined future. For Edelman (2004), Western culture is obsessed with an imagined "Child," a metonymic embodiment of our hopes and dreams, a figural release from both the darkness of the past and the frustrations of the present: "Historically constructed . . . to serve as the repository of variously sentimentalized cultural identifications, the Child has come to embody for us the telos of the social order and come to be seen as the one for whom that order is held in perpetual trust" (10–11). While his critique is centered on the ways this idealized Child stops queer liberation from being realized, as queers in this configuration are a constant threat to the nuclear family's focus on reproduction and linear self/familial continuation, Edelman's theoretical challenge is pertinent to writing studies: How does our imagined assessment model (our idealized futural Child) stop us from reimagining writing as processes and products? What happens when students fail to reproduce the writing construct we've mapped out for them, when they realign themselves and their work along sideways trajectories, when their passions, interests, and values resist being normed and aligned to our disciplinary and pedagogical goals?

In this chapter, we open with a brief look at one of education's most persistent and troubling monoliths, the bell curve, in order to demonstrate the ways that despite significant changes in our disciplinary knowledge about writing, and despite a long history of statistical and social critique, certain models and metaphors about human capacity and ability continue to be reproduced in our classrooms/programs and across our campuses. This seemingly endless reproduction of forced mediocrity often prevents us from imagining other types of assessment frameworks; however, we contend that a QVI model can help us challenge these existing frameworks in order to produce assessments that value additional elements of our writing construct like *dissensus* and *radical justice*. If you already know the history of the bell curve, of course, we encourage you to skip the next section and move right to our examples involving contract grading/digital badging and the oversampling of specific populations, but if you exist on a campus where this model continues to prevent certain types of innovative work in writing assessment, we hope this discussion of some of the problems in bell-curve models will provide you with at least a few arguments to use when advocating for more just and expansive models of assessment.

BELLS, BELLS, BELLS: ON REPRODUCING NORMATIVE DISTRIBUTIONS

For far too many of us, our grading practices remain haunted by the specter of the bell curve, whether we recognize it as we sit down to read a set of papers or not. Despite its having been continually debunked as neither a fair nor ethical practice, the bell curve has persisted in higher education as a framework for rationalizing a particular normative grade distribution in individual classes and across programs, even if only in faculty's and administrators' minds. Yet bell curves promote and demand deficit models of learning that advance white-supremacist agendas and work to dehumanize large numbers of students in our classrooms and schools (Ladson-Billings 1995; Moll et al. 1992; Sharma 2016). As we recount in chapter 1, we don't have to look too far back in our history to see the surge of deficit models within basic writing, writing labs/clinics, and first-year writing "inoculation" models for students on the wrong side of the curve. While we imagine a time in which we set aside the pseudoscience of the bell curve in favor of more robust discussions around learning and assessment, any casual perusal of current college classrooms demonstrates that time is not yet realized. The bell curve still emerges as the primary shape in most of our minds when we discuss grades and normative distribution models, even if it does so as something we feel our grades are somehow deviating from. Recently, Colleen Flaherty (2019) reported on a study that suggests STEM courses should use the bell curve to "equalize average grades across classes," which, in turn, would help close the gender gap. Despite the fact that the data Flaherty reported on showed women in STEM having, on average, higher grades than men, the solution for underrepresentation of women in STEM became a suggestion to curve their grades to Bs. Rather than addressing larger cultural issues that impact women's decisions to study STEM or prevent women's success in STEM fields through microaggressions and other "pushout" practices (Morris 2018), the report opted to pick low-hanging fruit by recommending bell-curve-based grading practices to change the numbers on the page. Despite grade-based numerical data to the contrary, Flaherty assumes women don't pursue STEM disciplines because they are "too hard."

The bell curve consistently focuses our attention on numbers over human beings, and our own writing programs are not immune to this practice of valuing grade distributions over the very bodies impacted by such elisions. It's not uncommon to hear that graduate student instructors at many institutions are required to submit grade-distribution charts to their WPAs in order to prove they are not inflating grades or being too lenient, all under the guise of teaching the graduate students as some sort of professional development linked to assessment. This sense of surveillance on graduate student teachers, as well as contingent/NTT faculty, often cultivates feelings of fear and resentment toward grading and assessment, especially when these teachers are familiar with the flawed nature of the bell curve and know their distributions may impact continuing employment. Over our many combined years, we have seen scenes like the following play out repeatedly. A faculty member in some discipline is frustrated with their students' writing; that person complains loudly and frequently wonders, "What are they doing over there in English (or writing and rhetoric)?" Eventually their department chair or the college dean corners the English department chair and parrots that very question, may even come with data that show large numbers of A grades in gen-ed writing courses. "You need to do something about this," the chair is told. They then repeat this to the WPA or bring it up at a faculty meeting. "The dean expects gen-ed courses to have grades that look like the bell curve. They're worried about grade inflation." Faculty take this in, many deciding for themselves that the dean is right and deciding to grade harder, be more rigorous. Others, particularly contingent faculty, hear this as a warning: get your grades aligned with a normal distribution; your next contract may depend on it. Graduate student instructors hear from the WPA that they must provide their grade distributions each semester as evidence they're really not inflating those grades. In this context, it may matter little that the bell curve has been debunked; the effects of its mythic norm keep working away, often at those instructors with the least job security.

But we know our resistance to the bell curve as a normalized practice for aligning bodies isn't without cause. After all, there is nothing particularly *normal* about norm-referenced grading, which is sometimes referred to as *grading on a curve*. If we think about the success-and-failure binary referenced in chapter 3, norm-referenced grading falls squarely into that narrative. Students' grades are based upon the grades their classmates get, *not* on their individualized learning or performance (e.g., criterion-based measures). Students are forced to succeed or fail—or worse, some might say, be deemed merely average. Forcing a predetermined range of scores, as the bell curve does, reproduces skewed notions of the average student. It forces student bodies to align with preestablished distribution criteria in which only 5 to 10 percent of the course can *earn* an A even if 30 percent of the students meet the learning goals. Again, we see Halberstam's (2011) conception of success/failure under late capitalism in practice, where success must be reserved at all costs for a select few regardless of value, merit, or labor. Similarly, in *Testing Testing: Social Consequences of the Examined Life*, F. Allan Hanson (1993) argues that "the most repugnant aspect of the competitive system of testing and grading is that it requires that some fail, if only to identify, by contrast, those who succeed" (219). Can we even imagine a system in which everyone succeeds?

Historically, the bell curve holds the assumption that most things happen in the middle, with a few outliers above and below. Mathematically known as the Gaussian curve, the bell curve was initially used by Carl Friedrich Gauss to confirm astronomical measurements and planetary positions (Elliot 2005; Fendler and Muzaffar 2008). The Gaussian curve was rooted within the mathematical construct of probability. Rather quickly, however, the Gaussian curve left mathematics and entered statistics, where eventually various disciplines across the social sciences picked it up as a way of understanding phenomena from less objective contexts (Fendler and Muzaffar 2008). Over time, the bell curve became the literal shape of eugenics movements wherein, since the majority of the population had only average intelligence, an elect few (usually, in the global West, members of the white race) were then constructed as being naturally superior (Elliot 2005; Herrnstein and Murray 1994). If we have a statistical model that seems to show us a refined notion of nature, or rather to show us nature as those in power want/think it should be, then those in power can point to this model and claim it is natural when, in reality, it's merely that very modernist construct of "Nature methodized" Alexander Pope once satirized in his poem "An Essay on Criticism."

With historical roots in mathematics and statistics, the bell curve has become a prominent fixture in Western societies in large part based on the common assumption of "that's just how things work" in nature, science, and education; this common-sense framework is particularly evident in what Norbert Elliot (2005) has called the "rhetoric of disenfranchisement." The literacy crisis referenced in our introduction—"Why Johnny Can't Write" (Sheils 1975)—prompted an accountability movement grounded in bell-curve logics:

> Whatever abilities existed were overshadowed by the students' failure to achieve excellence. In that distribution was required—student scores had to be distributed across a scale according to the Gaussian (normal) distribution—it was logically impossible for the majority of students to achieve scores at the very highest ends of the scale. (Elliot 2005, 341–42)

In tracing this trend throughout our disciplinary history, Elliot reminds us why we often find programs in which graduate teaching instructors and other contingent faculty are still asked to submit grade distributions, despite the fact that criterion-based measures would provide more socially just ways to approach grading and learning. Even when WPAs and department administrators can break out of the seductive logics of a norm-reference curve, they can still find themselves on campuses where eugenicist logics of intellectual ability/aptitude hold sway. As Lynn Fendler and Irfan Muzaffar (2008) write, "Under a bell curve, teachers are expected to direct their lessons to a fiction called the Average Student, despite the fact that no student actually embodies the characteristics of that statistically generated average" (67). Those of us invested in students and their learning understand the unjust and inappropriate use of the bell curve in the classroom, as well as the ways that framework is maintained across not only our college campuses but also our broader society. We recognize grading occurs after a period of learning and thus isn't randomized, one of the core features of the bell curve. By its very nature, teaching disrupts the curve (Potter and Baker 2011)—as it should!—sometimes flattening it and other times creating hyperspatial geometric patterns in the data. In the astronomical model that birthed the bell curve, Gauss was studying elements of the natural world, not human beings who were consistently being intellectually nudged and prodded by teachers who were, in kind, working to help students learn and modifying their instruction moment by moment based on what did or did not seem to be working.

Likewise, admissions criteria in place around the United States do not create any sort of truly randomized sample; instead, they create a student body already marked by various tests and other instruments as having a particular level of intelligence—or rather, as having tested in a particular way at a particular time given particular constraints. Consider the impact of what this means when we reduce the population from all US students aged sixteen to eighteen, or even all matriculating students in a given year, to only those in a particular class: in courses where there are fewer than sixty students, there are not enough data points to construct any sort of statistically relevant bell curve (Fenwick and Parsons 2000, 124). In writing studies, the likelihood that our courses would ever approximate a bell-curve distribution is even more fraught, as our courses rarely contain more than thirty undergraduate students, with NCTE/CCCC recommending course sizes closer to twenty students for a traditional first-year writing course and fifteen to eighteen students for ESL writing courses and for courses framed as developmental. Quite simply, given that we want small course sizes for the individualized nature of writing, response, and revision, the bell curve should never be part of our conversations about grade distributions. It also should not be part of the ongoing surveillance of contingent labor on our campuses.

In discussing the failure-oriented principles of QVI, we can't help but return to the bell curve once again to look at it askance: after all, this model structurally demands failure as part of normal scoring and sorting. As long as we continue to value the logic of normal distribution, we must recognize we are intentionally building systems that require some students to fail—whether they want to or not—and that means we need to better understand how failure works in our discipline and our culture. Halberstam (2011) highlights the way this conundrum is linked to larger capitalist systems, where failure is not only necessary for success but *must make up the larger portion of our outcomes*. More important, perhaps, this binary framework acts on and through affective economies to link success and failure to individual desires rather than to the larger systems that require them:

> Indeed believing that success depends upon one's attitude is far preferable to Americans than recognizing that their success is the outcome of the tilted scales of race, class, and gender. . . . While capitalism produces some people's success through other people's failures, the ideology of positive thinking insists that success depends only upon working hard and failure is always of your own doing. (3)

It's no surprise the bell curve has developed alongside Western capitalism, as both work hegemonically in tune with each other; both work to uphold a certain model of the state as an organizing and orderly construct where a very few succeed and have the money and power to control the means of production, determine what is and is not valuable, and enact the laws that further accumulate money and power to the very few—all while exploiting the labor, talents, and abilities of the masses. Turning toward failure, however, as we note in chapter 3, means turning toward "more local practices of knowledge, practices moreover that may be less efficient, may yield less marketable results, but may also, in the long term, be more sustaining" (Halberstam 2011, 9). By turning toward affective economies that privilege nuanced notions of failure, we approach normative distributions differently, diffractively, in order to imagine sideways trajectories that disrupt the heteronormative, reproductive loop that seems central to much assessment theory and practice.

We argue here that beyond the ways the bell curve functions at the center of both eugenicist and capitalist logics of success and failure, it also engages another trope central to Western imperialist logics, that of reproduction. As with many other assessment practices, the bell curve places our work within a reproductive loop that keeps us from noticing other possibilities. Within confined systems of thought like those produced and sustained by the bell curve, from the start we not only assume what we are going to learn but also how the data will align so we can seek an answer established in our construct from the beginning.

Failure-oriented practices, however, would revel in the intensities and folds (Deleuze 1993) of new sites of assessment research—open-ended, indeterminate spaces with endlessly diffractive potentiality. QVI asks us to privilege what we don't expect, what we might not seek out, to disrupt the linear, reproductive loop, and that disruption will lead us away from the comforts of the known toward the anxieties of the unknown. This is about getting us off the hamster wheel of going endlessly in circles to close the assessment loop and imagining different loops that are iterative, that move outward across lateral planes like Slinkies being stretched and rolled. Failing to reproduce, in other words, requires us to question the expectation that we always do what we've always (already) done in writing assessment. It requires that we unpack the social and cultural barriers to women's success in STEM courses rather than merely realign bodies on a preexisting curve. We must question what is hidden underneath and/or beside our traditional practices. How might posing that question challenge statistical work that assumes normative (cis, white, middle-class) assessment practices? For example, by purposefully seeking out a systematically biased sample to overrepresent a population of students typically disadvantaged by assessments, we can create different statistical distribution shapes that allow us to analyze the nonnormative spaces of demographic data in order to better understand the "long tails" of skewed data. Where traditional statistical models require us to ignore those aberrant bits of data or to explain them away, a QVI framework encourages us to welcome those bits of skewed data, perhaps to build whole assessment stories around those parts that are unfriendly, even hostile, to the normative bodies of our assessments. Through QVI, we can intervene in reproductive frameworks by creating alternative formulas, privileging bodies marked as different, and changing sample populations.

As the image at the start of this chapter demonstrates, we've now turned our Pyraminx so identities is on top, sitting at the front of our thinking. We can see affectivities and materialities as well, and our assessments are being shaped by having our attention focused at these particular levels. At the back, just outside our attention, remains failure. We know it's there and we know it is impacting how we engage the other parts of our model, but as teachers and administrators, we're focused on building something right now, on how we might work with students to create (in the writing classroom) and to imagine (in terms of experiences with writing). But rather than limit our thinking about identities to only the demographic categories into which contemporary human beings are being sorted each day by institutions, what if we imagined identities more broadly? Both race/ethnicity *and* role? Both sexuality and desire? Both gender and motivation? Both class and interest? Or all of the above, or a selection of the above? In the first example we present in this chapter—digital badging—we show how we have engaged the scholarship in writing studies around labor-based grading contracts in order to connect labor/activity with individual and shared interests, desires, and motivations, all of which are affective experiences rooted in how people performing as student-writers imagine themselves. An assessment model that's built to engage the affective and performative elements of writing may be one way we can provide a space for student writers to bring their whole selves to the writing situation without fear of retribution (grades) and inequitable distributions.

GRADING CONTRACTS: FAILING TO (RE)PRODUCE QUALITY

So how might we break up the quality-focused performance of writing and the ongoing reproduction of a success narrative that always requires failure in our assessment ecologies? For some writing teachers and assessment scholars, labor-based grading contracts have been a path for moving assessment laterally toward alternative goals. In fact, if we were to continue Kathleen Blake Yancey's (1999) waves metaphor for understanding the major shift in writing assessment, we might be tempted to name our current moment the *social justice (fourth) wave*, in which grading contracts are poised to be a key classroom assessment intervention. In the recent pivot toward labor-based grading contracts, writing teachers have initiated what seems to us a significant intervention in more traditional classroom-based assessment frameworks that forward narrow (racist, sexist, ableist) notions of quality over more robust and ample constructs of writing like the ones we are trying to capture through the examples in this book. While we have some concerns about the ways grading contracts may eventually be commodified as they are with the 6+1 Trait® Writing Analysis, which we examine in the previous chapter, at the moment, as teachers and students are engaging this new assessment framework in generative ways, we see potential for how such contracts work to queer normative (reproductive) assessment models.

While Peter Elbow (1993, 1997, 2000) mentioned grading contracts around the turn of the century, as a fully articulated assessment ecology, they were not introduced broadly to writing studies until Jane Danielewicz and Peter Elbow (2009) published "A Unilateral Grading Contract to Improve Learning and Teaching"; over the last two decades, grading contracts have become yet another option in a long line of interventions that center on our ongoing affective concerns about evaluating student writing (see also Tchudi 1997). Danielewicz and Elbow (2009) build their idea of the grading contract on Ira Shor's (1996) learning contracts: "We give up as much power over grading as we can manage, but we keep full power over course requirements. Note, however, that we don't hold back on teacher evaluation and judgment" (247). By retaining power over course requirements, Danielewicz and Elbow can maintain a focus in their writing classes on what they understand the writing construct to be, so their contract names activities like the following: attending class regularly, meeting all the due dates for projects set by the instructor, participating in class activities, providing feedback to peers on drafts, and copyediting final drafts (245–46). In addition to these activities, the contract also names far more subjective concepts/ dispositions like the following:

- give thoughtful peer feedback during class workshops and work faithfully with your group on other collaborative tasks (e.g., sharing papers, commenting on drafts, peer editing, online discussion boards);
- sustain effort and investment on each draft of all papers;
- make substantive revisions when the assignment is to revise—extending or changing the thinking or organization—not just editing or touching up. (246)

While the grading contract is intended to be a transparent agreement between teacher and student, it's worth noting that the language here—*thoughtful, faithfully, effort, investment, substantive*—represents highly subjective concepts that seem to speak to the dispositions named as important for success in two of the primary guiding documents of our field, the WPA Outcomes Statement (Council of Writing Program Administrators 2014) and the *Framework for Success in Postsecondary Writing* (Council of Writing Program Administrators, National Council of Teachers of English, National Writing Project 2011), and which have been critiqued significantly by Daniel M. Gross and Jonathan Alexander (2016) and Asao Inoue (2014) when they have been taken up without a more theoretical and nuanced understanding of what they might entail.

More recently, in *Labor-Based Grading Contracts: Building Equity and Inclusion in the Compassionate Writing Classroom,* Inoue (2019) has constructed a full assessment framework and justification for grading contracts in order to forward a writing and assessment construct that does not simply privilege values around *quality* that are ultimately a front for white-supremacist language practices and pedagogies. "Grades," Inoue argues, "represent one judge's ranking of a written document, but they say little to nothing about the substance of the performance of writing, the actual labor of writing that produced the document" (148). At the center of Inoue's project is dislodging in our disciplinary imagination any belief that students' written products are direct assessments of their learning or ability; to us, this is a major intervention into the ways teachers and writing programs tend to imagine their respective scenes of assessment:

> A document is not the actual learning, but we often treat it as such. It is an outcome of learning. It only represents indirectly learning to write. While writing programs usually consider the written products of students to be direct evidence of learning in assessments, they are not exactly that. They are not a direct measure of learning to write. They may be the most direct measure a program uses in an assessment, but they are not the *actual learning to write.* (148)

By advocating for labor-based grading contracts, Inoue calls our attention to the ways we are rarely assessing what we think we are assessing; more often, we are assessing a simulacra of something we fail to name or define accurately. When we shift our understanding about the relationship between finished products and assessments, we can begin to recognize that "getting students in a program or classroom to produce a certain kind of written product does not mean that anyone has learned anything in particular. It means they've been able to reproduce a certain kind of document in those circumstances" (149).

To counter this project, Inoue has built his grading contracts out of Danielewicz and Elbow's earlier work and examples in an attempt to acknowledge all students can labor on a project, even if they do not all start at the same place in terms of experience, knowledge, or acculturated writing ability. Likewise, similar to our larger argument in this book, Inoue believes contract-based grading allows for and encourages "productive failure" (157; see also Inoue 2014, 2020, 339). While we are suspicious of forcing failure to perform "productively" (and reproductively), we recognize, like Inoue, that failure is "necessary" (157) as part of learning, and that failure experiences can show us (sideways) "places to grow" (158). More important, and similar to Halberstam (2011), Inoue argues that failure also demonstrates a larger system is at work, that failure is not only or fundamentally an individual experience: "While writers can control much of what they do as writers and learners, *the nature of failure in ecologies is equally produced by those ecologies themselves,* and failure can have value and worth to the writer in those ecologies" (Inoue 2019, 159; emphasis added). Where grading contracts turn attention away from grade grubbing and the constant fear of not measuring up (for some) or needing the top mark (for others), they represent an important break in writing classrooms and programs merely reproducing the same flawed, quality-obsessed writing and assessment constructs.

As teachers, we have also been drawn to grading contracts since first reading about them in Danielewicz and Elbow (2009), and like they and Inoue (2019), we have explored their possibilities, both as B normed with A grades reserved for exceptional quality and as B normed with additional labor required for the A. For Danielewicz and Elbow (2009) and Inoue (2019), the grading contract has typically been constructed so all students who complete a certain amount and type of labor can expect to earn a B, no questions asked. These scholar-teachers sketch out the activities, behaviors, and dispositions they think represent appropriate labor for a writing course. Inoue (2019) frames the move from B to A for his students as follows: "The grade of B (3.1) depends primarily on behavior and labor. Have you shown responsible effort and consistency in our class? Have you done what was asked of you in the spirit it was asked? Higher grades than the default, the grades of 3.4, 3.7, or 4.0, however, require more labor that helps or supports the class in its mutual discussions and examinations of language" (136). After this statement, he lists a series of activities (e.g., revising projects, completing additional projects, creating a class presentation) students can complete to move their grade from B to A. While Danielewicz and Elbow (2009) frame their A as based on quality—"The grade of B does not derive from my judgment about the quality of your writing. Grades higher than B, however, do rest on my judgment of writing quality. To earn higher grades you must produce writing—particularly for your final portfolio—that I judge to be of exceptionally high quality" (246)—Inoue's contract maintains labor as the assessed variable throughout.

Having worked with grading contracts for many years, we found our-selves ultimately landing near Inoue: for us, labor remains the variable for grading though we are less apt to count labor as minutes/hours of work than as projects completed. In a more recent response to a pure-labor approach, Ellen Carillo (2021) is critical of the differential impact counting labor can have for students, particularly those with disabilities who remind us time spent on task is not a universal or value-neutral assessment model. But even so, we worry about the ways we continue to struggle with articulating a writing construct and assessment framework that does not either obviously or tacitly rely on highly subjective con-cepts hard to enumerate or name but which, well, we surely know when we see them. Danielewicz and Elbow's (2009) more subjective categories are ultimately mirrored in Inoue's (2019) as he explains the normal B grade to his students.

> In a nutshell, if you do all that is asked of you *in the manner and spirit* it
> is asked, if you work through the processes we establish and the work
> we assign ourselves in the labor instructions during the quarter, if you
> do all the labor asked of you, then you'll get a "B" (3.1) course grade.
> It will not matter what I or your colleagues think of your writing, only
> that *you are listening to our feedback compassionately.* (145–46; emphasis
> added)

"In the manner and spirit" strikes us as a difficult set of dispositions/behaviors to name in the same granular way we may name numbers of projects required, or numbers of hours required for work, or types of projects/genres. Danielewicz and Elbow and Inoue—and certainly our own attempts to use contracts over the years—demonstrate how diffi-cult it is to remove all quality judgments from the writing construct or from our assessment paradigms. But our investment in affective strains of queer rhetorics also cautions us against creating an assessment frame-work purely centered on countable items (time, pages, documents, genres, etc.).[1] After all, our broader writing construct is filled with intan-gible elements essential to *effective* writing. Our critique here isn't to sug-gest we should jettison those elements as part of our assessment model but to show that grading contracts, just like rubrics and other assessment technologies, are not necessarily going to be free of the more subjective (i.e., affective) elements of writing and assessment. And because of that, we cannot assume a move to labor-based grading contracts alone will right many of the oppressive frameworks that shape our beliefs about writing and success. We do wonder, however, how labor-based grading contracts allow students to engage their identities more fully in an as-sessment ecology. We've seen in our own classes how students clamor for the identity of an A student or a good writer. Labor-based contracts permit students to set those identities aside (if they so choose) and engage in a different set of identities they may never have been encouraged to explore in the classroom. And yet, these identity explorations also come at a cost. Not all students have the ability to set aside their identities in hopes of exploring learning for the sake of learning. Gender, race, sexuality, and class shape the ways students can engage classroom labor. As archaeologist Stephen W. Silliman (2006) argues, "Labor is a multiply experienced relation and a multiply relational experience—it is not always about only class or capitalism; it can also be about bodies, gender, and identity" (161). One way we have tried to move closer to the labor-based ideal, however, has been through the use of contract-based digital badging frameworks, which allows us to consider the subjective and affective elements of the writing construct while still acknowledging student labor as a core component of engagement and learning.

EMBRACING LATERAL ASSESSMENT
TRAJECTORIES: DIGITAL BADGING

In their respective writing foundations courses, Stephanie and Will made the switch from traditional grading contracts to digital badging around 2014, as both were intrigued by the disruption to narrow notions of quality that grading contracts embodied and both were also working on some microcredentialing projects with the National Writing Project. By the time they started imagining digital badging as part of a classroom-based assessment ecology, Open Badges had been on the scene for a few years (starting around 2010) and was being touted by many, along with MOOCs, as a "revolution" in education (IMS 2020). Naturally suspicious of such silver-bullet fixes, Stephanie and Will nevertheless found the promise of customization, individuation, and collaboration central to the development of badges extremely appealing, as those values were also central to their writing pedagogies. The born-digital Open Badges framework that had emerged through a partnership with Mozilla and the McArthur Foundation, and which was already by 2014 being used by numerous internet start-ups like Cred.ly and Badgr, allowed creators to design visual images reminiscent of scouting merit badges; to those badges, creators could attach various activities individuals could do to earn the badge (credential). Because creators could make as many badges as they wanted, it was easy to design multiple badges and even to create levels/learning pathways within each badge. Part of a constructivist learning paradigm, Open Badges seemed especially salient as a way of naming discreet parts of writing processes and production, linking them in open and connected ways and then awarding them to students so they could track their progress through the course without necessarily making each activity/process or product about a particular grade. For Stephanie and Will, then, this represented yet another way for their course-based assessment ecologies to eschew a focus on teacher-determined quality and to forward student choice, self-direction, and labor-based frameworks.

For example, in his English 2201: Writing about Education course, Will used digital badges to allow students to "choose their own adventure" in the course and to work on the numbers and types of projects that met their own goals for the course. The course is intended to support sophomores as a bridge between a more introductory college-level writing course and the students' majors; in this case, the students were likely to be intended education majors, so Will worked to design projects/badges that would be particularly relevant to that audience. Likewise, since the students were then currently or would soon be studying educational theories and histories, Will highlighted that labor-based grading contracts and digital badging were both emerging ideas in education, intersecting with ongoing discussions of gamification, and created spaces for students to study and reflect on these practices while participating in a pedagogy that used them.

In line with "you must do X amount of work" to achieve a particular grade, Will asked himself what the essential elements of the course were—in terms of his personal and professional course outcomes, programmatic outcomes, and national outcomes for college writing—and then he asked himself, "What experiences and abilities do I imagine are a baseline to achieving those outcomes?" From that, he decided all students would need to complete the multilevel work of three badges in order to earn a C for the course and that after they had thus passed the course, they could do additional labor and learning to justify a different grade:

- F = 1 or no required badge completed
- D = 2 required badges completed
- C = 3 required badges completed
- B = 3 required + 1 optional badge completed
- A = 3 required + 2 optional badges completed

Each badge involved at least three levels of activity, each level progressively more difficult or time consuming and involving greater degrees of intellectual engagement. The Fundamentals badge focused on a

Figure. 5.2. English 2201: Writing about Education badges

significant portion of the (often invisible) early labor in any course: students had tasks related to reading the syllabus and asking questions about policies, goals, and so forth, familiarizing themselves with the various badges, and developing their individual plans for how many badges they would complete and what order they wanted to work in (see figure 5.2). Because students could choose projects in a modular fashion after completing the Fundamentals badge, during any week in the course, some number of students might be engaged in each of the badges; therefore, some class meetings involved sorting students into badge-based groups so they could help each other through common activities like providing peer response and feedback, while other times, heterogeneous groupings made more sense.

Much of this course was centered on the Connected Learning framework developed by the Digital Media and Learning Research Hub at the University of California Humanities Research Institute (Ito et al. 2013), which focuses on interests, relationships, and opportunities as key elements of successful learning experiences. These are also affective elements of our identities, parts of what names and shapes who we are as people, in addition to more common demographic markers. Our passions, connections with others, and the ability we have to be part of different groups or events all become part of how we identify ourselves and understand ourselves in a relational framework. As such, the Connected Learning framework seemed to fit well with the work we were beginning around queering assessment practices. Likewise, given the success Stephanie had with badging in her courses, Will developed badge-based projects for his course with the goal of engaging students around their interests while encouraging them to explore relationship building both inside and outside the course (e.g., community partners, other instructors, nonclassroom literacy educators) and to explore opportunities that might not be normative in more traditional college courses. For example, students who chose to complete the three-level Making Literacy badge began by watching videos and reading online articles that would help them think about literacy less as autonomous or functional abilities and more as ideological and sociological practices of reading, writing, doing, and understanding. Level two asked them to learn to make/do something they didn't already know how to do and to pay attention to how they learned to do something new; they also were asked to identify a mentor who might help them, either a real person they could work with or a set of mentor texts (printed or online), and to reflect on how these mentor projects helped them (or didn't). Finally, in level three, they were challenged to take on a more sophisticated project related to what they had learned. One African American male student in the course used this project as a way to connect with his grandmother in Brooklyn, New York: he chose to teach himself to crochet, and he knew his grandmother knew how. This student's reflection on his project showcased how much he learned from both print-based texts and online videos but also how limited those sources could sometimes be, requiring him to turn to his grandmother's vast years of experience with yarn, needles, and patterns to help him understand more individually how to hold his crochet hook, why he might want synthetic rather than cotton or wool yarn, and how to read some of the more difficult parts of the pattern he was using to create a lap afghan. The student wrote thoughtfully about his experiences learning a new literacy, noting that if we understand literacy only as "saying words," we miss out on all the embodied ways we learn about what words really mean, particularly when those words are connected to people we care about and to projects that matter to us.

This student was also extremely proud of the lap throw he crocheted—in Pittsburgh Steelers' colors—when he brought it to class to demonstrate what he had learned and what he had created as part of completing the three levels of activities and earning his Making Literacy badge. Was his final "make" an expert (e.g., high-quality) example of crochet? Certainly not—though it was impressive for only a couple of weeks of work, and it did function as a lap throw. Likewise, the instructions/pattern the student wrote that would allow another user to replicate his work did not look as polished as the mentor texts he had found online and annotated as part of his learning process, but the student was also able to explain parts where another crocheter would know what was going on from experience. In short, he was able to demonstrate how *crochet literacies* are more complex than simply "saying words" or "writing words," that they are also about how those words, symbols, and images interact and leverage user experiences in order to work. This project activated many of the dispositions and values central to the *Framework for Success in Postsecondary Writing* but did so without forcing a success/failure binary onto the writing and learning experience. Similarly, because the student was allowed to choose the badge pathway most meaningful to him at a particular moment, rather than follow a preestablished pathway determined by the teacher, this project allowed for sideways growth centered on intentionality and opportunity rather than mastery. The end result was that the student got extensive experience with learning a new craft while also learning a lot about how literacy works across different (e.g., non-school-based) spaces and gained significant experience with different written genres and writing/research practice that have both in-school and out-of-school value.

In neither Will's nor Stephanie's writing-foundations courses, where digital badging and a labor-based contract system worked together to engage student-selected interests, relationships, and opportunities, did they see a reproduction of the bell curve in the final grades. While one student in Will's course chose early on to earn a C and complete just the bare minimum of required badges, the other twenty-four sought and earned Bs or As based on the labor they chose to expend that semester. No single genre of writing was reproduced again and again, nor was each piece written for the teacher-audience. But the most important thing they failed to reproduce was the normative construct of school-based writing as represented through a quality-focused assessment ecology. Lots of high-quality work emerged, certainly, and as Will and Stephanie reflect on those experiences now, they see students over the last six years who have created as many high-quality products as they ever did in more traditional quality-focused classrooms, but what shifted are the affective economies that allowed for and encouraged quality as an outcome of activity and engagement rather than the cart that we consistently put in front of the horse on the path to a particular predetermined outcome.

It is also important to point out that the badges, both types and levels, and the granular products and activities tied to those badges were built for each course Will and Stephanie taught. We certainly recognize that microcredentialing frameworks run the risk of being hypercommodified and then hyperreproduced. Because they can be built in a modular fashion, much like MOOCs, there are no doubt many ways neoliberal economic values can make particular badges and badging frameworks into marketable digital tools that would be counterproductive to the queer rhetorical work we seek to do in our courses. Of course, the same can be said of grading contracts more generally, which is perhaps one reason Inoue does not adopt Danielewicz and Elbow's contract wholesale. Nor, in fact, did Will and Stephanie adopt any of the contracts they read about without also making modifications based on local needs and contexts. But because contracts and badging frameworks allow for classroom teachers and students to collaboratively negotiate labor and activity, as well as various affective valences around composing, we believe these frameworks have the potential to activate alternative and ultimately subversive writing and assessment models across writing studies.

We also argue, based on our experiences across multiple sections of writing-foundations courses over the last six years, that labor-based assessment frameworks can point to another important failure: grading contract models can also fail to reproduce whiteness as the normative model of experience. Multiple scholars have found that BIPOC students and lower-middle-class students are far more interested in engaging with digital badging in the writing classroom than are their white, affluent peers (Inoue 2015; Inoue and Poe 2012a; West-Puckett 2016). In earlier work critical of grading contracts, researchers at the University of Akron found their students viewed grading contracts as largely irrelevant because these students had come to expect that the amount of work they invested in their courses would automatically be reflected in their course grade (Spidell and Thelin 2006). While these scholars do not focus on the racial makeup of their campus, it is worth noting the University of Akron is around 75 percent white. For this group, most already perceived a connection between their labor and their grade: the more work they put in, the better their final course grade should be. The extra labor of negotiating the contract, then, seemed to these white students to be a waste of time, as the students already assumed the educational system was fair for all participants. These researchers feel the negotiation of grading contracts ultimately creates not only frustration and futility but also a kind of disillusionment. For students from marginalized backgrounds, however, this assumption regarding the return on investment for more labor in the form of a higher grade doesn't seem to hold. In the racist and classist spaces of both K–12 and higher education in the United States, students from marginalized backgrounds have often found their hard work has not always yielded better grades, as often grades are linked to white-supremacist and other reductive disciplinary models of language use, discursive organizational patterns, and rhetorical style. As such, these students may not believe this implicit assumption, one that does seem to function as an implied white social contract in most of our classrooms. Like Inoue (2015, 2019), we have found that making these implied grading contracts explicit, concrete, and tangible to all students—regardless of prior educational preparation, experience, and assimilation into white middle- and upper-class discourses—can foster trust and a sense of agency in the writing classroom. These affective frameworks are essential to developing a socially just notion of fairness in writing assessment. In chapter 7, we return to fairness and how we can move beyond facile notions of fairness that operate across our campuses.

LOOPING BEYOND THE WRITTEN PRODUCT

The speed with which many compositionists have taken up labor-based grading contracts is a testament to the pedagogical and academic freedom many of us still enjoy in higher education. However, when we move beyond the classroom, the amount of pushback can be staggering, as multiple stakeholders engage assessment processes from so many different points of view. When funding streams and resources are tied to those assessments, it can become even more difficult to work beyond traditional models of success. In 2010, when Will became director of the University Writing Program at East Carolina University, there was a tiny budget for supporting various WAC initiatives and a small staff to manage professional development and the campus writing center. While everyone on campus seemed to know there was a writing center to support student writers, almost no one understood the "writing center"—at a university of then nearly twenty-seven thousand students—was one round table in the lobby of the campus library. Given hours of operation and staffing budgets, it was nearly impossible to host more than two thousand face-to-face and online writing conferences in an academic year. With the possibility of several million dollars in campus funding being redirected to support our then-upcoming reaccreditation initiative, it seemed a no-brainer to put forward writing as a key learning outcome to track and improve across campus (Sharer et al. 2016). With that added attention came the understanding that what ECU really needed was a large, supportive writing center to be the hub for much of this work, and they needed to hire a highly qualified writing center director.

Over the course of ten years, ECU University Writing Center came to embody the typical success narrative we often tell through usage statistics. In the first three years of the new and expanded center, for example, student usage increased by 265 percent. As program and center directors, Will and Nikki were thrilled by such growth but also recognized this aggregate percentage offered a limited view of success: they still wanted to know more about the students who comprised those usage statistics, which also meant they wanted to know who wasn't feeling welcomed and supported (yet) in the center. The writing center registration form provided for the typical student demographics—class level, gender, race, ethnicity, and major—and had been in use for years. However, as they continued to bring diversity concerns to staff meetings, the writing center student consultants pointed out they had no clue about what role, if any, sexuality played in writing and who did or did not use the writing center. After meeting with the leadership from the Dr. Jesse R. Peel LGBTQ Center on campus, as well as a student affairs educator who also focused on assessment, Will and Nikki realized one way to be committed to social justice on campus was to add a question about sexuality to the writing center registration form, to move beyond the male/female binary on the gender question already in use, and to recognize the need for better student pronoun acknowledgments. Unfortunately, the campus diversity office and the university attorneys were less excited to see the addition and through a host of phone calls and meetings worked aggressively to have us remove all demographic information from our form, arguing that none of it pertained to the services the writing center provides and that only the campus registrar's office should track such data.

Will and Nikki pushed back. They argued demographic information is pertinent to larger assessment designs in knowing who is being served and how well their needs are being met. When one university attorney suggested that other departments and programs meet their students' needs without asking about sexuality, Will responded, "How do you know that?" The fact that no other campus office collects information regarding sexuality as part of their assessments does *not* mean LGBTQ students do not have any concerns; nor does it suggest this population has had space to be critical of their experiences. In fact, Will and Nikki believed the lack of information made their desire to collect the data even stronger because they truly did not know if their writing center services were meeting the needs of LGBTQ students. Did LGBTQ students feel welcomed in the ECU University Writing Center? The university was comfortable with a Don't Ask, Don't Tell model of assessment. For example, while national surveys like the Community College Survey of Student Engagement (CCSSE) and the National Survey of Student Engagement (NSSE) ask questions about sexuality and gender/sexual orientation, ECU did not purchase the results of those questions, choosing instead to limit the demographic data requested to categories of race/ethnicity, family income, and binary gender identities. Eventually, because the program and center directors were respected and valued administrators on campus, the then-provost stepped in to support them by suggesting they seek IRB approval and consider this collection of data research rather than assessment—a vexed distinction, at best, but one that seemed to assuage the powers that be and provide some degree of protection for ongoing data collection and analysis. In the context of ECU, the writing center's desire to collect nonnormative assessment data marked the space and its directors as assessment killjoys. It didn't matter that they were going to report the data in aggregate, as the writing center had always done. It didn't matter that they were going to ask critical questions about the work they were doing to see if they could do that work better. What mattered was that they wanted to queer programmatic assessment at the university both by privileging queer students and by disrupting the assessment categories the university promoted.

Around the same time, Will and Nikki took up the questions they posed to the university attorney as broader research and assessment questions. Who is coming into the writing center space, and are we supporting their writing needs? To find answers to that question, they connected with the Peel Center on campus to recruit LGBTQ students into focus groups and interviews in order to discover where writing assessments and LGBTQ lived experiences had intersected (or not) in these students' educational experiences. In the end, only gay male students volunteered to participate in the initial focus groups, which was itself a powerful reminder of how and why marginalized bodies may resist inclusion in research if they are uncertain about who is asking the questions and how their stories will be used (possibly against them). But this problem of overrepresentation, Will and Nikki realized, was also meaningful: so often in our research, we collapse LGBTQ folks into one megacategory of identification, as though all these folks share the same experiences. They realized that by focusing on one subgroup of LGBTQ people at a time, they might get very different answers than if they did a more traditional aggregate data analysis across these groupings. They also realized that before conducting large-scale studies about LGBTQ students' GPAs or how LGBTQ persistence/retention aligned with other demographic markers, they needed to talk to students to understand how to develop identity taxonomies and what data to collect. After all, is LGBTQ even still the most appropriate set of markers to use? And what counts as writing and assessment when we ask students who may never have been allowed to write about their sexuality and gender identity before? Focus-group methodology provided one way to gather student input on designing studies that include LGBTQ students as a demographic category. And, when we think about that "grade" moment in the writing classroom, listening to students in these focus groups unpack their own affective and embodied negotiations regarding how and when to write about certain topics under the guise of "can I get a passing grade for this" becomes a key moment we should consider more intentionally as we design and implement assessment prompts and activities (Caswell and Banks 2018).

For this particular assessment study, Will and Nikki conducted two IRB-approved focus groups with a total of five students who identified as gay. Both focus groups were audio and video recorded. The focus groups employed a semistructured interview script with five questions designed to elicit students' experiences and stories with writing assessment both in and out of the traditional classroom. The first focus group included two undergraduate cis-male students: Michael, a white junior transfer student, and Marcus, an African American senior. The second focus group included one undergraduate student and two graduate students, all white males: Jason, a senior; Matthew, a first-semester master's student; and Steven, a third-semester master's student. All participants have been given pseudonyms. The first focus group lasted about forty-five minutes, whereas the second focus group was closer to seventy-five minutes. Will and Nikki initially attributed this difference in time to having three participants in the second focus group, but as they listened to the audio recordings, it became clear that participants in the second group demonstrated a greater sense of personal awareness and confidence as gay men and as students more generally, likely owing to the fact that two of them were in graduate school. Following transcription, Will and Nikki engaged in inductive, emergent coding (Kelle 2007) to preserve the students' experiences and to think through how those experiences shape the ways we approach researching and writing about LGBTQ students and assessment. Three key codes emerged as they read through the transcripts:

affective markers (e.g., teacher/classmate behaviors that suggested LGBTQ topics were welcomed); *curriculum markers* (e.g., presence/absence of LGBTQ topics in syllabi or assignment directions); and *identity markers* (e.g., students negotiating coming out in college or high-school contexts; demographics). These minor codes led to their major code that writing assessment for LGBTQ students is emotionally risky.

At the university level, the participants had to negotiate how and when to come out to classmates, teachers, and friends/family alongside students' typical concerns about writing (e.g., What does the teacher want? What does the rubric say? How do I phrase this?). For LGBTQ students, choosing to write about their personal experiences or an LGBTQ issue for a graded assignment becomes both a grade-based choice and a political choice, as well as one filtered through multiple issues around personal growth and development, and unfortunately still involves concerns about personal and academic safety. Aside from just wondering what the teacher wants or the writing context demands (e.g., organization, citation style, length, or type of sources), student writers may also need to consider the political leanings of their instructor, classmates, and university community. When the participants did elect to write on LGBTQ topics, it was because they felt it was somehow permitted. Marcus told a story of how he wrote two different versions of an assignment before he could discern whether it was safe to submit the one that outed him to his teacher and classmates. He ended up submitting his assignment late as he sought out cues for which one to submit, but the fact that he was enrolled in a face-to-face five-week summer course meant the time it took him to decide whether it was safe to hand in the writing he wanted to hand in meant he lost valuable time before moving to the next project and also lost points for late work. Would mentioning what was going on in his composing process and his anxiety be understood by the teacher as complaining or making up excuses? Where in our assessment frameworks do we understand the complex affective work that goes on with writing assignments and deadlines, particularly among marginalized and/or minoritized students? While the writing construct Edward White, Norbert Elliot, and Irvin Peckham (2015, 75) provide in *Very Like a Whale* gestures toward some of these broader contextualizing elements, we also recognize that there remain significant affective dimensions in the writing processes of the queer students Will and Nikki interviewed that are not centered in this or other common writing constructs that operate in our field.

In addition to adhering to the assignment guidelines, LGBTQ students must read the political and affective aspects of the teacher and classroom (Cox 2016). In the example above of Marcus, we see assessment practices are directly related to composition practices: for one student, the emotional work of articulating a self in text (Banks 2003; Hindeman 2003) was significantly different from other types of "personal" writing (Newkirk 2002) and in this case impacted the time it took for the student to finish the project and turn it in. Unlike the often-innocuous stories of favorite childhood toys, summer vacations, or family traditions that pop up in a number of both test-based and classroom-based narrative assignments for students from kindergarten to college, coming out as topic and trope remains one students in classroom settings have little experience writing, receiving feedback on, and revising. Recognizing the affective impact such writing has is important. For example, should Marcus's late paper lose points? Marcus may have done twice as much labor as his peers because the paper he wanted to write and the paper he thought safer to write were at odds. Both those experiences suggest some LGBTQ students may struggle more with certain writing assignments or activities as they attempt to negotiate their own sense of safety in a classroom or assessment setting. As we recognize above, in a labor-based assessment paradigm, there may be ways to account for Marcus's labor, both physical and affective, but doing so requires teachers to engage with an expanded writing and assessment construct.

Unfortunately, these emotional readings of professors and syllabi may not figure into our traditional notions of the writing construct. While they represent real, lived experiences students are negotiating while writing for our classes, they become invisible in our assessments and assessment reports. The focus group didn't forward a notion of programmatic writing assessment administrators are used to seeing. There were no charts in the report. There were no statistics. Instead, there were narratives. And a bulleted list of options Will and Nikki chose to implement based on what they learned from this group of students, students they are very grateful to for taking the time to speak and think with them about their experiences with writing and assessment.

On the most basic level, we think it is also still worth noting that simply engaging students as part of our assessment practices may represent a queer approach to assessment, one that pushes against the simple repro-duction of rubrics, evaluative guides, and other prefabricated assess-ment instruments that work to constrain the writing construct and the work students are permitted to do in writing classrooms. Unfortunately, far too often our attempts to engage students in assessment practices occur in spaces where their assessment activities are more performative than embedded in the process. Through writer's memos on portfolios, as we note in previous chapters, we run the risk of asking students to demonstrate their work in a prefabricated writing construct they had no hand in building.

HIDDEN UNDER SOME NUMBERS

The question of who we are serving has continued to haunt the ECU University Writing Center. As program and center directors, Will and Nikki have watched the racial, sexual, and gendered demographics of the writing center staff shift over any given semester. Similarly, as the staff shifts, so too do the students who seek out the writing center. It wasn't too hard to draw the conclusion that representation in the space contributes to students' desire to enter the writing center—or to go elsewhere. As Nikki was sharing her thoughts on who is and isn't using the writing center during an end-of-semester staff meeting, consultants began to share their experiences with who they saw coming in and going out of the writing center. One consultant shared, "As someone who works nights, I tend to see and hear from Black students who like to come to the writing center in the evening because there's less of a felt sense of being 'on display'[2] to their peers." That insight kept creeping into Nikki's thoughts as she worked through end-of-semester usage data. With WCOnline, the scheduling platform the center uses, it would be easy to analyze usage data and demonstrate that the numbers matched that consultant's experience, but Nikki didn't feel that was necessary. She trusted the stories the staff was sharing and felt reporting data in that way would erase the lived experiences of the staff.

Instead, Nikki turned to ECU's institutional data office to analyze writing center usage data. Rather than look at demographic categories as individual markers, Nikki was interested in an intersectional approach to usage data. In particular, she recognized that budget concerns on campus continued to occur at various levels, and many programs were working to show ever-increasing usage data as a metric of value. While she wasn't thrilled with using usage data to justify the existence of the writing center, Nikki did believe an intersectional approach might provide some of that usage information while also queering the report so as to put different bodies and experiences in front of higher-level administrators on campus. As mentioned above, the UWC collected voluntary data on sexuality as a demographic marker, but ECU as an institution did not. Therefore, to do an institutional-level writing center usage analysis, sexuality was removed as a category because the institutional office couldn't create a comparison cohort from the student body.[3] The demographic categories Nikki had access to were race, gender, and socioeconomic status: three markers routinely used to predict students' likelihood to persist or graduate. In a move to resist simple reproduction of demographic categories, however, Nikki asked whether the institution could run more intersectional analyses because students might hold multiple identity markers that complicate statistical formulas for persistence and graduation, or for learning support.

In writing assessment, when researchers attempt to respond to calls for more fluid understandings of identity markers, those projects don't always integrate fairness into the research process. When crafting sampling plans and deciding on what evidence to gather and analyze, researchers tend to focus on the relationships across categories (after running statistical models) instead of the interactions of those categories during or before the statistical models.[4] While single-gender and demographic category analyses leave the complexity of student bodies invisible and limit our understanding of how demographic markers influence the ways students experience college and learning differently, we don't argue it is simply a numbers or models issue. Rather, we need research designs that consider fairness from the onset so that as evidence is collected, we are attending to the multitude of ways students engage learning. To integrate fairness into the research process, the UWC advocated for a usage assessment that attended to issues of intersectionality (Crenshaw 1989) within statistical models (Zuberi and Bonilla-Silva 2008). One way to engage in intersectionality within statistics is through QuantCrit methodology (López et al. 2018). QuantCrit methodology grounds itself within a critical race theory that privileges the experiences and ways of knowing and being for students of color and actively challenges white-centric frameworks and ideologies. QuantCrit methodology is enacted through quantitative methods that advocate for statistical models attending to intersectional demographic markers. Following Nancy López, Christopher Erwin, Melissa Binder, and Mario Javier Chavez's (2018) intersectional analysis of that achievement gap at a large public institution using QuantCrit methodology, Nikki and the institutional data office at ECU began to construct an analysis of race, gender, and socioeconomic status of writing center users and compare one-year retention rates and four-year graduation rates to those who didn't use the writing center.

Their analysis focused on a cohort of 780 first-year students who used the writing center in fall 2013 (Caswell 2020). Usage data was collected by the writing center and shared with the institutional data office, who then constructed representation within the 4,453 total first-year-student cohort, configured socioeconomic status, and ran distributions of visits across social location (SocLoc) usage to calculate retention and graduation rates. SocLoc refers to the constellation of race, sex, and need level (López et al. 2018) and captures the "configurations of inequality" among the student body (McCall 2001, 6). Race and gender data were easy to access, but given what institutional data were available, financial-need level was used as a proxy for family income/class. High-need students applied for financial aid and were awarded a Pell Grant. Midneed students applied for and were awarded financial aid but not a Pell Grant. No-need students did not apply for financial aid. Focusing specifically on fall 2013 usage data, Nikki compared the retention and graduation rates of the first-year students' SocLoc who used the writing center in fall 2013 to those first-year students' SocLoc who did not use the writing center. The sample initially had Hispanic, American Indian or Alaskan Native, Native Hawaiian or Pacific Islander, nonresident aliens (international), people who identify as two or more races, and people with no reported race or ethnicity as individual race or ethnicity data points, but because of small sample cells, these groups were combined into underrepresented minorities.

Through the intersectional approach of SocLoc, demographic data revealed possible inequalities between student usage that would have otherwise been erased in aggregated gender and race data. Results indicated high-need males and females (table 5.1) used the writing center more frequently than no-need males and females (table 5.2). Focusing on female usage, only 13 percent of high-need white females used the writing center compared to the 29 percent of high-need underrepresented minority females, 25 percent of high-need African American females, and 23 percent of high-need Asian females. The largest percentage gap was between the 23 percent of high-need Asian females who used the writing center at least once in fall 2013 and the 14 percent of no-need Asian females who used the writing center at least once in fall 2013. No-need white females were more likely to use the writing center (21 percent) than high-need white females (13 percent). When race is removed as a variable, the same proportion of high-need females used the writing center as no-need females. One-year retention rates were higher for high-need (92 percent) and no-need females (90 percent) who used the writing center compared with those who did not (79 percent high-need females and 85 percent no-need females). High-need females with no writing center visits in fall 2013 had a 47 percent four-year graduation rate compared to high-need females (63 percent) who used the writing center in fall 2013. No-need females who used the writing center had a slightly higher four-year graduation rate (66 percent) compared with no-need females who did not use the writing center (64 percent).

The intersectional approach holds true for males even though there is a small usage difference between high-need males (13 percent) and no-need males (18 percent). The writing center had already identified males (in general) as an outreach demographic, but this analysis narrowed the outreach demographic to no-need Asian, African American, and underrepresented minority males. High-need (4.2 percent) and no-need (9 percent) Asian males were the least likely to use the writing center compared to other groups. No-need African American males (40 percent) were more likely to use the writing center than high-need African American males (13 percent). One-year retention rates were also higher for high-need (86 percent) and no-need (98 percent) males who used the writing center compared with those who did not (73 percent high-need males and 77 percent no-need males). The four-year graduation rate for high-need males who did not use the writing center was 33 percent, whereas the four-year graduation rate for high-need males who did use the writing center was 44 percent. The four-year graduation rate for no-need males who did not use the writing center was 44 percent, whereas the four-year graduation rate for no-need males who did use the writing center was 63 percent.

These results do not reflect a causal relationship between writing center usage and graduation/retention rates. While an intersectional approach provides a different look at the demographics of who is using the writing center, it does not account for other student characteristics (such as motivation) that might make it more likely for them to graduate sooner.

Prior to this intersectional analysis, the UWC believed it was mirroring the ECU student body by looking at race as a single demographic marker. By simply considering class level, writing center usage went from mirroring the racial breakdown of campus to 69 percent of first-year white students using the writing center compared with only 16 percent of first-year African American students. By looking deeper and intersecting race with gender and financial need, larger usage disparities emerged. For example, 13 percent of high-need Black males used the writing center compared to 40 percent of no-need Black males who used the writing center. While financial need as a single demographic marker does not appear to be a defining feature of students using the writing center, it does appear to illuminate differences when layered with race and gender. As a regional institution with a large first-generation population, the writing center should be paying attention to financial need as part of a students' SocLoc. This also means we must be asking ourselves what affective barriers the UWC may be throwing up for high-need Black male students, in addition to questioning what other social and economic barriers may exist for this group at the university.

What this study showed was that initially the UWC had a normative distribution of singular identity markers that aligned with campus demographics. Because the UWC usage mimicked the campus demographics, no office encouraged the writing center to do anything different. By all accounts and purposes, since the UWC was reproducing other (accepted/normative) campus demographics, everything was assumed to be fine. When Nikki disaggregated the data, the usage evidence no longer aligned with this argument. The UWC was not mimicking campus demographics. Although we do not yet know why, what we do know is what groups of students were not accessing the writing center. In this study, queer validity inquiry pushed us to ask different questions and look to see what was behind the single demographic markers. By making the unseen more visible, the UWC identified the ways it was failing to meet student needs. To engage in a more just model of assessment and impact, the UWC must continue to oversample those demographic groups in order to understand *why* questions rather than merely engage in target marketing.

IMAGINING ALTERNATE DISTRIBUTIONS

Part of what our experiences with queering assessment practices have provided us is a way of thinking differently about the distribution patterns that have become normative both in education and across US culture more broadly. Among statisticians and economists, there are normative distributions that account for probability and predictability, like the Gaussian or normal distribution we reference briefly earlier in this chapter.[5] These distributions—the platykurtic, the mesokurtic, and the leptokurtic—offer three relatively similar visual models for how systems measure their own excesses. The platykurtic is represented by the bell curve we tend to know well, with a large mass in the middle and fairly short tails on either side that represent a low probability of extreme outliers. The mesokurtic distribution follows the same model with even less probability of outliers, looking almost parabolic in nature, but with a slight sloping outward at either side. And the leptokurtic distribution represents far longer tails and suggests the higher probability of extreme outliers. All three distributions are normative because they assume a

Table 5.1. High-need student populations writing center data

		Writing center visits			
		None	*Single*	*Two or more*	*All*
		% (N)	% (N)	% (N)	% (N)
SEX	**RACE GROUP**				
F	Asian	76.6% (36)	12.8% (6)	10.6% (5)	100.0% (47)
	Black or African American	74.4% (215)	13.5% (39)	12.1% (35)	100.0% (289)
	Underrepresented minority	70.7% (94)	14.3% (19)	15.0% (20)	100.0% (133)
	White	86.1% (410)	7.6% (36)	6.3% (30)	100.0% (476)
	All	79.9% (755)	10.6% (100)	9.5% (90)	100.0% (945)
M	**RACE GROUP**				
	Asian	95.8% (23)	0.0% (0)	4.2% (1)	100.0% (24)
	Black or African American	87.2% (150)	4.1% (7)	8.7% (15)	100.0% (172)
	Underrepresented minority	86.1% (99)	8.7% (10)	5.2% (6)	100.0% (115)
	White	86.5% (230)	10.2% (27)	3.4% (9)	100.0% (266)
	All	87.0% (502)	7.6% (44)	5.4% (31)	100.0% (577)
All	**RACE GROUP**				
	Asian	83.1% (59)	8.5% (6)	8.5% (6)	100.0% (71)
	Black or African American	79.2% (365)	10.0% (46)	10.8% (50)	100.0% (461)
	Underrepresented minority	77.8% (193)	11.7% (29)	10.5% (26)	100.0% (248)
	White	86.3% (640)	8.5% (63)	5.3% (39)	100.0% (742)
	All	82.6% (1257)	9.5% (144)	8.0% (121)	100.0% (1522)

mass middle of (statistically) similar data, outcomes, findings, and so forth: they are Lake Wobegon gone average. But economists also study a fourth distribution they refer to as "black swans," or events so rare and

Table 5.2. No-need student populations writing center data

		Writing center visits			
		None	Single	Two or more	All
		% (N)	% (N)	% (N)	% (N)
SEX	RACE GROUP				
F	Asian	85.7% (6)	14.3% (1)	0.0% (0)	100.0% (7)
	Black or African American	76.9% (10)	15.4% (2)	7.7% (1)	100.0% (13)
	Underrepresented minority	74.2% (23)	16.1% (5)	9.7% (3)	100.0% (31)
	White	79.4% (255)	10.6% (34)	10.0% (32)	100.0% (321)
	All	79.0% (294)	11.3% (42)	9.7% (36)	100.0% (372)
M	RACE GROUP				
	Asian	90.9% (10)	0.0% (0)	9.1% (1)	100.0% (11)
	Black or African American	60.0% (6)	20.0% (2)	20.0% (2)	100.0% (10)
	Underrepresented minority	82.6% (19)	4.3% (1)	13.0% (3)	100.0% (23)
	White	87.1% (249)	8.0% (23)	4.9% (14)	100.0% (286)
	All	86.1% (284)	7.9% (26)	6.1% (20)	100.0% (330)
All	RACE GROUP				
	Asian	88.9% (16)	5.6% (1)	5.6% (1)	100.0% (18)
	Black or African American	69.6% (16)	17.4% (4)	13.0% (3)	100.0% (23)
	Underrepresented minority	77.8% (42)	11.1% (6)	11.1% (6)	100.0% (54)
	White	83.0% (504)	9.4% (57)	7.6% (46)	100.0% (607)
	All	82.3% (578)	9.7% (68)	8.0% (56)	100.0% (702)

unpredictable they cannot be accounted for in advance, only studied after they occur (Taleb 2007). While these black swans are extremely rare, they are still part of a normative binary framework statisticians and economists consider. What strikes us about this somewhat granular model is that it imagines two extremes: the utterly normative (with acceptable variations) and the extremely rare. But the reality of our classrooms and writing programs, as we discuss at length throughout this book, is that they do not look like either of these things. They are neither large enough and diverse enough to meet any requirement for a statistically normative distribution, nor are they catastrophic events.

As teachers and program administrators, what we need instead are visual/thinking models that help us meaningfully reimagine our assessment distributions. We conclude this chapter, then, by imagining with you, our readers, at least one distribution shape we believe better represents writing assessment as a queer praxis, one rooted in valuing dissensus and radical justice as part of our writing construct. To do so, we invite you to join us in leaving behind the two-dimensional plane of the bell curve to unflatten how we imagine the distribution of data, bodies, and affects. For such a model, we turn to nonlinear, nontraditional geometries, or perhaps to the movements, intensities, and folds represented in models from fluid dynamics and non-Newtonian fluids more generally. Imagine the image in figure 5.3: fluid assessments as a classroom or even just a single assignment, where a writing activity starts at rest in a fluid mass of possibility, undisturbed, perhaps, until the assignment or activity is presented to the students. The teacher/assignment initiates an agitation, but one that strikes the fluid at different rates in different places; the agitations created by the assignment and its affects, histories, and resonances create different tensions in the fluid/classroom, different experiences for each writer. Some writers will be pulled up by this special, momentary combination of forces, seeming to take off on the project, while others will find the topics, the context, the genre conventions, the linguistic expectations overwhelming, frustrating, anxiety producing, possibly even debilitating. Those writers will respond differently, create different movements or none at all. But all these writers and their differential responses to the stimulus of this assignment/activity will still remain part of the larger ecology. Some will shine at peer review even as they struggle to write their own response; others will shut down, generating negative or resistant affects in the space. Rather than a linear grade model in which there must be a certain number of As, Bs, Cs, and so forth, what if our classrooms and programs were spaces where we noticed what the work does, how it does it, other ways it might do that same and/or different work, spaces where we value the peaks and valleys, successes and failures alike? Rather than a mere comparative model of ranking and sorting, what if we saw what each writer's process and

Figure 5.3. Non-Newtonian fluid plane.

product does both on its own and in connection with the larger system? What if we could share that noticing and make it part of our classroom and programmatic assessment ecologies? How might engaging students in this sort of relational system create a different affective and epistemological assessment paradigm, one not rooted in competition and individual success but in the awareness that writing and meaning making are fundamentally social and shared projects?

Here we are using our own fairly pedestrian ideas about non-Newtonian fluids, which experience different levels of viscosity, fluidity, and resistance based on the ways they interact with stimuli both internal and external to the system. Children in school often make a substance from cornstarch and water called "oobleck" as a way of learning about such fluid systems and how they differ from Newtonian fluids, whose viscosity does not change based on external stimuli. We think this is a helpful metaphor for us in terms of assessment, as we've been thinking about how so much of what happens in and around writing is fluid, moving, shifting, adjusting based on a range of affective and material experiences. The need to grade, evaluate, or assess, then, can become an external stimulus that affects the "viscosity" of our students' writing systems: some texts become resistant, while others open up to external analysis. But in a non-Newtonian fluid plane, the movements of external stimuli, applied differently and in different ways, may cause different parts of the fluid to respond differently, some becoming thick and viscous while other parts remain loose. We invite you to imagine how such a plane might allow for another, less hierarchical, less linear image of assessment to emerge.

Rather than reproducing a linear model that requires failures and nets large averages in order to mark certain products at certain times as exceptional, we imagine a queer distribution model, perhaps one that is fluid like in figure 5.3. That's the model that emerges when we engage in the descriptive collaborative assessments from the previous chapter or when we make use of the learning stories we discuss in the next chapter. Or we might also imagine one that is rhizomatic, or another that is crenelated like the hyperbolic geometries of a coral reef, which are "characterized by an almost organic excess" ("Hyperbolic Space," n.d.). These are the sorts of distribution patterns that emerge when we reject mastery, expertise, and quality as the sine qua non of our writing and assessment constructs. In models that acknowledge the role of dissensus and radical justice in our writing processes and products, represented in this chapter by the nonlinear flows of digital badging and contract grading, learning emerges along curving folds that shift and change with both time and tide: as students engage with composing and making through the Connected Learning framework, for example, they activate their interests/passions and connect with others; they follow some paths, stop, change direction, follow other paths; they build connections across networks; they abandon some things, pick up others. Our traditional assessment frameworks and grade-distribution models cannot capture the moments of intensity and flow central to such a diffractive, sideways pedagogy or writing construct. When we cannot imagine other distributions, we run the risk of shoehorning our teaching practices into untenable containers. Continuing to do so means ultimately never really enacting the capacious writing construct most writing studies professionals desire for the writing classroom.

But classrooms do not happen in isolation from larger contexts that serve to act on them, so our classroom practices will always be in conversation with broader institutional and cultural paradigms. To that end, we also hold that a recognition of dissensus and radical justice in our writing construct means we must challenge large-scale studies of data by welcoming the opportunity to oversample individual demographic groups and disaggregate normative data sets. When we imagine the larger writing construct or assessment ecology as fluid in the ways figure 5.3 suggests, we see how each arcing vector becomes part of the larger picture we're trying to understand through our assessments. QVI pushes us to understand that while lateral trajectories may not intersect with our current project, they are still part of the larger, undulating system; they will still have impacts even if those impacts are not obvious or quickly perceived. In the next chapter, we demonstrate through learning stories and playful methods some ways we can continue to disrupt the mechanized approaches to writing and assessment that work to reproduce and maintain such normative assessment distributions.

6
FAILING TO BE MECHANIZED

We concluded the last chapter by sketching out a vision for lateral assessments metaphorized through the (seemingly) chaotic embodiments of fluid dynamics. The flows and movements of soft masses across that plane resist the sharp edges of the norming ruler.[1] In such a model, the success or value of each part is not measured against the other parts of the system; instead, they work in tandem, some growing large while others diminish, only to find themselves pulled back to equilibrium at another point so other parts can rise or swell. The success of movement and change in this model isn't measured by its ability to replicate or copy other parts but by larger materialities: the qualities of the fluid, the pressures exerted, the shear strength, the locations of those pressures, the ways the system feeds back into the system and shifts those pressure points. These parts do not compete against each other for dominance and ranking but interconnect and interanimate each other. This is a system of relationality.

We evoke the metaphor of the non-Newtonian fluid plane primarily as suggestive; after all, none of us writing this book are physicists, nor are we experts in the ins and outs of the complex mathematics involved. Instead, when we tried to imagine a metaphor to stand against the ruler and other linear and unidirectional frameworks for imagining assessments, we appreciated the ways the visuals we found related to fluid movements and shifts, not unlike the crenelated planes of hyperbolic geometry, and seemed to capture the chaotic nature of composing and meaning making in the writing classrooms we've taught in over the last several decades. In these spaces, most of what we find as the joys and frustrations of teaching writing seem to disappear completely when it's time for assessment. In the print-based age of portfolios, when students compiled drafts in their three-ring binders, even though we hoped to capture the nuances and complexities of the process itself, the organizing principles of that binder still seemed to ask students to move in a linear fashion from first to final draft. For many writers and writing

https://doi.org/10.7330/9781646423705.c006

Figure 6.1. QVI Pyraminx rotated to the side labeled materialities

teachers, the digital age did little to disrupt this pattern, as students often revised over previous drafts so earlier versions were no longer available for writerly self-analysis (metacognition) when it was time to turn in their portfolios of work. Once the assessments left our individual classrooms, as we note throughout this book, those ebbs and flows of meaning, attention, value, connection, and so forth drifted further from the assessment scene, usually lost completely in the assessment reports that fed back into the systems we taught in.

In this chapter, we concern ourselves with the ways so many of the assessment scenes writing teachers participate in work to normalize our classrooms and students. These practices, while useful for telling us certain things about writing, also feed back into our pedagogies and programs in ways that mechanize (dehumanize, derhetoricize) not only our assessments themselves but also our work as readers and writers. We turn our Pyraminx, then, toward *materiality*, bringing into our focus the ways bodies, objects, spaces, technologies, and larger systems work together through affects and identity/agency to create *writing* and to engage with assessments of and around writing. More specifically, we turn to learning stories and other playful assessment methodologies we have used to disrupt more mechanized assessment practices and to attend more meaningfully to the lived experiences of composers and the ways our embodiments impact writing and reading. This focus on bodies and experiences in/with/among composing objects and contexts as part of our writing construct may serve as a corrective to the overly mechanized models of materiality Laura Micciche (2014) critiques as part of writing studies. By failing to embrace the more mechanized models of assessment, the assessment killjoy works to resist hypernormativizing models in favor of assessments that embrace what we value as the messy, complex, and exciting work of writing.

AFTER NORMATIVITY: QUEER(ING) MATERIAL AFFECTS IN THE ASSESSMENT SCENE

In order to situate our sideways assessment examples that make up the bulk of this chapter, however, we think it is important to highlight some of the normativizing constructs against which these assessments were built in order to frame our own work in terms of queer materialities that challenge those normativizing tendencies. As writing teachers, writing program/center administrators, and writers ourselves, we often feel caught between the values and commitments that are central to the writing construct additions we've been addressing throughout this book and the assessment models we learned in graduate school or have inherited at our institutions. These models, typically originating outside our experiences and those of the students we teach, favor a mechanistic understanding of writing (and assessment) that tends to ignore *processes* and *experiences* in favor of direct assessments of *products*. Despite significant advances in educational measurement and writing assessments over the last two decades, including important advances to enlarging the writing construct and in attending to broader sociocultural elements we highlight throughout this book, in our day-to-day lives as teachers and administrators, we are far more often met with limiting assessment practices we have struggled to interrupt. In these assessments, the students' finished-for-now drafts serve a metonymic function: they stand in as stable representations of students' abilities as writers.

While writing studies and writing assessment scholars more specifically have challenged that spurious connection, the reality for many writing teachers at colleges and universities across the country is that we must often wrestle with that damaging construction of what writing is and what writing does in our daily work. A still-common programmatic assessment scene, for example, may involve criterion-referenced assessments that faculty are asked to perform on large samples of student writing. When ECU was up for reaccreditation in 2018 by the Southern Association of Colleges and Schools Commission on Colleges (SACSCOC), for example, we were part of a then-new initiative that required schools to envision a Quality Enhancement Plan (QEP) that

1. includes a process identifying key issues emerging from institutional assessment,

2. focuses on learning outcomes and/or the environment supporting student learning and accomplishing the mission of the institution,

3. demonstrates institutional capability for the initiation, implementation, and completion of the QEP,

4. includes broad-based involvement of institutional constituencies in the development and proposed implementation of the QEP, and

5. identifies goals and a plan to assess their achievement. (SACSCOC, n.d.)

Because this multiyear initiative had to be completed in time to be part of the university's final report in 2018, we had to begin seven years earlier with those initial steps. From 2011 to 2013, faculty leadership at ECU used previous assessments and data from faculty around campus to create a plan we called Write Where You Belong (ECU, "Writing Across," n.d.; ECU, "University Writing," n.d.). During the five years from 2013 to 2018, writing leadership at ECU implemented a host of curricular changes (e.g., moved the second composition courses to the sophomore year to make it more WAC/WID focused, changed the WAC program to an outcomes-based framework) and structural changes (e.g., created a large writing center, developed extensive professional-development opportunities) and then assessed the impact of those changes. Given the campuswide nature of this project, there was a long list of stakeholders, all coming to the writing assessment table from vastly different methodological, ideological, and epistemological backgrounds. The size of the assessment and the limited window for creating a workable plan encouraged the leadership of that initiative, of which Will was a key member, to fall back on more statistically viable and familiar models that involved norming readers on particular criteria from the QEP outcomes rubric and moving assessors through thousands of student writing samples generated in more than four hundred writing-intensive courses from across campus. As *Reclaiming Accountability: Improving Writing Programs through Accreditation and Large-Scale Assessments* (Sharer et al. 2016) demonstrates, this sort of large-scale, criterion-referenced assessment activity is a common feature in national QEP re/accreditation projects.

And yet the whole time he was involved in the assessments, which happened each summer as faculty from around campus were provided with additional stipends to do that work, Will never felt as though they were really assessing writing, or rather he felt that wasn't the meaningful impact of their shared work each summer. In fact, as is not uncommon in such projects, the real value seemed to be in how faculty were experiencing student writing: faculty in those assessment scenes discovered that the assignments in their courses or programs were not really effective at helping students meet the ECU Writing Outcomes (ECU, "Writing Across," n.d.), that their assumptions about student writing practices were perhaps too parochial, and ultimately that student writers were better than faculty had thought when they looked at the work with greater distance than course-based evaluations had provided. These revelations and experiences were not part of our impact report to ECU or to SACSCOC, but they are the things WPAs and faculty who participated still talk about as meaningful in that assessment. If Will were to ask faculty or administrators on campus, it's unlikely anyone could really tell him the numbers/statistics recorded in the report, and yet the epistemological framework that enabled and required that report persists.

In critiquing the mechanized approach of criterion-referenced assessment and rater norming, then, we are not necessarily arguing these are prima facie flawed assessments, nor are we suggesting these models cannot produce meaningful understanding of validity, reliability, and fairness. We are also not suggesting these types of assessments should be abandoned altogether, though we may no longer ourselves have much interest in participating in them. Rather, we are concerned with the ways this particular assessment shibboleth prevents us from engaging with and advocating for assessments that capture the parts of the writing construct that are difficult or impossible to capture through such a limited notion of empirical inquiry. Throughout those summer writing assessments at ECU, as faculty pairs reviewed sets of undergraduate essays, multiple times each day they asked questions about the writing sample not matching the rubric criteria in a particular way. In those moments of friction, the faculty members most often advocated for the student writer, who they felt was somehow disenfranchised or harmed by asking their writing to do work it was never intended to do. One example that happened each summer involved the use (or not) of secondary sources. Outcome One states students will "use writing to investigate complex, relevant topics and address significant questions through engagement with and effective use of credible sources," but not all writing samples submitted required secondary sources. Selections from math classes, for example, involved explaining proofs/formulas. Was the proof/formula a secondary source since the writer did not create it but was simply trying to articulate its logic? Some raters offered thoughtful arguments that those proofs/formulas were secondary sources, while others felt they were not in terms of how the outcomes seemed to be expecting source use. As facilitators, Will and his colleagues allowed the group to decide how best to frame the work, but in those moments of disagreement or uncertainty, different groups of raters during different summers assessed those components differently. There was internal consistency for that particular moment of assessment but not across the years, which means the impact report had to explain that phenomenon as a key limitation in the data.

But what if our focus could have been less on running the student work through an assessment mill and more about engaging those projects, frictions, affective differences, and contextual challenges in the moment? For the QEP leadership, there was both campus-based and external pressure to stick with the original assessment plan and not make adjustments so as to preserve a particular notion of validity and reliability, but the more we think about those moments of dissensus and disagreement, the more we see how limited are the uses of large-scale assessments we and our colleagues are most familiar with. Where they work and where there is perfect alignment among the writing construct, the writing activity, the written product, and other parts of the assessment scene, such models can offer a meaningful internal consistency and provide a certain type of understanding. But in our experiences as writers, writing teachers, and writing program/center administrators, that sort of scene is nearly impossible to construct out of the complexity and chaos of the contemporary university.

Instead, moments like those with the QEP summer assessments continued to call us out of a world where raters are normed against particular criteria, or perhaps where raters are not even normalizable, and toward assessment scenes rooted in queer materialities, moments when what most interests us as stakeholders in the assessments are the ways our reading of student work and engaging with student writers challenge us to shift our intellectual model from nomothetic to more idiographic frameworks (Windelband 1980). We discuss this shift in chapter 2 when we set up our additions to the writing construct Edward White, Norbert Elliot, and Irvin Peckham (2015) created in *Very Like a Whale: The Assessment of Writing Programs*, in which they also base their writing construct on a reading of Wilhelm Windelband's dichotomous model. As we note in chapter 2, our construct additions—agency, consent, vulnerability, dissensus, radical justice, embodiment, and lived experience—grow out of a queer materialist understanding of writing and affectivity that speaks to the more idiographic elements of writing, those parts that are unique, contingent, or highly contextual/cultural.

In chapter 2, we highlight the queer and feminist theories of affect/ivity that have influenced our thinking about writing assessment, in particular the ways these theories challenge the commodification, reproduction, and mechanization of writing practices and assessments. Through our embracing of the feminist killjoy (Ahmed 2010a), we have taken a turn toward affective domains we contend both shape and are shaped by our entanglements with the materials of writing: bodies, technologies, emotions, objects, contexts, and so forth. These materials have been part of the ways many in our field have come to understand writing studies as deeply entangled with new materialist theories of writing. Central to this work is the recognition that nonhuman bodies have the capacity to make things happen, to shape their surroundings and the human bodies that interact with them. As such, they can serve a traditionally agentic function in their environments, though one that traditional human-centered rhetorical theories have struggled to understand fully or to engage constructively in a full-scale theory of rhetorical action/engagement (Boyle 2018; Cooper 2019; Dobrin 2015; Mays, Rivers, and Sharp-Hoskins 2017; Reid 2022). One problem Micciche (2014) has identified with the ways we've often taken up new materialisms and other object-oriented ontologies is that in doing so we tend to "substitute talk of bodies, identities, and differences with the materiality of texts. In the grips of this approach, writing becomes an effect of tools and technologies, an activity that is unteachable, a ghostly production, and the province of theory and men" (491). In the hypermechanized assessment practices common to criterion-referenced assessments and rater norming, in which the idiographic particulars/uniquenesses of writing are often factored out of human readers so they read more like machines than deeply affected individuals with different reading needs and values, the supremacy of textual materiality tends to win out. What we are advocating for here is a turn to those seemingly unteachable and "ghostly" elements of writing and meaning making that exist among and between complex materialities. We need assessment practices that also seek to capture those parts of writing too often left on the cutting-room floor of the normativized (and normativizing) assessment scene.

One way to do this is to recognize as part of our writing constructs and assessments what Karen Barad (2007) refers to as "agential realism." In ways perhaps too complex to fully unpack here, the evaluation and assessment of writing probably suffers too much from an overreliance on representationalism, the idea that words "naturally have the power to represent preexisting things" (133). Barad recognizes representationalism as an ideology that positions human actors (teachers, administrators, assessors) somehow "above or outside the world we allegedly merely reflect on" (133) and instead calls on us to imagine the entangled and interanimated materialities of the world as fundamentally performative:

> Hence, in ironic contrast to the misconception that would equate per-
> formativity with a form of linguistic monism that takes language to be
> the stuff of reality, performativity is properly understood as a contesta-
> tion of the unexamined habits of mind that grant language and other
> forms of representation more power in determining our ontologies
> than they deserve. (133)

A move (even if only temporary) away from representationalism to performativity can work to shift our questions about assessment toward
"matters of practices, doing, and actions" (135). Barad names such a
shift "agential realism," which "allows matter its due as an active participant in the world's becoming . . . [and] furthermore it provides an
understanding of *how* discursive practices matter" (136).

By shifting our focus in this chapter away from the representationalist
frameworks that have been de rigueur in writing assessment, we engage
key lenses from our Pyraminx—materiality, affectivity, and identities—in
order to demonstrate how a performative framework for writing assessment can allow often-valued but ignored parts of the writing construct
to bubble up and be valued in the larger assessment scene. In the case
of the examples here, we focus on how *embodiment* and *lived experiences*
emerge as construct values when we consider the broader performative
elements of writing assessments.

TOWARD AFFECTIVE ECONOMIES FOR WRITING
ASSESSMENT: CONSTELLATING STORIES

One of the ways we can fail to be mechanized, that we can embrace failure
as a resistant move against the ways automated essay scoring and other
standardizing projects work to make us reading and rating automata, is
to embrace the various and complex subjectivities inherent in writing and
reading and to engage with these affective economies in order to imagine
a more humane writing construct for higher education. When programmatic assessments are focused on the analysis of individually produced
student artifacts to determine larger patterns of student performance, the
assessment scene becomes dominated by previously produced products,
offering an assumed stable moment of knowing what student writers can
and cannot do with writing. In line with market logics and corporatized
approaches to education, these sorts of assessments attempt to quantify
learning performance and celebrate achievement as the result of individual merit. In a recent writing-across-the-curriculum assessment Will participated in, for example, one of the first questions to come up was how
to handle group projects; beyond that, the group wondered, in sampling

a class, what if two writers from the group submit the same group project and different raters assign different scores—how might that unsettle our rater reliability and the assessment itself? In the end, perhaps primarily in the service of efficiency, the group decided to treat the texts as being no different from those submitted by one writer and thus assessed each as a sample of that writer's individual ability. Since the projects were treated in the aggregate, it was decided these anomalies would simply blend in; the group doing the assessment decided to just make a comment about this issue in the limitations section of the report. In the end, what we privileged was a type of automated, machine-like scoring coded into the rubric and our understanding of the assessment itself. Such a focus over-privileges certain types of reliability measures and dehumanizes learners and assessors. As Tom Drummond and Kayla Shea Owens (2020) argue, these practices conceal the situated and contextual work of teaching and learning and focus on learning as a state of being, rather than an inde-terminate, dynamic, and continuous set of processes enacted through engagement with others.

In contrast to such individualistic, static assessment measures, *rela-tional assessments* allow educators to document and examine learning as emergent social activities among students and themselves by engaging assessment as a form of professional development. Relational assessment considers the learning and meaning-making behaviors that emerge among a host of human and nonhuman actants in a learning commu-nity. These actants can include students, instructors, support staff, peers, texts, drafts, conceptual models, rhetorics, technologies, affective flows, and other materialities that are part of the learning context. Relational assessments can work to connect the dots among these bodies, constel-lating learning and meaning making as a dynamic, shared, sociocultural practice. As such, relational assessment is well suited for teaching and learning in the humanities because it refuses objective tendencies to stress the external elements of cognition and performance, focusing instead on collaborative and cooperative peer-to-peer learning and "a rediscovery of the solidarities we share in being human" (Drummond and Owens 2020). Relational work seems particularly important in writ-ing studies, where students from a host of linguistic and cultural back-grounds are too often measured against the same stick in our classes, which, as Esther Milu (2021) suggests, can lead to a flattening of differ-ence that diminishes students and their work.

As we discuss, particularly in chapters 1 and 2, social activities like writ-ing, learning, and assessing are always already interlaced with emotional valences. When we acknowledge and modulate our emotions, we can create sideways pathways for remembering, activating, transferring, and bridging new experiences and information to what has come before. When the act of assessment (and of writing, for many) is shrouded in negative emotions, we see fight-or-flight emergency responses by faculty continually confronted with the expectation or responsibility to evaluate and assess. As we've argued, this response has led many educators to flee the assessment scene as quickly as possible. To return takes a kind of embodied resistance we have gleaned from the figure of the assessment killjoy. The killjoy, as a collective ethos, can provide a productive means of dealing with anxiety, fear, frustration, or shame, a means to develop other kinds of relationships with other assessment stakeholders. In fact, relationships form the primary means by which we regulate our emotions. Humans perceive activities we must complete, such as writing, learning, and assessing, as more difficult and resource depleting when we must do them alone. This social baseline theory points to the ways collaborative assessment can function as a way to help us safeguard our energy stores, reduce the demands of affective labor, and create sustainable assessment ecosystems that fail to be mechanized (Beckes and Coan 2011; Proffitt 2006).

In her dissertation study, for example, Stephanie used relational methods to assess connected learning frameworks in two informal student learning initiatives: (1) a massive, open online science literacy program and (2) a paracurricular makerspace at a local high school. Stephanie and Will served as co-PIs on the grants that funded both these initiatives, while Stephanie served as the project director who worked intimately with teachers to design, implement, and assess both programs. Because these programs were experimental in nature and took place in paracurricular contexts, there were no predetermined measurable outcomes to assess; however, the teacher teams created a host of informal curricular pathways with intentionality. Teachers used the Connected Learning framework (Ito et al. 2013; National Writing Project n.d.) and its design principles to create learning activities for young people that were interest driven, production centered, peer supported, openly networked, and academically oriented. In addition, both programs enabled teachers, students, and community partners to self-select into groups based on shared interests in science, technology, and language/visual arts. This self-selection created shared purpose across generational, disciplinary, and institutional contexts.

Stephanie's study sought to better understand the relational underpinnings of this Connected Learning framework in action by tracing the affinities and aversions that drove composing behaviors. Stephanie drew from feminist and queer scholarship to build an interdisciplinary research methodology for investigating how meaning moves with, around, and through affective currents and material bodies in writing and making communities (West-Puckett 2017). As opposed to isolating texts in the hopes they might tell us something meaningful about the networks in which they were produced, Stephanie traced the intensities and flows of meaning making, investigating how writers and makers got stuck and unstuck, how they accelerated and decelerated through time, how they moved across conceptual and physical space, and how they gathered up a host of others along the way. Thus, she turned to the metaphorical practice of constellating, which is rooted in practices from cultural rhetorics (Bratta and Powell 2016; Cedillo et al. 2018; Cobos et al. 2018; Powell et al. 2014,). Constellating calls attention to the embodied and material structures, practices, objects, orientations, and relationships made and remade in communities. According to Malea Powell, the concept of a constellation "allows for all the meaning-making practices and their relationships to matter. It allows for multiply-situated subjects to connect to multiple discourses at the same time, as well as for those relationships (among subjects, among discourses, among kinds of connections) to shift and change without holding a subject captive" (quoted in Bratta and Powell 2016). In this way, constellations are fluid, flexible, and open to multiple approaches as participants orient toward an assemblage in particular ways depending on their own positionality over time. Constellated rhetorics prompt us to consider how bodies and objects (including texts) emerge and reemerge through material and affective relationships.

To better understand the constellated meaning-making patterns in these two learning networks, Stephanie developed assessment research methods that enabled her to approach the networks laterally, moving alongside participants as they made sense of their experiences. Drawing on John Law's (2004) and Caroline Dadas's (2016) articulations of "messy methods," Stephanie made use of both conventional and nonconventional data sets to understand composition as movement. The more conventional sources, such as anonymous interviews conducted by the funding agency, were useful in providing a large-scale view of composing practices in the network; however, these methods and the resulting data fell short in helping Stephanie explore the microrelationships among facilitators and students, among participants and tools, and among participant groups. Furthermore, as a project director, her relationship with participants was already figured as both an organizer and a coparticipant/partner-in-the-making; thus, adopting an objectivist

Figure 6.2. Educators making origami fortune tellers

institutional position seemed to undercut existing interpersonal relationships with the program facilitators and participants. Similarly,
the use of overly precise and out-of-the-box research instruments like
structured or semistructured interview questions and two-dimensional
paper-based surveys also seemed unfitting for participants who had been
writing and making with a host of three-dimensional composing tools,
media, and objects.

For these reasons, and in keeping with the "maker" *ethos* of the
communities, Stephanie designed an origami fortune-teller game that
prompted research participants to document the material dimensions
and microcollisions of meaning making (see figure 6.2). So what did this
look like in practice? Many readers are no doubt familiar with the hand-
held fortune tellers elementary and middle schoolers have constructed
for generations as playful ways to figure out who likes them or who their
true love is or whether they will be rich and famous or what sort of job
they might have. Game play usually involves hiding names or occupa-
tions several layers down and then going through rounds of spelling

colors and/or counting numbers as users manipulate the fortune teller and eventually can unfold it to reveal the future (Joe_Tutorials, n.d.). In Stephanie's riff on the game, classroom teachers, informal educators, and students identified tools, materials, media, people, places, practices, and affective orientations important to their experiences of composing, and they wrote the names for those things on various parts of the fortune teller. They were also asked to rate their highest levels of frustration and disorientation while participating in those networks. Then, through interactive game play with these coded fortune tellers, which involved using the numbers from their rates of frustration/disorientation, participants manipulated the fortune tellers to create aleatory configurations of tools, materials, media, people, and places (see figure 6.3). Then participants wrote short relational narratives about what mattered most to them in their composing community by using the objects, people, places, and affects that emerged during game play. By using the materialities that emerged through the game, participants were pushed to connect elements they might have ignored as trivial or less important. Instead of framing their past experience with the story that was "ready to hand" (Ahmed 2006)—the rehearsed story, the stock story of experience—participants were pushed to explore alternative stories of those experiences and to make less expected or hoped for connections.

The origami fortune teller and its accompanying rules for game play demonstrate a playful, transgressive, queered orientation to collecting assessment data. Games have the potential to underscore the dynamic nature of relationships in a given gaming phenomenon as players make and remake their identities based on new rules and structures, redistributions of material objects, and affective responses to the practices of game play. In each instantiation of game play, players refigure rules of play, their relationships, and thus their identities, suspending often-unnamed social rules and hierarchies existing outside the game (deWinter and Vie 2015; Salen and Zimmerman 2003). In playful contexts like makerspaces, data-collection and interpretation games can serve this democratizing function, creating more informal opportunities for unscripted sharing of experience data, addressing problems with disclosure Cynthia Selfe and Gail Hawisher (2004) note are exacerbated by formal interview protocols that maintain a careful distance between interviewer and interviewee. In effect, these material practices of game play can transgress proper intimacies (Ahmed 2006; Chen 2012; Payne 2014) that maintain clear distance and boundaries in a research setting, creating new opportunities for collaborative, collective, queer relationships and relational knowledge making.

Figure 6.3. Sample fortune teller

Furthermore, game play often produces an excess of emotion, as we experience joy, frustration, accomplishment, failure, and other structures of feeling as our positions to others change over the time and space of gameplay (Juul 2013). As we've demonstrated, assessment research method/ologies too often ignore the affective experiences of students and teachers, valuing the "extreme usability" (Dilger 2007, 48) of discrete methods that privilege simplicity, efficiency, and error-free interaction. Game play, on the other hand, can approach two often overlooked features of usability—pleasure and memorability—acknowledging that structures of meaning can't be divorced from structures of feeling (Cvetkovich 2003; Stewart 2007), whether we explicitly acknowledge the connection in our assessment practices or not. With its ability to restructure the terms of knowledge reproduction, as well as elicit affective transactions among players, game play can resist mechanization, particularly when the games are not overly rule bound or forced to follow overly mechanized rules. In this way, we can work against telling the expected or normative story in assessment scenes, reorienting ourselves away from the well-traveled lines our assessments have taken. Interestingly, the participants in Stephanie's research resisted strict adherence to the guidelines or rules for game play, intervening in the methods to resist hyperlocal mechanization. This was a powerful reminder that users always hack a system when the system doesn't meet their needs, and we, as researchers, teachers, and assessors, can either punish that resistance or engage it. The larger system of game play made the hacking feel welcomed, and participants didn't worry about the failure or success of their stories. The goal wasn't to tell the right story or the most impactful or emotionally manipulative story—narrative patterns we all know well—but simply to tell a story of the experience. By engaging in different interactions of this game, participants found they could tell many different stories, not all of which were bound by frameworks of success or accomplishment.

Drawing on the logics of game play to design assessments, we are finding ways to resist the commodification of assessment protocols, the reproduction of normative data sets, and the mechanization of research processes and relationships. Here, we offer a story of what Stephanie and Will did to make sense from the data collected through that game-play scenario and trace the constellated nature of composing in both networks Stephanie was studying as part of her dissertation. This story further demonstrates how assessment researchers can resist mechanization by engaging practices of crafting assessment tools and procedures by hand.

Borrowing from work in grounded theory, Stephanie and Will (as co-PIs) engaged in three practices of data analysis: coding qualitative data, using coding memos to reflect on the coproduction of meaning, and creating 3D representations of the coding schemes. First, Stephanie and Will analyzed the game sets in aggregate using three types of coding practices: open, axial, and selective coding (Farkas and Haas 2012; Neff 1998; Teston 2012). Game sets included the fortune teller each composer made, as well as the game logs and relational narratives the composers created from their fortune tellers. Then Stephanie and Will used the codes—places, people, tools, activities—with which participants labeled fortune tellers initially to define the affective and material dimensions of each composing community. They read the relational stories participants wrote about their experiences for additional codes that emerged through the narrativizing of experience. Next, they created three-dimensional representations of each community constellation using everyday crafting materials—foam board, yarn, safety pins, construction paper, and the participants' original origami fortune tellers.

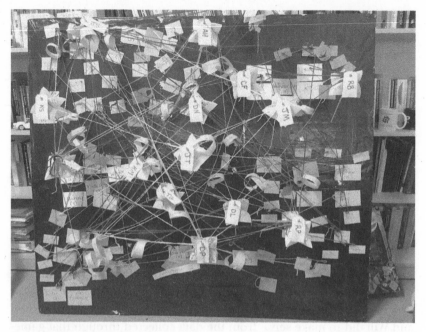

Figure 6.4. Three-dimensional representation of research data using everyday crafting materials

The construction of this data board took approximately fifteen hours, during which time Will tied loops of yarn around safety pins and slipped them over the bamboo skewers to which the origami fortune tellers were affixed (see figure 6.4). Stephanie read aloud the coded data, directing Will to string the yarn from this marker to that marker and telling him which yarns should be gathered up into an affective web, which he then stapled together and banded with orange construction-paper loops. Stephanie eventually produced an interpretive key that detailed the final coding scheme and demonstrated how they translated their qualitative coding practices into hand-built visualizations of composing practice in writing and making networks.

As researchers and assessors, Stephanie and Will approached these artifacts from spaces of embodied experience and happy affects. Creating the large board of linked stories and materials was time consuming, yes, but it also carried them back to other times, particularly Stephanie, who, as a preteen growing up before the large-scale availability of home computers and internet-connected personal devices, had spent many afternoons and weekends with girlfriends folding squares of paper into origami fortune tellers, little toys they referred to as "cootie catchers." On the triangular folds, they wrote the names of their future spouses, the brand names of cars they might drive, the number of children they could have, the places they might live, and the jobs they might have in the world. Through this process, they coded the material objects with the discourses that reproduced their young yet complex systems of desire and yearning for futural happiness. During each turn, they pushed and pulled along an imaginary Cartesian coordinate system, creating lines of possibility and potential horizons that remixed their present and future selves into bizarre constellations of object-oriented possibility. Through the processes of folding, the nodes on those prepubescent assemblages touched and rubbed against one another, smearing names written in colored markers, underscoring the permeability of boundaries. They wrote down the names of boys (and occasionally girls to give the game a queer twist), objects, times, and places that could combine and recombine infinitely across the folds as they manipulated the fortune-telling device. With this "silly object" (Berlant 1997), each turn was a first-person working of material logics and created a strange assemblage of materialities through which these friends enacted their anxieties toward and desires for a future that was in the making. They knew even then that some lines would offer a host of (positive) returns, yet they also pulsed with the possibilities of those that wouldn't. They didn't know that in Japan these paper fortune tellers were also known as *paku-paku*, which means, roughly, "gobble up," but they could somehow feel that the present, the there-ness of their presence as preteen girls, was imaginary, one that was under constant threat of being similarly gobbled up. They could feel the threat of an impending future whose course had been set through heteronormative and neoliberal lines of monogamy and marriage, representations of a successful middle-class existence with a house, kids, and a luxury car to drive them to a nine-to-five professional job.

We tell this object story of the assessment tools and materials in Stephanie's dissertation for two reasons. First, it demonstrates how queer or silly objects and procedures like game play can reorient stakeholders and unearth alterity through queer approaches to assessment data collection, interpretation, and representation. Second, we want to underscore the idea that materiality matters in queer validity arguments. Object stories like the one we tell about the fortune tellers, yarn, safety pins, and bodily actions (Will's kneeling, stringing, gathering, looping) provide space for people to (re)attach stories to the material objects disembodied from people and cultures through processes of commodification, reproduction, and mechanization. As we note in our examples throughout the book, disembodied narratives of failure and success separate bodies from their social and cultural learning contexts and practices, often with the same goal of predicting young peoples' futures that Stephanie's "cootie catchers" had. Stephanie's story of the "cootie catcher" grounds the assessment of intentionality in writing networks through a feminized technology—a playful thing *she made and she continued to make* as a way of making meaning at the intersections of her and others' material and discursive lives. Unlike the processes of commodification, reproduction, and mechanization we describe in these last three chapters, a materialities framework can help us resist fetishization, as well as the ready-to-hand uncomplicated usage of tools like 6+1 Trait® Writing Analysis rubrics, semistructured and structured interviews, and standardized admission tests. Materiality frameworks prompt us to consider how assessment objects and technologies constellate around, entangle with, extend, distend, accelerate, and decelerate bodies. While commodification, replication, and mechanization erase cultural and material histories and ignore the affective experience of writers and makers, constellated material practice takes seriously these human and nonhuman entanglements and the affective currents they produce (Barad 2007). QVI provides a method to surface these alterities of writing and writing assessment that machines and automata cannot compute.

LEARNING STORIES FOR RESISTING MECHANIZATION

Another example of relational assessment is the learning story. Learning stories move beyond simple documentation/confirmation of performance by integrating context in order to narrativize students' learning experiences. Learning stories typically include four parts: (1) background on the learner/writer, which can include dispositions, challenges, and strengths; (2) one or more learning stories that focus on progress toward a key competency; (3) next steps for continued development of the key competency; and (4) a reflective section that analyzes stories, connects to effective pedagogies, and includes open-ended discussion questions to engage with audiences (Carr 2000). Unlike ostensibly objective measures, such as rubric scoring or automated essay scoring, learning stories prompt educators to embrace their positionality as expert narrators of learning and make themselves present in the construction of the learning story. Likewise, learning stories do not make comparisons between learners or among groups of learners but focus on individual experiences. While learning stories avoid making comparisons among students, they do connect student learning to competencies, just not to a static set of standards-based outcomes. Instead of measuring proximity to some a priori or external standard, learning stories illustrate a diversity of lateral and multidimensional learning behaviors students exhibit in relation to those key competencies. The goal here isn't so much to line students up and see how they match these preestablished outcomes or competencies as to engage the students and their learning relationally across a host of trajectories that may be moving in multiple directions at once.

To date, much of the scholarship on learning stories has investigated early-childhood learning environments where different kinds of disciplinary knowledge are integrated and where children tend to work at the intersections of content areas such as the arts, physical education, mathematics, and technologies. To connect student performance to competencies across knowledge domains, learning stories use a layered approach that begins with the student at the center of a set of concentric circles. Given our focus on sideways learning and assessment patterns, we understand these circles as rippling outward and back, providing an epistemological framework for understanding learning and, in this case, writing experiences across flows that move in more than one direction, often simultaneously. The first layer beyond the student moves out to key competencies such as critical thinking or developing global perspectives. Moving out again, the next layer links key competencies to particular knowledge domains such as science, English language arts, or technology. An additional layer links features of effective pedagogy such as providing rich, repeated opportunities to learn, using reflection as a means of prompting awareness of learning, and supporting an inquiry-based approach to knowledge construction. There may, of course, be additional layers we would want to account for in a specific assessment scene. What's key here is that these layers are not progressive or developmental in nature; we are not suggesting one of these layers indicates levels of accomplishment, as one layer is not necessarily more sophisticated than the others. They are layers of meaning making and understanding that link to each other, that rub up against each other, that create friction and promiscuous meaning making (Payne 2014). Where mechanized assessment practices focus on sorting, ranking, and evaluating discrete parts of student learning, learning stories are messier, less neatly ordered, but also far richer and more complex. They bring nuance and sophistication to how we understand writers and their work across various domains. While it may be seen as inefficient in several learning economies and scenes of assessment, storying student learning provides the sort of qualitative deep dive that is central to QVI.

Learning stories can serve as relational objects that engage multiple audiences for different purposes. Teachers benefit from learning stories because they are able to focus on particular moments of everyday class-room practice and better understand how a particular student or group of students, working and learning at a particular moment in history, is embodying a key competency like relating to others. In addition, teach-ers have reported that learning stories help them reimagine students as "more competent learners" and engage pedagogies that support contin-ued growth and development (New Zealand Ministry 2007, 10). Unlike many traditional assessments, which report *on* but rarely ever *to* learn-ers, learning stories are shared with the learners themselves, enabling them to return to these represented learning moments and reflect on their experiences and changes in their learning over time and across contexts. These stories can also serve decolonial practices by focusing on relationality and on our shared responsibilities to each other that can disrupt traditional classroom hierarchies and capitalist values. These stories are not one and done necessarily but remain open so students can engage them at different times and in different ways. For many students, the learning story is something to be proud of, as they are able to see themselves as capable learners, develop their self-esteem and a sense of belonging, and build the resilience necessary to take on new and more difficult learning challenges (9). For us, such stories resist the move to define students by deficits but instead as part of cultures of abundance (Gutiérrez and Rogoff 2003; Ladson-Billings 2021; Lee 2007; Muhammad 2020; Paris and Alim 2017; Yosso 2005). In K–12 contexts, learning stories have also addressed parents, families, and community members, bring-ing them into the teaching and learning context as powerful partners. Those outside formal classroom contexts appreciate the accessibility of learning stories, as storytelling is a meaning-making activity common across cultures. In addition, learning stories rely on visual modes to communicate, as educators take photographs of students engaged in the activities they story. By avoiding jargon and communicating through the immediacy of images, learning stories enable families and community members to understand some of the purposes and practices of learn-ing and to pair home and community learning activities with in-school instruction. In some contexts, family and community members also write learning stories, making assessment a distributed practice of negotiating what it means to learn as interpreted through different kinds of expertise and across formal and informal contexts (New Zealand Ministry 2007, 9).

Some educational researchers, however, have called into question the validity and accountability of learning stories (Blaiklock 2008; Perkins 2013; Zhang 2016). Arguments against the widespread use of learning stories include concerns related to observational duration; the labor-intensive nature of crafting detailed stories; a perceived focus on dispositions as opposed to skills and competencies; a concern that the "data" cannot be transparent or objective, as it is storied and thus "interpreted" prior to sharing with other stakeholders; and the generalizability of findings, as learning stories take a hyperlocal focus that makes it difficult to trace discrete learning across different temporalities and contextual situations.

These concerns with validity provide an effective test case for QVI. Instead of working to conceal power and privilege inside the algorithms of automated/machine-based essay scoring or mechanizing readers to be raters, learning stories embrace a failure to be mechanized. They embrace the messy baggage of learning—what Ken Blaiklock (2008) understands as hyperlocal contextual information, which is grounded in particular times and places and with particular people and tools. They ask teachers not to be raters but to be readers and writers with a host of subjective perspectives. They call into question the inherent value we place in the standardized practice of norming assessors and instead engage an antinormative approach to meaning making. This type of narrative assessment draws on the expert analysis of those closest to the moments of learning—teachers, staff, learners, and their families—and leverages those important bodies and experiences as necessarily partial and interested components in the assessment scene. QVI constructs this familiarity as an affordance rather than a constraint; it reimagines expertise and mastery as not belonging exclusively to those with certain academic degrees but to those folks *and* others. What's more, in writing studies, we know knowledge does not transfer in neat and predictable ways (Wardle 2007; Yancey, Robertson, and Taczak 2014); as such, the argument against a hyperlocal focus is rendered inconsequential. Instead of looking for discrete evidence of knowledge application in multiple contexts, or what Elizabeth Wardle (2007, 69) calls the apples that have already been made into apple pie, we might work to trace competencies and dispositions across contexts, further developing our capacities to notice and identify the plethora of ways learners might embody and apply habits of body and mind as they engage new tasks and contexts.

Ultimately, we recognize that relational assessment methods generally, and learning stories specifically, are time-consuming, community-based activities. It takes both time and resources to humanize assessment practices, but if our institutions do not invest meaningfully in resources, assessment will continue to be regarded by teachers, learners, and community members as little more than an exercise in bureaucratic power. Beyond that, we believe teachers and WPAs inhabit particularly rich spaces for developing ongoing learning stories that can be ready when outside assessment folks come calling. We've seen program after program scramble to find data and figure out what to say about it when those large accrediting bodies show up every few years or so and ask for evidence of effective teaching and learning. This sort of reactive culture of assessment leads too easily to reporting on only the most reductive measures of success, and because an outside body is asking the questions, we can feel tremendous pressure to be *successful*, to construct a narrative that says, "Everything is fine here, well, except this one little thing over here that we will plan to fix right now." In these mechanized frameworks, department-level administrators and faculty alike feel pressured to simply submit to whatever they're told to do, to just get it done and get it over with, aware that virtually nothing they discover will actually be useful to them, their programs, or their students. While we do not want to shame anyone's assessment kink, feminist and queer theorists remind us continually that consent matters, that consent is effective to good kink. As such, we want writing studies to imagine assessment as consensual, as pleasurable, as desirable rather than as the ongoing abusive relationship it has become in both K–12 and higher education contexts.

Learning Stories in Higher Education: A Case Study from URI Writing and Rhetoric

Having highlighted learning stories as an assessment methodology we've seen operating in pre-K settings and similar emergent literacy contexts, we turn our attention now to work with narrative assessment that has been picked up in higher education contexts with some surprising and exciting results. Drummond and Owens (2020), for example, have demonstrated how learning stories can be used to assess general education courses, specifically in their context foundations-level chemistry courses, to uncover the mechanics of sociocultural learning. Their multileveled assessment project included the following: (1) videotaping learning moments as they emerged through in-class peer-to-peer group activities and discussions; (2) preparing clips for those same groups of students to review and analyze; (3) sharing clips and analyses with program faculty, as well as state-level leadership responsible for institutional development; and thus (4) allowing for deeper analysis through multiple perspectives. In this assessment paradigm, Drummond and Owens were able to represent learning that moves laterally away from a transmission or banking model. Instead, they were able to document and analyze how learning, and in this case discipline-specific learning, is part of an interactional, progressive change in the ways students construct, approach, and solve problems, both individually and collaboratively, and also confront *unknowing* as a necessary corollary of knowing. Addressing their alternative approach to assessment, Drummond and Owens write,

> Our work is a departure from the dominant discourse of accountability-driven assessment, where a delineation of agreed-upon outcomes guides a subsequent effort to gather information about learners' performance on those outcomes. . . . We have demonstrated how dialogue based on that documentation enables educators to move beyond objectivism and relativism into a new kind of rational endeavor, a conversation grounded in our caring. The examination of traces of events in the classroom creates the space for dialogue, disagreement, and the emergence of complexities, so it can grow our schools—through participation and willingness to risk—into amiable spaces where we create a community of equals, a sense of public freedom, and a rediscovery of the solidarities we share in being human.

Given the experiences Drummond and Owens have had with learning stories, as part of its 2019 Student Learning Outcomes Assessment (SLOA), the Department of Writing and Rhetoric (WRT) at the University of Rhode Island (URI) enacted a similar relational assessment of student learning. Like Drummond and Owens, URI faculty video recorded dynamic classroom learning interactions and used a collaborative method to engage students and faculty in the interpretation and evaluation of student learning interactions. Specifically, the program wanted to better understand what it means to analyze rhetorics of identity, culture, and power; to reach this understanding through cross-cultural dialogue; to determine how WRT might refine its curricular and pedagogical approaches to teaching students to analyze identity, culture, and power (ICP); and to better enact and embody a cultural rhetorics praxis across their program.

The assessment team began by working to understand the context of the classrooms where this student learning outcome (SLO) was being reinforced and emphasized, and they then video recorded small group discussions in which students were prompted to analyze how rhetorics of ICP impacted their thinking and their textual production. The WRT assessment team produced a video that featured these clips by category and invited other WRT faculty, WRT student majors, and Harrington School of Communication and Media (HSCM) faculty outside WRT to preview these clips and engage in an open discussion to negotiate interpretations and evaluations of them. Initial findings indicated analysis of ICP is highly subjective, explicit examples are rare, and WRT student majors and WRT faculty do not view analysis as a means to an end; instead they tend to view analysis as most valuable when applied in real-world contexts. A key discovery in this assessment was that URI students find value in analysis but mostly when it is integrated into critical world-making praxis.

As a department in motion, turning toward the ideological and material practices of community and cultural rhetorics, WRT faculty and administrators identified this outcome as foundational to assessing the larger program's development. Thus, this assessment project sought to clarify the outcome for all stakeholders in the department by documenting and collaboratively examining

- student analyses of embodied identities;
- student analyses of how identities are shaped by the shared impulses, habits, and customs of culture;
- student analyses of the dynamics of power, which include authority dominance and capacity to act within systems of control;
- students' connections among and applications of these analyses to their behaviors and actions both in and beyond the classroom.

How did WRT do this work? In what follows, we showcase the methods Stephanie and her colleagues at URI used to enact this alternative assessment project. We then look at their initial findings. While this project does not represent the sort of mechanized, bean-counting assessments higher education personnel outside writing studies might think they want when the assessment train comes barreling into the station, by having this engaged, rigorous, carefully validated model of assessment as part of regular practice, URI's Department of Writing and Rhetoric has adopted a proactive model that means it begins any future assessment with a large supply of critical data around writing and learning. But first, let's look at how WRT accomplished this assessment project by highlighting the ten distinct levels of systematic inquiry that made up WRT's multilevel relational assessment project.

Level 1: Identification of Learning Opportunities

Working with instructors in WRT 360: Rhetoric for Writing Majors and 495: Advanced Digital Writing and Rhetoric to identify opportunities for collaborative student analysis, negotiation, and application of rhetorics of identity, culture, and power, as well as reviewing assignment parameters and goals with instructors. Participants: assessment coordinator and course instructors (which included WRT department chair). The assignment guidelines for both classes are summarized below:

WRT 360: Rhetoric for Writing Majors

Asking students to prepare a multimodal definition for a rhetorical term they had covered in class. Students could use tactile or digital materials, but they were required to combine two or more of the different modes—linguistic, visual, aural, spatial, or gestural—to communicate their definition. In class, students were asked to present their multimodal definitions in small groups and to explain how these definitions were inspired by their study of cultural rhetorics. In particular, students were prompted to discuss how their definitions involved or described rhetorics of identity, culture, and power.

WRT 495: Advanced Digital Writing and Rhetoric

Challenging students to imagine they had been selected as a finalist for a job at their dream company, one with a reputation for being both brilliant and unorthodox. To move to the interview stage, the company sent them a simple request: send us your desktop wallpaper image. In class, students were asked to discuss their wallpaper choices, to reflect on how recasting themselves for hiring committees made them reevaluate rhetorical choices that may not have seemed significant before. In addition, students were prompted to discuss how their coursework prepared them to negotiate rhetorics of identity, culture, and power, as well as how their thinking about these constructs changed (or didn't) as a result of this desktop wallpaper assignment.

Level 2: Recording Experience

Video recording small groups of students performing analyses of rhetorics of identity, culture, and power through these collaborative in-class assignments and activities. Video was captured during the duration of one class period in each course. Participants: student production-lab intern, course instructors, and selected groups of students from both courses.

Level 3: Analysis

Examining classroom video footage and selecting a representative sample of clips from both courses, which fell into three categories: analysis explicit, analysis possible, and analysis expected but absent. Participants: assessment coordinator and department chair.

Level 4: Building the Assessment Artifact

Producing and editing an eighteen-minute video and publishing it to YouTube as "unlisted." The video explains the outcomes assessment project purpose and goals, describes the assignments, and presents video clips categorized by three codes: *analysis explicit, analysis possible,* and *analysis expected/absent.* Participants: assessment coordinator and department chair.

Level 5: Noticing within the Program

Conducting a focus group with WRT faculty to review the video and participate in an hour-long open discussion of the clips, including ways the clips were categorized, as well as assessments of how students in the clips were or were not engaging in analyses of identity, culture, and power. Handwritten notes were taken to document participant responses. Participants: assessment coordinator and three additional full-time faculty members in WRT who were familiar with or had taught WRT 360 and WRT 495.

Level 6: Noticing with Students

Conducting a focus group with WRT student majors who volunteered (and were compensated with pizza) to review the video and participate in an hour-long open discussion of the clips, including ways the clips were categorized, as well as assessments of how students in the clips were or were not engaging in analyses of identity, culture, and power. Handwritten notes were taken to document participant responses. Participants: assessment coordinator and four upper-division majors in WRT, some of whom were enrolled in the recorded 360 and 495 courses but not featured in the selected video clips.

Level 7: Noticing with Campus Stakeholders

Conducting a focus group with the Harrington School of Communication and Media (HSCM) to review the video and participate in an hour-long open discussion of the clips, including ways the clips were categorized, as well as assessments of how students in the clips were or were not engaging in analyses of identity, culture, and power. Handwritten notes were taken to document participant responses. Participants: assessment coordinator and three full-time faculty members representing the departments of Public Relations and Communication Studies in the HSCM.

Level 8: Storying the Assessment, Part 1

Anonymizing and summarizing focus-group conversational data and analyzing focus-group conversational data to note agreement and disagreement about clip categorization among the three groups, identifying themes that surfaced in conversations across groups, and locating insights that might assist departmental faculty in clarifying, introducing, reinforcing, and emphasizing this outcome. Participants: assessment coordinator.

Level 9: Storying the Assessment, Part 2 (Summer)

Completing the program outcome assessment report and sharing it with focus-group participants as well as WRT faculty. Participants: assessment coordinator and department chair.

Level 10: Looping Assessment Feedback (Next Academic Year)

> Using the outcome assessment report to design and integrate read-
> ing ladders (Lesesne 2010) to scaffold analyses of identity, culture,
> power, and their entanglements, and developing additional assign-
> ments and activities that prompt students to connect and apply
> these analyses to their behaviors and actions both in and beyond the
> classroom.

This complex learning assessment ecology was neither easy nor
efficient but involved the kind of relational work and commitment to
community building characteristic of cultural rhetorics research and
constellated assessment practice (Powell et al. 2014; Cedillo et al. 2018;
Hidalgo 2021; Osorio 2021). During these meetings, stakeholders were
encouraged to approach the classroom video footage and the learning
activities contained therein from their different subjective, disciplinary,
and organizational positions. As a result, the findings were rife with
differences of opinions and perspectives that were not smoothed over
or brought to consensus through reader norming. Instead, findings
from this study suggest that what counts as analysis of identity, culture,
power, and their relationships is highly subjective. The different assessment groups agreed when analysis of ICP was absent, but they did not
agree on what counted as "textbook examples" of analysis or where the
acts of proto- or emerging analysis start. Findings also suggested faculty
outside Writing and Rhetoric held different expectations of analysis
than did WRT faculty and majors. Harrington College faculty took a
more objectivist approach to analysis, one that favors the examination
of parts to understand the whole. WRT majors and faculty, however, did
not construct objective analysis as a desirable end goal. Instead, they
expected analysis to provide the groundwork for critical approaches to
rhetorics of identity, culture, and power, as well as practical, real-world
application of this critical rhetorical analysis. Table 6.1 captures some
of the rich discussion students generated in response to watching and
categorizing these classroom video clips. While the final assessment
report totaled more than twenty pages, this chart is representative of
the ways Stephanie and her colleagues translated the multivocal, multilayered, distributed assessment inquiry into a more traditional format
mandated by URI's Division of Student Learning, Outcomes Assessment
and Accreditation. In chapter 7, we consider the labor involved in
translation or bridging the gap between what we want to know and what
institutional assessment offices want to know, and we offer suggestions
for creating an "assessment double boon" that alleviates some of the
burden of assessment labor.

Table 6.1. WRT assessment report excerpt

University of Rhode Island Upper Division Majors, Writing and Rhetoric			
Analysis Explicit Clip Category	Analysis Possible Clip Category	Analysis Expected/Absent Clip Category	Overall Findings
Clip 1 Agreement: Majors agreed that this clip included explicit analysis of identity, culture, power, and their entanglements. Majors noted that the student expanded on her analysis by providing explicit examples of how dominant culture shaped embodied identities.	Clip 1 Disagreement: Majors argued that students in this clip make blanket statements about Writing and Rhetoric majors and do not question their cultural biases when they seem certain that no other majors on campus have the capacity to objectively analyze cultural patterns and behaviors. Two majors were annoyed that the students did not recognize the politics of borderland encounters at work in their narratives.	Clip 1 Agreement: Majors note a lack of analysis or discussion of rhetorics of identity, culture, and power. Many noted that they felt like outsiders as the student assumed shared cultural knowledge with others.	1. Majors argue that discussion of culture, particularly popular culture, is often prevalent and that students demonstrate an understanding how culture puts pressure on individuals to assimilate and adopt particular identities. They noted, however, that the students seemed to lack a sophisticated vocabulary to discuss the relationships among culture, rhetoric, identity, and power. 2. Majors found that students seemed to be able to identify dominant cultures and rhetorics; however, they were unable to analyze the rhetorical patterns that operate in dominant rhetorics. Similarly, they note that students, including themselves, are struggling to understand the cultural patterns that structure marginalized cultural practices. 3. Majors argued that students are displaying simplistic, binary understanding of traditional and cultural rhetorics and reducing them to traditional=bad and cultural=good. 4. Majors noted that students seem to lack an understanding of larger cultural contexts, making it difficult to see how meaning-making practices are both influence by and influence culture. Student believe that a tool for helping them think contextually about people in different times and places, cultural practices and attitudes of those people, and how rhetorical productions/objects were circulated and how audiences were impacted by those productions/objects. 5. Majors are eager for more classes in cultural rhetorics.
Clip 2 Disagreement: Majors disagreed that the students were analyzing the rhetoric of survivance, noting instead that they were circling around the rhetorical concept without providing concrete connections to culture, power, and hegemony or examples of patterns.	Clip 2 Disagreement: Majors noted that the students discussed brand identity, digital authorship, and networked power, but they do not explicitly state the allusions they are making to a culture of impermanence. In addition, they do not critically reflect on how individuals and groups are impacted differentially by digital rhetorics and cultures.	Clip 2 Agreement: Majors agreed that this clip lacks analysis as the student discusses personal characteristics and style without reflecting on identity or the cultural trends that influence style. Students noted that the "it doesn't matter" statement at the end of the clip undercuts any attempt the group may have made to analyze visual rhetoric or to connect with concepts of identity, culture, and power.	
Clip 3 Agreement: Majors argued that this clip is the strongest example of analysis of identity, culture, and power because the students identify a dominant narrative about professionalism, analyze and critique how professional rhetorics work to include some and exclude others, and apply that analysis to the visual rhetoric in their portfolios.	Clip 3 Disagreement: Majors note that the students focus on a single identity marker—Writing and Rhetoric Major and most, with the exception of one student, do not consider how other identities intersect with the performance of this identity. Students note that the conversation seems to be skimming across the surface without delving deeper into analysis.	Clip 3 Agreement: Majors found that students in this clip were identifying rhetorics of culture and power, but they hadn't make the jump from identification to analysis and application in their projects.	
Clip 4 Agreement: Majors agreed that this clip demonstrated explicit analysis by naming the ways that their impulses and behaviors were influenced by dominant culture. They also noted that the students were applying this critical analysis to their decision-making both in- and out-of the classroom.			
Clip 5 Disagreement: Majors noted that the student identified a cultural rhetoric and discussed a particular reading but did not connect the marginalization of Hispanic rhetorics to cultural hegemony in the United States.			

FAILING AT WRITING (ASSESSMENT): RESISTING MECHANIZATION

While Stephanie and her colleagues received a Faculty Senate award for excellence in program assessment, the SLOA office called the findings into question based on a normative expectation in mechanized assessment design: sample size. Central to statistical frameworks, sample size is used to promote confidence in assessment findings. The better the sample population matches the total population under study, the higher the confidence in the findings in the statistical model. If the sample is too small, there may be too many outliers in the data. These outliers can skew the findings, as they are not a fair representation of the larger group. On the other hand, if the sample is too large, the assessment project can become unwieldy because assessors are unable to collect, manage, and interpret the data in systematic ways. The Writing and Rhetoric program at URI was advised that its sample size was too small; therefore, high confidence couldn't be placed in the findings. In this particular context, confidence comes in large-scale, mechanized assessments, not in human-focused, anticolonialist storying paradigms. Assessment killjoys spoil confidence.

When confidence is based on statistical models, these critiques are important, as assessors want a fair and representative sample of the population under study. When confidence is based on humanistic models that value relationships and trust, however, these critiques are not very helpful. Case studies shared in writing studies scholarship, such as Jennifer D. Turner and Autumn Griffin's (2020) "Brown Girls Dreaming," highlight how we can attend to anticolonial paradigms while engaging in storytelling. What's key in both these paradigms is the way inferences are generalized beyond the study. Regardless of sample size, studies make sense when readers are familiar with the population being studied. Bias is built into our everyday experiences, and we carry that bias into how we read, interpret, and design assessment studies. Yet in Stephanie's case, the assessment office privileged a particular paradigm regardless of how the study was designed. As we discuss in chapter 5, oversampling can get at the particular experience of students from marginalized backgrounds and resist their erasure in statistical models. Stephanie was reminded of this in the WRT program assessment project as well. During the student focus-group session, participants discussed the particular importance of honoring the experiences of students of color, even though those students might be statistically insignificant at a predominantly white institution (PWI)—and even more so in an overwhelmingly white writing major. Students took particular note of a moment in the class recording when a senior writing major who identified as Latinx discussed analysis. The student stated that during her upper-division rhetorics class, as she read Gloria Anzaldúa's (1987) *Borderlands* for the first time, she saw herself reflected in the course content and recognized herself as a serious rhetor. To coldly dissect and objectively analyze Anzaldúa's words in that space with her classmates felt to her like a personal violence. The participating focus-group students noted this analytical pedagogy could be another colonizing move that serves not to empower but to disempower students from marginalized backgrounds. Without oversampling and amplifying this student's voice in the assessment context, Stephanie and her colleagues could ignore how analysis of identity, culture, and power is perceived and felt differently depending on one's constellation in that ICP matrix.

Similarly, the learning stories we examine in this chapter demonstrate how undersampling can provide opportunities to develop other models of confidence. Through the lens of QVI, we argue that confidence can also be achieved in nonnormative ways such as making assessment work public, involving diverse stakeholders, creating assessment paradigms that attend to both access and accessibility, and approaching data through practices of rhetorical listening. As Krista Ratcliffe (2005) argues, rhetorical listening requires a "stance of openness that a person may choose to assume in relation to any person, text, or culture" (17). This openness, we believe, is central to developing constellated approaches to writing assessment. As opposed to norming readers or assessors under objectivist paradigms of good writing, rhetorical listening allows for a different kind of confidence to emerge, one based on shared responsibility among students, teachers, programs, and institutions. As we demonstrate in this chapter, to resist mechanization, we must make space for stories of writing and writing instruction to collaboratively and relationally emerge. These stories move beyond a simplistic success/failure binary and help practitioners better understand how we might create more culturally responsive and relevant opportunities for the relational praxis of writing instruction and assessment.

To do that, we must remember *lived experiences* and *embodiment* are key affective (in)competencies that should be an integral part of our writing constructs. Focusing in on materiality (along with affectivity and identities) as we do in this chapter creates a space for different stories of writing (processes and products) to emerge and to have a more central space in our discussions of what we value. As important, only through validity models that reject disidentified and disembodied writing artifacts as the norm in our assessments will we be able to connect student writing, student learning, and our teaching practices in ways that will meaningfully feed back into our classrooms and programs. This work is not efficient, easy, or labor free by any stretch of the imagination, but as we point out in the next chapter, embracing the assessment killjoy and the antinormative assessment paradigms we suggest throughout this book can have long-term savings for faculty and students alike: it can reduce the wasted labor we spend on assessments that mean little or nothing to students and teachers while helping faculty and program administrators frame their work in more meaningful ways for institutional assessment offices and external accrediting agencies.

7
ASSESSMENT KILLJOYS
An Invitation

Even with the examples we share in this book, we know it's hard to start queering writing assessment, and we realize you might be thinking, "Okay, yeah, I'm on board with this idea, but how exactly do I get started?" We recognize that engaging in queer validity inquiry will require new or perhaps quite different emotional and mental labor from you. Unlike the quick fixes marketed by textbook companies and educational-testing groups, the examples we've shared are not ones you can box up and drop into your own teaching and administrative contexts. You'll have to read more about learning stories, digital badging, onboarding and professional development, and intersectional data analysis if you want to adopt such an approach for your classroom or institution. Depending on your level of interest and commitment, this can be big work; we won't pretend otherwise. Our examples provide a snapshot of how we've used these approaches, but they don't provide a roadmap for adoption. That's intentional. QVI is messy and time intensive because writing is messy and time intensive—and our assessments should probably mirror the work they are evaluating if we want them to be valid and fair. The allure of commodified, mechanized, and reproductive assessments is that they can seem fast and easy to implement. You don't have to invest emotionally in the process, and you certainly do not have to wrestle with the ways they so often build on and reproduce the unfairness and inequities in our current systems.

However, when you decide to embrace the assessment killjoy, you also choose to invest affectively and materially in changing the writing construct and the assessment ecologies of your classroom, program, and campus. These are big and important commitments that connect with so many of our disciplinary and personal values. To that end, we want to end our discussion of queering assessment (for now, at least) by turning toward spaces in assessment that may be creating yet another imaginative limitation on writing teachers and writing program administrators

https://doi.org/10.7330/9781646423705.c007

seeking to pursue more localized and equitable assessments, namely campus accreditation practices that call out for us to embrace the assessment killjoy as a resistant strategy of disidentification. In this chapter, we look at how institutionalized assessment practices create a double burden on faculty who are invested in meaningful assessment, and we offer ideas for how we all might disidentify with local interpretations of assessment practices established by larger accrediting bodies.

ASSESSMENT'S DOUBLE BURDEN

We know from our own experiences, as well as countless conversations with colleagues at other institutions, how mentally and emotionally taxing it can be to commit to justice-oriented work when institutions seem focused primarily on checking boxes and limiting the impact of assessment to easily controlled and managed practices. In this context, these commitments to justice-oriented work can feel like a double burden because on the one hand, faculty and program administrators are beholden to an institution whose job it is to succeed by delivering a quality educational experience and demonstrating that quality to its accrediting bodies. Particularly at public institutions, this sort of accountability is important, as taxpayers and citizens invest time, energy, and financial resources in making sure educational institutions deliver on the promises of those investments. Likewise, the data from our writing classrooms and programs are often an essential part of that narrative of success, particularly given the role foundational writing courses tend to play in general education initiatives. To that end, we must invest in the labor of designing and implementing assessments that contribute to that externally established vision of assessment. On the other hand, we recognize that these designs and data may have marginal use value in understanding the complex cognitive, social, and emotional work of writing—and assessing writing—and may offer little opportunity to pursue educational and social justice. This recognition motivates us to create "second-shift" assessments like the ones we've shared in previous chapters that perform the care work in our writing communities. After we've finished that first job of performing assessments for the institution, our sense is that most of us then sign up for an additional work shift to get the more meaningful assessment labor done. Borrowing from Arlie R. Hochschild and Anne Machung (1989), we argue that this bifurcated practice disadvantages those who do the care work of assessment because they are engaging in not only the formal, recognized, and paid practices of writing assessment but also in the informal, invisible, and unpaid labor of queer and femininized assessment care work. In short, the system we work in levies an assessment tax that unfairly burdens the assessment killjoy.

If we are to alleviate or eliminate this assessment labor tax, we might borrow from labor-policy analysts working to alleviate the double burden of paid work and unpaid care work. They advocate a three-pronged approach: recognition, reduction, and redistribution (Sengupta and Sachdeva 2017). Such an approach, they argue, can create a "double boon" that offers reasonable paid work that both "empowers . . . and provides support for their unpaid care work responsibilities" (1). In writing assessment ecologies, institutions might also pursue practices that create an assessment double boon by offering reasonable opportunities to demonstrate success for accreditors while simultaneously enfranchising assessment laborers and providing support for alternative assessment practices that support democracy, equity, and justice. As Monica Stitt-Bergh, Catherine M. Wehlburg, Terrel Rhodes, and Natasha Jankowski (2019) argue, assessment as a public good rejects notions of individual competition and gatekeeping and instead focuses on using assessment as an opportunity to make transparent the work of classrooms, programs, and institutions. It requires a radical shift from thinking about assessment as a way of "chas[ing] ever-shifting external accountability goal posts" (45) to a collective recognition of the social, public, and civic value of assessment. Collective recognition at the institutional level would allow assessment laborers to pursue projects that can both satisfy accreditation requirements *and* transform the teaching and learning of writing.

Institutions could also reduce the labor of institutional assessment by curtailing the number of required assessment reports and better coordinating assessment initiatives across the university. Yearly or biennial reporting leaves little time to design assessments, engage in practices of validity inquiry, and use the results of assessment meaningfully at the classroom or programmatic level. Given the well-documented test fatigue that has occurred in K–12 settings (Hart et al. 2015), colleges and universities should certainly enter into the assessment scene with greater trepidation. With such short cycles, assessment becomes a burden with little or no pedagogical value. Furthermore, faculty are often pulled in different directions by multiple institutional assessment demands that are poorly and negatively correlated. For example, faculty and program administrators in writing studies are often engaged in learning outcomes assessment for both program review and general education course evaluation. Although less common in our field, writing studies faculty may also participate in accredited program assessment, particularly if they are located in a school of journalism and mass communications. In our experiences, these different assessment initiatives and their regulatory offices do not collaborate effectively with one another to integrate their various institutional assessments. This lack of orchestration means assessment laborers end up duplicating efforts and missing ripe opportunities to analyze data sets and evidence through multiple lenses.

Ultimately, to redistribute assessment labor, we need a better understanding of who our assessment laborers are in terms of race, gender, and faculty status. University committee work falls disproportionately on marginalized faculty, particularly those who are of color, women, queer, and from working-class backgrounds (Arkolakis et al. 2018; University of Oregon 2017). While the labor demands generally, and the invisible labor of assessment more specifically, are explored in scholarship (Champagne 2011; Singer-Freeman, Robinson, and Bastone 2020), we know of no studies at present that analyze the disproportionate burden of assessment labor on particular faculty groups. This is an example of what Mya Poe (2021b), borrowing from Mimi Onụọha, calls missing data sets in assessment. Missing data sets are empty spaces where data *should* but *do not* (yet) exist. Those empty spaces stand in for that which is overlooked, ignored, and deemed unimportant by institutions (see also Caswell and Banks 2018). While looking for this missing data at her institution, Stephanie found the student learning outcomes assessment office does maintain a record of faculty assessment coordinators. However, in many cases, the named assessment faculty "lead" is the department chair, not the faculty member(s) who are conducting and reporting on assessment. These inaccuracies work to skew that data because white men remain in control of higher education leadership positions such as the role of the department chair. In several instances in which the tenured chair is listed as assessment lead, the actual faculty assessors are women in contingent faculty positions. Thus, an initial step toward redistributing labor is filling in those missing data sets. Once we understand who is doing the assessment labor, we can push for incentives meaningful to different faculty groups. In doing so, we might take up fairness as a value for both students and faculty in an assessment ecology. Of course, this is also assessment-killjoy work.

THE POWER OF FORBIDDEN ASSESSMENT KNOWLEDGE

Creating the conditions for an assessment double boon requires systematic change, but institutional change is a slow and frustrating process

(Porter et al. 2000). Institutional assessment offices have created their own policies and procedures to manage the institutional work flows of assessment with good reason. These offices must process an enormous amount of data to prepare their accreditation reports, and having standardized practices undoubtedly makes the workflow more efficient. When faculty and program administrators push back on these standardized approaches, assessment officials sometimes throw their hands in the air and blame the accrediting body for such unproductive requirements and mandates: "It's not up to us. Our office is just enforcing SACSCOC (or NECHE or HLC or MSCHE) requirements!" Complicating the issue, of course, is that these offices are typically staffed by nonfaculty employees whose relationship with and responsibilities to the institution are dramatically different from those of research-oriented faculty. In our experiences as assessment laborers, however, we've learned that at least some of these double assessment burdens are created artificially at the institutional level. They are not, in fact, mandated by our accrediting bodies; instead, they are quite often sedimented assessment practices within local university cultures. As we demonstrate below, some of these sedimented practices are the result of a conscious desire for efficiency, while others are sustained un- or semiconsciously by narrow interpretations of the accreditors' requirements. Thus, we argue, familiarity with your university's accreditation standards can help you (to paraphrase Porter et al. 2000) rewrite institutional assessment policy through rhetorical action, thereby becoming a more empowered and effective assessment killjoy.

We owe this realization of the disconnect between institutions and accreditors' approaches to assessment, at least in part, to Poe (2021b). In spring of 2021, Stephanie's college invited Poe as a faculty keynote speaker to share her research in writing assessment and social justice. Initially, Poe had planned to ground her talk in a review of assessment guidelines provided by the New England Commission of Higher Education (NECHE), URI's regional accrediting body, in order to demonstrate how assessment as social justice was embedded in NECHE's recommendations for linking outcomes assessment to university mission statements. Poe thought faculty would appreciate that the institution's mission statement provided a clear justification for this work, as the statement includes "creativity and scholarship; diversity, fairness, and respect; engaged learning and civic involvement; and intellectual and ethical leadership" as its core values (University of Rhode Island 2006). When university assessment officials learned Poe's talk was making these local connections, they feared the keynote was turning into an unauthorized assessment consultation and asked to review her presentation materials.

Poe was encouraged to strike this material from her talk and focus only on her published research. Campus assessment officials argued faculty didn't need to know about NECHE or engage with its resources because faculty answered to the institutional assessment office, not the accreditor. This campus office saw itself as assessment intercessors; they would communicate externally and would interpret the goals, values, and materials for faculty. From our perspective, however, they were performing less as intercessors who open up communication than as the Great and Powerful Oz, projecting back to faculty an omnipotent and controlling force that "owned" assessment and controlled what it did or could mean—but all, of course, for the good of the little people involved. This level of oversight and interference in the research presentation of an internationally recognized scholar in our field was unexpected and escalated preexisting tensions around assessment on campus. It seemed Poe might be playing the role of Toto in this drama, as some feared she was about to pull the curtain back for faculty whose belief in the omnipotence of URI's institutional assessment office should not be shaken.

Using NECHE's forbidden knowledge base (forbidden, at least, in the context of her institution) has enabled Stephanie and her colleagues to push back on two institutional assessment mandates: the frequency of assessment cycles and the types of evidence required to measure progress toward student learning outcomes. First, the institution requires that programs complete a learning outcomes assessment report biennially. Part of the report includes articulating a plan for closing the loop by putting the results of assessment into practice. This is an impossible task given that as soon as the assessment report is completed, it's time to begin collecting data for the next cycle of assessment. The pedagogical implementation is given short shrift and usually amounts to the articulation of a plan that is never enacted. Essentially, it amounts to a pedagogical performance for the sake of accountability similar to what we discuss in chapter 3 with the state-mandated writing portfolios. What we've learned by scouring NECHE's materials is that student learning outcomes assessment must be regular; however, there's no requirement to report every two years. With support from their college deans, Stephanie and her colleagues are pushing on assessment officials to extend the reporting cycle to a three-year period. This change would open up opportunities to work over the course of the third year with faculty-development specialists who could guide faculty in using the assessment data to improve classroom instruction and bolster the program's capacity to attract, retain, and provide better support for its students. Faculty at URI are making some headway here, as the most recent survey from the assessment office to measure the culture supporting academic program assessment included a question about faculty interest in moving from a two- to a three-year reporting cycle.

In addition to the issue of frequency, Stephanie's institutional reporting template currently requires that programs use direct evidence of student learning and lists indirect evidence as optional. While NECHE recommends the use of both direct and indirect evidence, the institution has unnecessarily narrowed faculty options for representing student learning. Direct evidence includes the review of artifacts such as student projects and performances, and, of course, students' written products. Direct evidence purportedly allows assessors to measure what and how much students have learned through a systematic evaluation of their work, which we and others in writing assessment have been critical of (see chapter 5; Inoue 2019). This systematic evaluation is almost always achieved through the use of a rubric as we describe and critique in chapter 4. Indirect evidence, however, provides insight into the affective valences, motivations, values, and perceptions of learners and others involved in the assessment ecology. Many of the QVI practices we share throughout this book give equal or increased weight to indirect evidence as a means of failing sideways toward a more robust writing construct. This is not to say direct evidence is not useful or, at times, more appropriate in some assessment designs. However, when we refuse the primacy of direct evidence, we open up lateral possibilities for investigating what writing can mean, construct, do, accomplish, and feel like to writers and to those who teach and assess it.

Being critical about what assessment offices and accrediting agencies mean by direct is another important way to be an assessment killjoy, to challenge the correlational relationships these groups have often constructed for writing by assuming the same processes and practices work across disciplinary or learning contexts. In fact, as we show through the examples in the previous chapters, by foregrounding indirect evidence, we can build more responsive frames for considering direct evidence of learning. Consider the example we share in chapter 5 of when we oversampled gay male students' experiences with writing assessment. Without understanding the ways Marcus negotiated identity performance in his writing, we would have little understanding of what Marcus actually learned about writing and himself as a writer—or what of that learning is transferable to other writing contexts. It was only through the indirect evidence provided by the focus groups that we were able to see a more complete picture of what Marcus was learning about writing, audience, purpose, and context with his writing and to create more humane assessment practices that keep these important elements of writing and assessment linked.

Similarly, Stephanie approached her most recent assessment cycle by leaning in to Halberstam's (2011) failure-oriented practice of "strategically forgetting" this requirement for direct evidence; instead, she used rounds of focus-group data to interrogate operational understandings of what students and faculty mean by "analyzing rhetorics of identity, culture, and power" throughout the undergraduate writing major, which we detail in chapter 6. While Stephanie's report was criticized for inadequate sample size, none of the assessment professionals mentioned the fact that only indirect evidence of learning was gathered and analyzed for the report. In fact, the URI Faculty Senate recognized Stephanie's report as an assessment exemplar, and she's been able to share her assessment work on campus with other faculty and thus encourage more use of indirect evidence as the most appropriate means of answering particular kinds of assessment questions. While she and other faculty members have taken on the frequency of assessment cycles directly by petitioning the student learning assessment office, this kind of institutional resistance is more . . . well, *indirect* . . . and subversive in nature. It's a good reminder that the assessment killjoy has tactical options and that the approach the killjoy takes should not always be head on into open battle, though that, too, can be an important option.

If arming yourself and your colleagues with forbidden (or at least seemingly hidden) knowledge of accreditation guidelines is not enough, you might seek out other partners in collusion. Unionized faculty might try calling in their union representatives to help redress the double burdens created by contemporary high-stakes accountability versions of assessment. Each of the three major faculty labor unions—AAUP, NEA, and AFT—recognize that faculty participation in assessment is both essential to faculty governance and central to academic freedom in the classroom; however, they also note that increasing faculty participation in assessment is challenging because of faculty knowledge gaps and the lack of visibility and compensation for assessment labor (Gold et al. 2011). Larry Gold, director of the Higher Education Department of the American Federation of Teachers, contends that a "critical need for front-line faculty and staff is for correct and up-to-date information about the range of accountability and assessment measures proposed or implemented so they can develop their own local capacity to respond and make constructive recommendations in this area" (15). He goes on to demonstrate how faculty unions can support more meaningful assessment work through mentoring, public advocacy, collective bargaining, and the collection and publication of resources for faculty related to assessment. In that same report (Gold et al. 2011), AAUP secretary Gary Rhoades argues further that unionized faculty contracts should explicitly address assessment work as a fundamental instructional practice that should be equivalent to serving as instructor of record for a course. Rhoades has pointed out that unionized faculty contracts often include supplemental salary or reassignment time to develop online courses; however, assessment labor has not been systematically considered as an extra assignment. According to Rhoades, as corporatized universities strive to decrease the cost of labor by driving up faculty credit-hour production, "It is important to advance a different conception of productivity—one defined in terms of learning outcomes attained and dropout rates reduced" (quoted in Gold et al. 2011).

Rhoades's comment frames assessment as a powerful tool for understanding that *working conditions are learning conditions.* As we note in chapter 1, we must be aware that moves to overly mechanize assessment are working to turn teachers into tools that can be leveraged and redirected for peak efficiency at the behest of an institution's self-sustaining initiatives, which do not always align with actually improving learning experiences for students. Instead, we must value teachers as professionals who write and teach and learn, and who work in relation with other writers and learners. Such a move could resist turning students into numbers rather than human beings engaged in learning, in writing, and in making meaning through a host of discursive and material-affective activities. If we are to pursue fairness as a key outcome of writing assessment, we must think about solidarity not just among faculty members but also with our students, their families, and our communities. Labor unions can be influential in establishing assessment public policy that works for those learning and laboring in writing classrooms.

FAIRNESS ENTANGLED WITH QUEERNESS

Throughout this book, we orient toward assessments that would lend themselves toward notions of fairness rooted in an equity mindset. Fairness allows us to achieve an ethical outcome (Elliot 2016) in our writing assessments. Following Norbert Elliot's definition of fairness that attends to maximum construction representation, our additions to the writing construct push us beyond simple product/process-oriented binaries and ask us to unpack the ways our assessments influence (and are influenced by) human behaviors. Thus, like Poe (2021a), we agree that "written communication is a deeply situated behavior, and to understand how that deeply human activity works, we must understand context as more than a flat surface against which writing happens" (20). Our QVI practices and lenses have worked to resist flattened notions of writing that imagine fairness as that which is superficially the same for everyone involved, choosing instead to relish in the peaks and valleys created by more fluid understandings of the assessment scene (as represented by figure 5.3). In chapter 3, we consider failure as part of our move toward fairness. We turn our attention to other kinds of assessment objects and stories that allow us to ask questions such as, What are we interested in? Why? Whose interests are served? In chapter 4, we resist the definition of fairness as sameness; specifically, we resist the commodification of isolated features of writing onto a rubric. Although we understand the desire and context-specific value for reviewers to operate from the same criteria, we wonder what might happen if we move toward more collaborative notions of assessments that generate shared knowledge bases. This, too, is an equity move that imagines success, achievement, and opportunity as a lateral project, one that allows difference to be valued and celebrated on its own terms rather than as simply a trait on a scale.

We see QVI as not only permitting an equity orientation toward fairness but, in fact, demanding that writing studies professionals continually orient in that direction. In doing so, we also recognize that fairness, like QVI, is an orientation toward futural horizons not necessarily achievable. To that end, we situate our project amid other assessment scholarship (Kelly-Riley and Elliot 2020) that see fairness as something not finally or easily attained but rather as an endless loop of seeking and trying that involves being careful and critical about the work we're doing. QVI allows us to work toward fairness but acknowledges that a Platonic notion of fairness is not achievable given how contextual fairness must be. The moment we create assessment structures we believe provide an opportunity for all to learn is the same moment we must reengage QVI to see what's happening beneath and beside those assessments. QVI asks us to always be thinking about how writing and assessment are ongoing, becoming, and aiming toward. Through QVI, fairness and queerness are enfolded and entangled—always becoming, but never quite there.

THE PLEASURE OF YOUR COMPANY: AN INVITATION

We close this book with an invitation to you to be part of that not-quite-thereness of queering writing assessment. Queering assessment involves a constellation of disruptive practices for unmaking the regimes of assessment that mark the bodies of students and teachers. It is a speculative methodology, not only in terms of risk and contingency but also in terms of theoretical ideation. It conceptualizes other ways of making knowledge about writing, writers, and writing communities by rejecting mastery narratives and their reliance on a success/failure binary. As we demonstrate across our chapters, it holds promise for developing assessment instruments, practices, and critical validity arguments that help us attune to the queer movements and moments of writers, writing instruction, and writing communities. As scholar-activists, we have held and nurtured this promise for the past five years, working in fits and starts as we moved our thinking in, around, behind, below, and above this project of theorizing queer assessment. We have published both individually and collaboratively on its theoretical dimensions, and we have thought with and followed the lead of queer scholar-teachers in our field as they imagine ways to broaden their writing constructs and then build assessment frameworks to ethically engage with those constructs. For example, we might look to Jacqueline Rhodes's (2004) "Homo Origo: The Queertext Manifesto" for some queer writing constructs. Here is a sampling from among Rhodes's fifty-six queertext resistances:

1. Textual conversations are human conversations; our textuality intersects our humanity at the point of our writing hands, our typing fingers, our seeing eyes.

2. There is nothing natural in text; there are, however, material considerations in text. The material of a queer text dances in the openness of the margin between Signifier (Sr) and Signified (Sd). . . .

10. We cannot win freedom, but can explode it, more fully inhabiting the liminal space of queertext by celebrating bodies and materialities of identity.

11. The discipline of our queer bodies includes the discipline of our speaking mouths and writing tongues. . . .

17. Words dominate our texts; a few Words dominate other words. They enact this dominance through grammar. . . .

24. We see the personal as already political, an insight drawn from radical feminists. We further add: The *personalpolitical* is already sexual and textual. . . .

26. We regard our bodily experience with language, and our feelings about that experience, as another component of language, albeit an often unspoken part. . . .

43. We can all be queered. That means you, too. (388–90)

More recently, Stacey Waite (2019) has offered their own version of the "failing, impossible, contradictory" acts of writing queerly. We've excerpted a few of these, as well, to give you a taste of how we might carry on the important work of queering the writing construct:

1. Commit rhetorical disobedience.

2. Write from a position of failure instead of writing from the position of what you think you know. Certainty is only queer when you are certain your knowledge is partial, failed, and fragmented. . . .

4. Don't stay "on topic." Drift gleefully off. Get lost.

5. Imagine your writing outside the bounds of binary understandings: critical and creative, academic and personal, theoretical and practical. All of these all at once, or none of these all at once, which is a binary so nevermind. . . .

10. Approach writing as an act of discovery and experimentation.

11. Be irrational, hysterical even. . . .

13. Show up in your writing as a body, an embodied force in the text, all while keeping your reader aware that even the body is a contradiction: both an idea constructed and a real material thing that impacts the world. . . .

15. Write with the knowledge this is all true, and all lies, all real, and all made up, which leads us to . . .

16. Write in queer voice(s). Contradict yourself. Queer writing "involves deliberately courting paradox" (Rhodes 2015).

17. Undermine your own authority, be certain in your uncertainty, develop a voice that can be trusted even as it is subjective, unreliable, and impossible to pin down, unless of course, you want to be pinned down in a sexy way.

18. Be promiscuous, neither married or monogamized to your discipline, your language(s). . . .

30. Don't be faithful or loyal to institutions, disciplines, or persons to whom others say you must be speaking. . . .

37. If there is not a word for what/who you are/mean/do, make one up: *queertext, genderqueer, bicurious, cisnormativity*. Words become words when we say, write, and circulate them.

38. Invent more words; we need them; more words for who we are/ do. . . .

40. Get disorganized, make a mess. (43–48)

There is really nothing all that radical here, when you think about it, and yet there is also massive radicality in what Rhodes and Waite suggest. Similarly, in *Teaching Queer: Radical Possibilities for Writing and Knowing*, Waite (2017) offers a powerful rationale for queering the ways we welcome students into writing:

> I think that what it means to introduce students to writing in the humanities is to ask students to consider that composition is not a moment when we decide one thing over another or take one side of a two-sided debate—rather, it is an act of wavering and careful consideration in which writers move fluidly through the complicated terrain of their own thinking and the thinking of others. (41)

To heed these calls from Rhodes and Waite is to remember the playfulness and excitement that can be part of our writing construct when we embrace both curiosity and exhaustion, passion and disgust, pride and shame, and a host of other seemingly disparate binaries—when we remember writing exists to make visible our desires, needs, and values—in short, when we remember writing is fundamentally an affective project of meaning making, meaning sharing, and meaning doing both in and with the world and others. When we remember this important part of writing, we realize very quickly that the ways we have been called upon by our disciplines, by our schools and universities, by our profit-desiring stakeholders to respond to and assess student writing have too often enacted a dangerous disconnect between our writing constructs and our assessment paradigms. It's time for these two things to communicate again, to work in tandem to build a better, more capacious, more joyful writing construct.

WHAT'S NEXT FOR QVI?

Now, we think it's important for us, and to the field at large, to shift from speculation to empirical research that extends, distends, and perhaps upends this constellation of practices we've traced out. We use the term *empirical* here to mean systematic, reflective, and analytical, and we recognize storytelling as an empirical methodology for decolonizing our discipline and our research (Battiste 2013; Kovach 2010; Patel 2016; Rhee 2021; Smith 2012). As we promise at the start of this book, we have brought together both quantitative and qualitative data, as well as direct and indirect evidence of student learning, in order to tell stories about writing assessment, and we have shared stories of our experiences. What we need more of now are your stories, your experiences with queering assessment and queer validity inquiry. We want to see your arguments, your contexts, your experiences. We want to feel the grooves and curves of your stories, to touch the crenellated edges of your meandering assessment narratives, and we want to edge along with you. We crave more stories of local, meaningful, affective, and embodied writing assessments that will overwhelm our discipline with alternative assessment scenes.

In taking up QVI as a methodology, we recognize how queer scholars have long been suspicious of using *queer* as a descriptor for normative and normativizing structures like pedagogy and administration (Banks et al. 2020; Banks and Alexander 2009; Rhodes 2015). We add assessment to these normative structures and agree they are quite possibly impossible to queer because they are disciplining mechanisms that preserve heterosexism, patriarchy, whiteness, colonialism, and elitism in educational contexts. To borrow from Michel de Certeau (1984), these normative structures can be understood as the very strategies that reproduce hegemony, that keep fairness as an always futural and utopic place. To queer assessment, then, we offer QVI as a failure-oriented set of everyday tactical moves that help us navigate the prefigured worlds of assessment as gatekeeping, as discipline, and as punishment. These improvisational tactics are means for developing collective agency as writing studies scholar-practitioners. They offer a language for naming what we feel in existing assessment scenes, and they provide a glimpse of what it could mean to refigure the worlds of writing assessment.

In such refigured worlds, queer assessors queerly assessing queer writers with queer rhetorics and queer measures could be perfectly queer . . . or not. Beyond the perfectly queer, however, there is space for imagining a host of improv-style *queer and* configurations and practices. Queer assessors can queerly assess straight writers with queer and inappropriate measures. Straight assessments can uncover queer moments among straight writers and teachers when subjected to queer rhetorical analysis. Straight assessors can queerly assess queer writers with straight tools. Intersectionally speaking, queer students of color can queerly assess straight "white-ing" programs with queer metrics. Queer crip rhetorics and rhetors can help straight assessors assess the accessibility of their assessments in ways that move beyond limited notions of access and fairness. To make it perfectly queer: we can queer a lot of stuff, and a lot of stuff can get queer(ed). And we might even find it both joyful and sustaining to get queer with our assessments.

Ultimately, we hope this book and the practices of queer assessment we sketch throughout the chapters can challenge you to

- take on the *ethos* of the assessment killjoy;
- make and hold space for a diverse set of nonconforming actors in nonconforming assessment scenes;
- build queer validity arguments that serve the needs of the diverse writers and writing teachers in your communities;
- use assessment tactically as part of the lived practices of writing and teaching writing; and

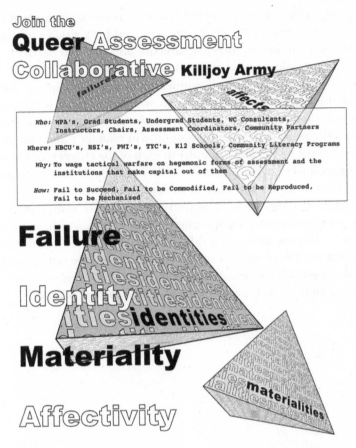

Figure 7.1. Invitation to join the Queer Assessment Collaborative Killjoy Army

- embrace failure-oriented moments and movements as alternative ways to write/do/say/be/value/believe in writing assessment as an investment in social justice.

If you're interested in this work, we offer you an invitation to join us in organizing and mobilizing a Queer Assessment Collaborative Killjoy Army. Our invitation is, of course, extended to writing program administrators, but we also want to extend a special invitation to writing teachers, graduate and undergraduate students, writing center consultants, and community members. We want to enlist those of you who think of yourselves as assessment outsiders, as we believe you have the most to gain and lose from assessment battles going on across campuses. As we've noted, you'll need to do more reading, thinking, maneuvering, and conspiring with others—so do we! However, if you fancy yourself crafty and willing to make, unmake, tinker with, and hack systems to respond to your own and others' pressing affective and material needs, you are exactly the people we need engaged in this work.

Finally, if you find yourself wondering how to take up the trajectories of this queer assessment work in your own research agenda, we invite you to design and implement empirical validation studies of the expanded construct of writing we outline in chapter 1 and that we add to through the stories and examples in each of the chapters of this book. Our experiences have been our own; they have been deeply embedded in our local contexts and have in each case been responses to broader assessment ideologies and values on our respective campuses, as well as in our departments and programs. We need to see these practices in other contexts, to see how different contexts, writers, and teachers can point out the places where equity and fairness are not yet realized, and where yet more sideways failures might lead to even better affective (in)competencies in the writing construct. Welcome, killjoys . . . come join us!

NOTES

CHAPTER 1: RISKING FAILURE

1. Throughout this book, we use the terms *neoliberal* and *late capitalist* somewhat interchangeably, and while we recognize there is some variability in how these terms are taken up in other contexts, each coming out of particular lines of intellectual inquiry, we do so here inasmuch as both point to ideological frameworks that have taken up a particularly pernicious place in the mindsets of contemporary academic cultures. Academic work spaces cannot resist prevailing ideologies that shape market forces in capitalist cultures like those in the United States, the United Kingdom, and most of Europe. To that end, we understand neoliberalism as an ideological imperative toward privatization and a disinvestment from public goods and services (Breu 2014; Burford 2015; Duggan 2002, 2003; Gilbert 2013; Mayor 2018; Wang 2021). As an ideology, neoliberalism represents a "procorporate, 'free market,' anti-'big government' rhetoric shaping US policy and dominating international financial institutions since the early 1980s" (Duggan 2002, 177). While working toward the "privatization of public assets, contraction and centralization of democratic institutions . . . [and the] active encouragement of competitive and entrepreneurial modes of relation across the public and commercial sectors" (Gilbert 2013, 11–12), neoliberal policies simultaneously advocate for increases in "spending on the military, police, and legal systems to secure private property rights" (Mayor 2018, 201). Neoliberal ideologies support a host of policies that advance individuals based on their economic value to the production of capital and demoralize individuals who do not enact key bootstraps models of self-improvement and success. As Christopher Breu (2014) notes,

> In neoliberal biopolitics, all social relationships are privatized and marketized; individuals are deemed investment worthy (a.k.a., employable) or disposable depending on the share of human capital they possess. As ugly as this rhetoric is, with its spoils go to the winner mentality, the rhetoric of human capital still articulates a vision of economic investment (although one targeted to the already well off and socially advantaged). In contrast, the rhetoric of austerity treats all laboring subjects (whether citizens or nation states) as indebted and guilty before the law of accumulation. It thus can be used to justify all kinds of cost-cutting, appropriation, and asset stripping, even in situations of marked productivity and efficiency. If "human capital" is the logic of neoliberalism in its expansionist periods, then austerity is its logic in periods of decline and divestment. (30)

Throughout this book, we return again and again to the ways we believe neoliberal/late-capitalist ideologies have become central to higher education in relation to writing and writing assessment, valuing those practices and activities that lead to success while punishing any deviation from that narrow path. In this worldview, universities overly invest in the administrative class and spend outrageous amounts of money on prepackaged assessments, frameworks, rubrics, models, and so forth that can be bought and implemented to push students and faculty along that narrow and myopic path of success. Rooted in efficiency at whatever cost, neoliberal assessment ecologies work against both teaching and student learning as a shared, relational set of activities and entanglements that lead to human empowerment and meaningful, critical self-awareness. Through this book, readers will notice we have developed a host of assessment practices we believe work against these moves at the local levels of classrooms and writing programs in hopes that faculty and students can find ways to resist the hyperprivatization of higher education.

2. We borrow our understanding of diffraction from Karen Barad's (2007) *Meeting the Universe Halfway: Quantum Physics and the Entanglement of Matter and Meaning.* Barad proposes diffraction as a nonhierarchical model for scholarship, one that recognizes ideas as entangled rather than requiring new ideas to prove themselves by passing through the restrictive lenses of past discoveries or ideas: "Diffraction does not fix what is the object and what is the subject in advance, and so, unlike methods of reading one text or set of ideas against another where one set serves as a fixed frame of reference, diffraction involves reading insights through one another in ways that help illuminate differences as they emerge: how different differences get made, what gets excluded, and how those exclusions matter" (30).

3. "Unthinking happiness"—that sounds like an insult we do not intend. Rubrics are assessment technologies that have been advocated for, in part, because they can help make writing expectations more visible to students and instructors alike; they can also seem to embrace fairness, as all students are being evaluated on the same clearly articulated values. And yet, we borrow from Ahmed's notion of orientations as well-trodden paths because part of what makes rubrics or any similar teaching technology so "nice" is that the more we use them, the more automated they become, and the less we have to think about where they came from, how they're working (or not working), or how students understand (or do not) their values in their writing processes. When we call them "unthinking," we mean not that the people using them are not smart people but that the technology is doing what it is meant to do: create a smoother, less frictive pathway toward shared happiness in the classroom-assessment scene. To risk that pathway is to invite concerns, bumps, potholes that can be jarring. We know that, and we think the risk is worth taking.

CHAPTER 2: QUEER VALIDITY INQUIRY

1. In a recent NPR *All Things Considered* story, host Michael Martin asked *The Atlantic* education contributor James Fallows (2021) about how we rank schools and why. As part of that talk, Fallows notes that *U.S. News & World Report* began ranking colleges and high schools back in the 1980s as part of a savvy business decision to increase sales of the magazine, sales that now keep the publication afloat far beyond the work of reporting news. Fallows goes on to express real concern that the publication will now be ranking elementary schools:

    > My honest reaction was, God save us all. These rankings have already done enough to the higher education ecosystem that, with all the problems public elementary schools and high schools have, they don't need this as well. The public school system in the US has been struggling with the eternal questions of equity—of having property tax differentials not be

the main thing that determine students' chances very early in life—and achievement. How can you make sure students are learning what they need to learn? And having a purported ranking system that tells you, this school in one part of Illinois is better than that school in the other part of Illinois is not really helpful. For example, I just learned that my elementary school in Southern California is allegedly No. 2,115 among elementary schools in California, whereas the one my sister went to a few miles away is, like, 600 places better, which is absurd information and doesn't help elementary schools with the very, very hard job they all have to do.

Our obsession with ranking items, schools, people, experiences, and so forth demonstrates the far-reaching ways ranking systems are both born out of and contribute to consumerist frameworks that move students from certain backgrounds and with marked material privileges ahead of others regardless of merit or ability—or context for both. There's a lot of money to be made in assessment and marking success for some at the expense of others.

CHAPTER 3: FAILING TO BE SUCCESSFUL

1. It's hard to read *productive* in our culture and not see it immediately tangled up in *success*, but the reality of writing is that we are always producing failure over and beyond the successes we produce. We produce words and images and ideas we then cut, or that the mythic Reviewer 2 tells us are irrelevant or irrational. We produce emotions and feelings that move alongside our work, or that thwart our movement. In the scene of writing, there is endless production, only a small part of which is easy to see, feel, touch in the materiality of a written product.

2. One argument that permeates each chapter of this book is that assessment in the "accountability academy" that has been produced by political and corporate trends over the last four decades too often becomes delinked from meaningful validity arguments and instead becomes located in various portable assessment technologies: portfolios, rubrics, standardized testing, and so forth. While most of these technologies grew out of meaningful assessments or assessment values, when institutions and governmental agencies invest in them, they do so because they believe they will scale up, become a technology that can solve large problems or demonstrate something is working across instructional contexts. We offer critiques of these technologies throughout this book not because each one is inherently flawed but because their values have been lost in the push to scale up and manage the often unruly and complex work of assessment, particularly, in our case, writing assessment. See also Brian Huot and Michael Neal (2006).

3. Empirical temporalities are central to the logics of writing assessment scholarship as they are with most Western positivist and postpositivist inquiry models; as researchers, administrators, and scholars, we also value what's "current," even at times at the expense of historical or older work. One of the generous reviewers of this book in manuscript form questioned why we would still include the Kentucky portfolio experiment given how much has happened with portfolios and assessment since then, and while we agree our knowledge of portfolios has shifted dramatically since then—and the critical-validity turn in educational measurement and assessment more generally has also shifted the way we frame assessments—part of engaging with queer time (Halberstam 2005) is to recognize that our pasts and past projects do not quit acting simply because we have "moved on," if indeed we can actually fully move on. Often, that moving on is built upon a reiterative rejection of what

came before, such that what came before ends up being a mere shadow of what it was, a straw argument or scenario we reference and then distance ourselves from. We've certainly made some of those rhetorical moves in this book. Conjuring Callahan's (1997, 1999) and Scott's (2005) work again through a failure lens, however, allows us to think about the ways failure operates in assessments and helps us make a larger argument throughout this book about the ways failure interoperates with success, change, progress, and other "happy" work. This particular return also speaks to the ways practitioner lore (North 1987) can remain in the system despite nuanced changes happening in the research literature.

4. That list included the following items: "predict an outcome," "defend a position," "solve a problem," "analyze or evaluate a situation, person, place, or thing," "explain a process or concept," "draw a conclusion," "create a model" (Callahan 1997, 329).

5. We know from our own classrooms, where we tend to make course outcomes, national outcomes like the CWPA's, and the *Framework* habits part of an ongoing conversation with students, students often have no idea what these particular items mean. To them, they're written in "teacher language" and do not communicate what writing is expected to do or be. Anne Ruggles Gere, Anne Curzan, J. W. Hammond, Sarah Hughes, Ruth Li, Andrew Moos, Kendon Smith, Kathryn Van Zanen, Kelly L. Wheeler, and Crystal J. Zanders (2021) have done important work to help us disrupt the idea that the outcomes/frameworks documents are static and immutable, but more clearly must be done in our classrooms and professional organizations. Recently, the CWPA put together a subcommittee to investigate antiracist languaging practices embedded in the outcomes document as a way of rethinking the organization's (and our field's) investment in white-supremacist languaging and writing practices. While the organization as of this writing has resisted the revised outcomes/frameworks the committee created, our reading of them in draft form (https://tinyurl.com/FYCGoalsStatement) suggests they could offer a powerful attempt to localize the language around key writing outcomes and thus could empower students and classroom teachers to cocreate more meaningful and enriching outcomes that may, themselves, move sideways along different trajectories than more traditional outcomes-as-standards models.

6. Given summer schedules and faculty availability, Will and the QEP director, Dr. Wendy Sharer, could not always perfectly connect or align assessors, but in general, when they assembled departments or programs for weeklong summer assessments, they tried to follow this model. For example, they might combine a department from the College of Allied Health Sciences with Health Education and Promotion and Biology; genres and research methodologies/frameworks might be similar and different enough that both discipline-based and extradisciplinary readers share disposition and frameworks for research. Similarly, they might combine anthropology, sociology, and criminal justice for the same week, or philosophy, history, and English for the same week. Over the years of working in WAC professional development, Will had found that methodological bias among faculty was often one of the strongest factors in disagreements about good writing, and the assessment leadership team hoped this attention to methodological/inquiry values would allow faculty assessors a jump start for focusing on the rubric and the student writing, reducing at least one type of "noise" in the assessment scene.

7. As a reminder, the ECU QEP Write Where You Belong was designed and implemented with a five-outcome framework, but when assessments began, the first outcome was divided into two separate outcomes. We still think of the University Writing Outcomes as five key elements, however, so we represent them and discuss them as five.

CHAPTER 4: FAILING TO BE COMMODIFIED

1. While it's possible to read the emoji self-assessments from the previous chapter as similar examples of reductive microassessments, we argue that context matters here as much as it does in any assessment scene. On Amazon, these star ratings are very public moments in which microassessments are meant to derail, defame, promote, adore, and so forth, products; these public performances are intended to advance the inexpert assessor as a valuable knowledge maker. In the emoji self-assessments, the goal is to allow writers to affectively frame their own work, to connect to the ways their work does or does not succeed at a particular moment.

2. For example, the Morrill Act of 1862, subsequently expanded in 1890, supported the development of land-grant public universities that would focus on practical sciences such as agriculture and engineering, while private philanthropists like Ezra Cornell, whose endowment supported the land-grant that would establish Cornell University, provided financial backing for many of these progressive institutions. With the growth of the economy and these learning institutions at the secondary and postsecondary levels, a bureaucratic strand of educational progressivism was also born.

3. Education corporations like Pearson were quick to enter and trade in this market, using the well-worn practice of trait analysis to develop machine (a.k.a. automated essay) scoring. Relieved of the burden of establishing interrater reliability among reliably unreliable human beings, as we discuss in chapter 3, machines could efficiently, if not effectively, rate textual features such as word count, variation in vocabulary, and sentence or paragraph length, as well as errors of punctuation, grammar, mechanics, and spelling. What the machines cannot do, as scholars in the field have thoroughly explained, is participate in a meaning-making relationship between writers and readers (see chapter 6 for more on machine scoring; also Anson et al. 2013; Ericsson and Haswell 2006; Klobucar et al. 2012; Perelman 2012). While writing studies scholars and practitioners, as well as our professional organizations, have been vocal in their censure of automated essay scoring, less attention has been given to other less pernicious but still problematic writing assessment technologies developed out of practices of trait analysis.

4. It's important to note here that pulling these artifacts away from their contexts of production, an activity we criticize throughout this book, was done with a very different end goal in mind. The examples we look at that decontextualize student writing for traditional assessment purposes seem inextricably rooted in deficit models of education and in observing lack so as to rank and sort the materials and their creators. With the descriptive assessment model Stephanie and her colleagues used for these multimodal projects, the point wasn't to observe what the projects lacked in order to justify a ranking; instead, they approached these from an abundance model that looked for what the creators were doing that went above, beyond, beside, in addition to what the teachers may have intended in creating the assignments. This decontextualizing move functioned to let readers see what they could see without a teacher's defending the artifact or justifying what was or wasn't there, assessment moves hard for teachers to shake given how much of their assessment worlds are built in finding blame for what's supposedly lacking in student work.

5. It's worth noting that this sort of connected learning and doing shows up in other examples in this book in which student writers seem eager to talk to parents, friends, classmates, and others as part of their learning. In chapter 5, for example, one student we report on uses a writing assignment as a space to connect to his grandmother, who is hundreds of miles away in another state. She has expertise around his project—learning to crochet—and by working with her, he's able to

increase his learning while simultaneously strengthening affective bonds he shares with a family member. So much of higher education is about stripping other attachments from students, asking them to be physically, emotionally, and intellectually present on our cloistered campuses. First-generation students often feel this detachment as particularly alienating, so when we can imagine writing and thinking projects that allow for greater connectivity across learning networks, we may find students bring more of themselves to their learning and, as a result, engage in deeper and more transformative learning experiences.

6. Campuses around the United States are increasingly investing in student-management technologies that allow faculty, advisors, and student affairs educators to track each student throughout the semester and provide interventions for "off-path students" (EAB n.d.). Starfish, now owned by EAB, is one such platform used at both URI and ECU. Through this tool, faculty are encouraged by email to report on students' successes and failures at multiple stages in the semester and to recommend interventions (e.g., the writing center, the general tutoring center, crisis counseling, etc.). In December 2020, a press release from Hobsons (then owner of the Starfish technology) noted that during the pandemic, its student-management platform had contributed to a 97 percent retention rate on campuses across the country: "During a period when many classes moved online, academic advisors and faculty members raised more than 1.79 million alerts in support of students, and the number of students reaching out for help through Starfish increased 300 percent from the same period in 2019" ("Starfish by Hobsons" 2020).

7. Perhaps a more common example to those in writing studies is the use of the Buckley Amendment waiver, whereby students of legal age can provide consent for their parents or guardians to speak with their instructors and others on campus about their academic records, including individual grades on individual assignments, attendance in class, and so forth. While on the surface this has become an innocuous and commonplace practice, we've watched at campus-orientation sessions when parents strong-arm their adult children into signing the form so they can supervise their grades and work. Consent in this case is more often coercion, as students may feel they have no choice if their parents are supporting them financially. From their first days on campus, their adulthood and agency are stripped away through multiple small but significant acts of surveillance and control.

CHAPTER 5: FAILING TO BE REPRODUCED

1. Recent work with "ungrading" practices (Blum 2020) like specifications grading (Nilson 2015) seems to fit this framework, where discrete, countable acts are named as part of the grading framework. Specs grading tends to work in a framework modeled after business practices in which clients receive work that either meets or doesn't meet expectations (specifications) and thus either passes or requires revision until it does. As we've seen it practiced, specs grading actually tends to work around fairly narrow notions of quality rather than supposed countable activities/products named. However, additional work with this framework might be needed to better understand its connections to labor-based contract grading.

2. We should note that while aesthetically pleasing, the writing center is an open-space design including clear glass doors. One consequence of the architecture is the sense of working in a fishbowl and a lack of student privacy in terms of who is in the writing center.

3. We think it is important to note that our failure orientation also highlights the ways we conduct research in systems often not designed to support social justice

research. When we ask individual researchers to be responsible for changing data sets and inventing new analyses, we also must recognize we are always already part of institutions and systems that may (perhaps passively) stand in the way of our work. When we were engaging with categories around race/ethnicity, binary gender, and income levels, we had institutional data to use comparatively in building our study; when we moved away from categories at least superficially valued by state and campus officials, we had to modify our work significantly. In this case, that means stepping back from sexuality as a code in the data analysis. This failure on the institution's part to collect diverse and comprehensive data also meant our ability to run broadly intersectional analyses was compromised, thus further limiting what we could do in our research and assessment.

4.   Writing assessment has made great strides in interrupting reductive research designs, and the social-location research we reference throughout the book builds on that tradition.

5.   It's important to note here that statisticians also recognize other distribution patterns, as well as the fact that some populations simply cannot be understood through normative distributions. For such groups/situations, statisticians have turned to models from nonparametric statistics like the Wilcoxon signed-rank test or the Mann-Whitney U test. We do not address these models here, as normative distributions remain central to (nonstatistician) faculty in writing studies and/ or English departments, who are often called on to justify their grade distributions. For additional information on nonparametric statistical models, we suggest Sheskin's (2011) *Handbook of Parametric and Nonparametric Statistical Procedures*, 5th edition.

CHAPTER 6: FAILING TO BE MECHANIZED

1.   The founding principal of the Illinois State Normal University (ISNU), Charles Hovey, once noted that the idea of the "normal" in the nineteenth-century normal (teacher-training) school comes from "the Latin word originally being a 'square' or rule used by carpenters; as applied to schools, it means a pattern, model or example" (quoted in Lindblom, Banks, and Quay 2007, 94). In their archival history of writing instruction at ISNU, Kenneth Lindblom, William Banks and Rise Quay note that "a normal school seeks to norm knowledge, the teachers of that knowledge, and the methods by which those teachers will teach that knowledge" (94), and thus this classical connection seems both descriptive and performative, recognizing what such schools were intended to do and also how they went about that work. We argue that the history of norming or squaring the amoebic boundaries of learning remains a part of teaching, particularly in K–12 environments, where common syllabi and standardized curricula often hold sway. In the world of assessment, the same squaring off of opaque, nonlinear, and complex elements of writing seems to be part of norming raters/readers to process large sets of writing in mechanistic and normalizing ways.

REFERENCES

Active Minds. 2020. Student Mental Health Survey. https://www.activeminds.org/active
-minds-student-mental-health-survey/.

Adler-Kassner, Linda. 2008. *The Activist WPA: Changing Stories about Writing and Writers.*
Logan: Utah State University Press.

Agboka, Godwin Y., and Isadore K. Dorpenyo. 2022. "Curricular Efforts in Technical Communication After the Social Justice Turn." *Journal of Business and Technical Communication* 36 (1): 38–70.

Ahmed, Sarah. 2004a. "Affective Economies." *Social Text* 22 (2): 117–39.

Ahmed, Sarah. 2004b. *The Cultural Politics of Emotion.* Edinburgh: Edinburgh University
Press.

Ahmed, Sarah. 2006. *Queer Phenomenology: Orientations, Objects, Others.* Durham, NC: Duke
University Press.

Ahmed, Sarah. 2010a. "Feminist Killjoys (and Other Willful Subjects)." *Scholar and Feminist
Online* 8 (3). https://sfonline.barnard.edu/polyphonic/ahmed_01.htm

Ahmed, Sarah. 2010b. "Killing Joy: Feminism and the History of Happiness." *Signs* 35 (3):
571–94.

Ahmed, Sarah. 2010c. *The Promise of Happiness.* Durham, NC: Duke University Press.

Ahmed, Sarah. 2012. *On Being Included: Racism and Diversity in Institutional Life.* Durham,
NC: Duke University Press.

Ahmed, Sarah. 2014. *Willful Subjects.* Durham, NC: Duke University Press.

Ahmed, Sarah. 2021. *Complaint!* Durham, NC: Duke University Press.

American Educational Research Association, American Psychological Association, National
Council on Measurement in Education. 2014. *Standards for Educational and Psychological
Testing.* Washington, DC: American Educational Research Association.

Andrade, Heidi L., Randy E. Bennett, and Gregory J. Cizek, eds. 2019. *Handbook of Formative Assessment in the Disciplines.* New York: Routledge.

Anson, Chris M., and Jessie L. Moore. 2016. *Critical Transitions: Writing and the Question of Transfer.* Fort Collins, CO: WAC Clearinghouse. https://wac.colostate.edu
/books/perspectives/ansonmoore/.

Anson, Chris M., Deanna P. Dannels, Pamela Flash, and Amy L. Housley Gaffney. 2012.
"Big Rubrics and Weird Genres: The Futility of Using Generic Assessment Tools Across
Diverse Instructional Contexts." *Journal of Writing Assessment* 5 (1). https://escholarship
.org/uc/item/93b9g3t6.

Anson, Chris, Scott Filkins, Troy Hicks, Peggy O'Neill, Kathryn Mitchell Pierce, and Mai-
sha Winn. 2013. "NCTE Position Statement on Machine Scoring: Machine Scoring Fails
the Test." Urbana, IL: NCTE.

Anzaldúa, Gloria. 1987. *Borderlands/La Frontera: The New Mestiza.* San Francisco: Aunt Lute
Books.

Arkolakis, Costas, Marla Geha, Marion Gehlker, Daniel Harrison, Brad Inwood, Ayesha
Ramachandran, Anthony Smith, and Carla Staver. 2018. "Report of the Committee
on the Economic Status of the Faculty: Academic Years 2016–17 and 2017–18." Yale.
https://yale.app.box.com/s/4jssznfahh704allnejjicyjdyns3loc.

https://doi.org/10.7330/9781646423705.c008

Arter, Judith A., Vicki Spandel, Ruth Culham, and Jim Pollard. 1994. "The Impact of Training Students to Be Self-Assessors of Writing." Paper presented at the annual meeting of
the American Educational Research Association, New Orleans, April 4–9.

Atwell, Nancie. 1987. *In the Middle: Reading, Writing, and Learning with Adolescents*. Portsmouth, NH: Boynton/Cook.

Baker-Bell, April. 2020. *Linguistic Justice: Black Language, Literacy, Identity, and Pedagogy*.
New York: Routledge.

Baker-Bell, April, Bonnie J. Williams-Farrier, Davena Jackson, Lamar Johnson, Carmen
Kynard, and Teaira McMurtry. 2020. "This Ain't Another Statement! This Is a Demand
for Black Linguistic Justice!" National Council of Teachers of English. https://cccc
.ncte.org/cccc/demand-for-black-linguistic-justice.

Bandura, Albert. 1997. *Self-Efficacy: The Exercise of Control*. New York: Freeman.

Banks, William P. 2003. "Written through the Body: Disruptions and 'Personal' Writing."
College English 66 (1): 21–40.

Banks, William P. 2016. "What Is the National Writing Project?" In *A Rhetoric for Writing
Program Administrators*, 2nd ed., edited by Rita Malenczyk. Anderson, SC: Parlor.

Banks, William P., and Jonathan Alexander. 2009. "Queer Eye for the Comp Program:
Toward a Queer Critique of WPA Work." In *The Writing Program Interrupted: Making
Space for Critical Discourse*, edited by Donna G. Strickland and Jeanne Gunner, 88–98.
Portsmouth, NH: Boynton/Cook.

Banks, William P., Matthew B. Cox, and Caroline Dadas. 2019. *Re/Orienting Writing Studies:
Queer Methods, Queer Projects*. Logan: Utah State University Press.

Banks, William P., Michael J. Faris, Collie Fulford, Timothy Oleksiak, GPat Patterson, and
Trixie G. Smith. 2020. "Writing Program Administration: A Queer Primer." *WPA: Writing Program Administration* 43 (2): 11–43.

Barad, Karen. 2007. *Meeting the Universe Halfway: Quantum Physics and the Entanglement of
Matter and Meaning*. Durham, NC: Duke University Press.

Battiste, Marie. 2013. *Decolonizing Education: Nourishing the Learning Spirit*. Vancouver: UBC
Press.

Bean, John C. 2011. *Engaging Ideas: The Professor's Guide to Integrating Writing, Critical Thinking, and Active Learning in the Classroom*. San Francisco: Jossey-Bass.

Beckes, Lane, and James Coan. 2011. "Social Baseline Theory: The Role of Social Proximity
in Emotion and Economy of Action." *Social and Personality Psychology Compass* 5 (12):
976–88. https://doi.org/10.1111/j.1751-9004.2011.00400.x.

Bell, Lee Anne. 2010. *Storytelling for Social Justice*. New York: Routledge.

Bennett, Jane 2009. *Vibrant Matter: A Political Ecology of Things*. Durham, NC: Duke University Press.

Berlant, Lauren. 1997. *The Queen of America Goes to Washington City: Essays on Sex and Citizenship*. Durham, NC: Duke University Press.

Berlant, Lauren. 2011. *Cruel Optimism*. Durham, NC: Duke University Press.

Berlin, James. 1987. *Rhetoric and Reality: Writing Instruction in American Colleges, 1900–1985*.
Carbondale: Southern Illinois University Press.

Blaiklock, Ken. 2008. "A Critique of the Use of Learning Stories to Assess the Learning
Dispositions of Young Children." *New Zealand Research in Early Childhood Education* 11:
77–87.

Blum, Susan D. 2020. *Ungrading: Why Rating Students Undermines Learning (and What To Do
Instead)*. Morgantown: West Virginia Press.

Blythe, Tina, David Allen, and Barbara Schieffelin Powell. 1999. *Looking Together at Student
Work: A Companion Guide to Assessing Student Learning*. New York: Teachers College
Press.

Boquet, Elizabeth H. 1999. " 'Our Little Secret': A History of Writing Centers, Pre- to Post-
Open Admissions." *College Composition and Communication* 50 (3): 463–82.

Boyle, Casey. 2018. *Rhetoric as a Posthuman Practice.* Columbus: The Ohio State University Press.

Brannon, Lil, Cynthia Urbanski, Lacy Manship, Lucy Arnold, and Tony Iannone. 2010. "The Ebay-ification of Education: Critical Literacy in a Consumerocracy." *English Journal* 99 (3): 16–21.

Bratta, Phil, and Malea Powell. 2016. "Introduction to the Special Issue: Entering the Cultural Rhetorics Conversations." *Enculturation* 21. http://enculturation.net/21.

Brereton, John C., ed. 1996. *The Origins of Composition in the American College, 1875–1925: A Documentary History.* Pittsburgh: University of Pittsburgh Press.

Breu, Christopher. 2014. "Against Austerity: Toward a New Sensuality." *Symploke* 22 (1–2): 23–39.

Breuch, Lee-Ann M. Kastman. 2002. "Post-Process 'Pedagogy': A Philosophical Exercise." *JAC* 22 (1): 119–50.

Broad, Bob. 2003. *What We Really Value: Beyond Rubrics in Teaching and Assessing Writing.* Logan: Utah State University Press.

Burford, James. 2015. "Not Writing, and Giving 'Zero-f**ks' About It: Queer(y)ing Doctoral 'Failure.'" *Discourse: Studies in the Cultural Politics of Education* 38 (4): 473–84. http://doi.org/10.1080/01596306.2015.1105788.

Butler, Judith. 1990. *Gender Trouble: Feminism and the Subversion of Identity.* New York: Routledge.

Butler, Judith. 1994. *Bodies That Matter: On the Discursive Limits of "Sex."* New York: Routledge.

Butler, Judith. 2004. *Undoing Gender.* New York: Routledge.

Calkins, Lucy. 1994. *The Art of Teaching Writing.* Portsmouth, NH: Heinemann.

Calkins, Lucy, and Shelley Harwayne. 1987. *The Writing Workshop: A World of Difference.* Portsmouth, NH: Heinemann.

Callahan, Raymond. 1962. *Education and the Cult of Efficiency.* Chicago: University of Chicago Press.

Callahan, Susan. 1997. "Tests Worth Taking?: Using Portfolios for Accountability in Kentucky." *Research in the Teaching of English* 31 (3): 295–336.

Callahan, Susan. 1999. "All Done with the Best of Intentions: One Kentucky High School after Six Years of State Portfolio Tests." *Assessing Writing* 6 (1): 5–40.

Carillo, Ellen C. 2021. *The Hidden Inequities in Labor-Based Contract Grading.* Logan: Utah State University Press.

Carpenter, Rowanna, and Yves Labissiere. 2020. "Accountability and Actionable Data: A Comparison of Three Approaches to Program Assessment Using ePortfolios." In *ePortfolios@edu: What We Know, What We Don't Know, and Everything in Between,* edited by Mary Ann Dellinger and D. Alexis Hart. Fort Collins, CO: WAC Clearinghouse. https://wac.colostate.edu/docs/books/portfolios/chapter11.pdf.

Carr, Allison. 2013. "In Support of Failure." *Composition Forum* 27. https://compositionforum.com/issue/27/failure.php.

Carr, Margaret. 2000. *Assessment in Early Childhood Settings: Learning Stories.* London: Paul Chapman.

Caswell, Nicole I. 2020. "What's Beneath the Demographics? Writing Center Usage and Inequality." *Intersection: A Journal at the Intersection of Assessment and Learning:* 25–29. https://www.aalhe.org/assets/docs/Intersection/AAHLE_spring_2020_intersection.pdf.

Caswell, Nicole I. 2022. "Resisting White, Patriarchal Emotional Labor in the Writing Center." In *CounterStories from the Writing Center,* edited by Wonderful Faison and Frankie Condon, 109–19. Logan: Utah State University Press.

Caswell, Nicole I., and William P. Banks. 2018. "Queering Assessment: Fairness, Affect, and the Impact on LGBTQ Writers." In *Writing Assessment, Social Justice, and the Advancement of Opportunity*, edited by Mya Poe, Asao B. Inoue, and Norbert Elliot, 355–79. Fort Collins: Colorado State University Press.

Caswell, Nicole I., Jackie Grutsch McKinney, and Rebecca Jackson. 2016. *The Working Lives of New Writing Center Directors*. Logan: Utah State University Press.

Cedillo, Christina V., Victor Del Hierro, Candace Epps-Robertson, Lisa King, Jessie Male, Staci Perryman-Clark, Andrea Riley-Mukavetz, and Amy Vidali. 2018. "Listening to Stories: Practicing Cultural Rhetorics Pedagogy." *Constellations: A Cultural Rhetorics Publishing Space*. https://constell8cr.com/pedagogy-blog/listening-to-stories-practicing -cultural-rhetorics-pedagogy/.

Champagne, John. 2011. "Teaching in the Corporate University: Assessment as a Labor Issue." *AAUP Journal of Academic Freedom* 2: 1–26. https://www.aaup.org/sites/default /files/files/JAF/2011%20JAF/Champagne.pdf.

Chen, Mel. 2012. *Animacies: Biopolitics, Racial Mattering, and Queer Affect*. Durham, NC: Duke University Press.

Clark, Irene, and Bettina J. Huber. 2018. "Argument Essays Written in the First and Third Years of College: Assessing Differences in Performance." *Journal of Writing Assessment* 11 (1). https://escholarship.org/uc/item/0j34r4n3.

Clark, J. Elizabeth. 2019. "What, Exactly, Are We Amplifying? A Decade of AAC&U's ePortfolio Forum." *International Journal of ePortfolio* 9 (1): 59–63.

Cobos, Casie, Gabriela Raquel Ríos, Donnie Johnson Sackey, Jennifer Sano-Franchini, and Angela M. Haas. 2018. "Interfacing Cultural Rhetorics: A History and a Call." *Rhetoric Review* 37 (2): 139–54.

Coe, Michael, Makoto Hanita, Vicki Nishioka, and Richard Smiley. 2011. *An Investigation of the Impact of the 6+1 Trait Writing Model on Grade 5 Student Writing Achievement* (NCEE 2012–4010). Washington, DC: National Center for Education Evaluation and Regional Assistance, Institute of Education Sciences.

Connors, Robert J. 1997. *Composition-Rhetoric: Backgrounds, Theory, and Pedagogy*. Pittsburgh: University of Pittsburgh Press.

Cooper, Charles, and Richard Lloyd-Jones. 1977. *Evaluating Writing: Describing, Measuring, Judging*. Urbana, IL: NCTE.

Cooper, Marilyn. 2019. *The Animal Who Writes: A Posthumanist Composition*. Pittsburgh: University of Pittsburgh Press.

Council of Writing Program Administrators. 2014. "WPA Outcomes Statement for First-Year Composition." *WPA: Writing Program Administration* 38 (1): 144–48.

Council of Writing Program Administrators, National Council of Teachers of English, and National Writing Project. 2011. *Framework for Success in Postsecondary Writing*. https:// wpacouncil.org/aws/CWPA/asset_manager/get_file/350201?ver=7548.

Cox, Matthew B. 2016. "Queering Student Participation: Whispers, Echoes, Rants, and Memory." In *The Rhetoric of Participation: Interrogating Commonplaces in and Beyond the Classroom*, edited by Paige Banaji, Lisa Blankenship, Katherine DeLuca, Lauren Obermark, and Ryan Omio. Logan, UT: Computers and Composition Digital Press.

Craig, Sherri. 2021. "Your Contract Grading Ain't It." *WPA: Writing Program Administration* 44 (3): 145–46.

Crank, Virginia. 2010. "When Process (Theory) Becomes (Consumer) Product: How the Six Traits Fails Teachers." *Wisconsin English Journal* 52 (2): 45–53.

Crenshaw, Kimberlé. 1989. "Demarginalizing the Intersection of Race and Sex: A Black Feminist Critique of Antidiscrimination Doctrine, Feminist Theory and Antiracist Politics." *University of Chicago Legal Forum* 1989 (1): 139–67.

Crowley, Sharon. 1998. *Composition in the University: Historical and Polemical Essays*. Pittsburgh: University of Pittsburgh Press.

Culham, Ruth. 2003a. *40 Reproducible Forms for the Writing Traits Classroom*. New York: Scholastic Professional Books.

Culham, Ruth. 2003b. *6+1 Traits of Writing: The Complete Guide Grades 3 and Up.* New York: Scholastic.

Cushman, Ellen. 2016. "Decolonizing Validity." *Journal of Writing Assessment* 9 (2). https://escholarship.org/uc/item/0xh7v6fb.

Cvetkovich, Ann. 2003. *An Archive of Feelings: Trauma, Sexuality, and Lesbian Public Cultures.* Durham, NC: Duke University Press.

Dadas, Caroline. 2016. "Messy Methods: Queer Methodological Approaches to Researching Social Media." *Computers and Composition* 40: 60–72.

Danielewicz, Jane, and Peter Elbow. 2009. "A Unilateral Grading Contract to Improve Learning and Teaching." *College Composition and Communication* 61 (2): 244–68.

Daniels, Harvey A. 1983. *Famous Last Words: The American Language Crisis Reconsidered.* Carbondale: Southern Illinois University Press.

Day, Michael. 2020. "Electronic Portfolios: Scaling Up from Programmatic to Inter-Institutional Articulation and Assessment." In *ePortfolios@edu: What We Know, What We Don't Know, and Everything in Between,* edited by Mary Ann Dellinger and D. Alexis Hart, 227–52. Fort Collins, CO: WAC Clearinghouse. https://wac.colostate.edu/docs/books/portfolios/chapter12.pdf.

de Certeau, Michel. 1984. *The Practice of Everyday Life.* Translated by Steven Rendall. Berkeley: University of California Press.

Deleuze, Gilles. 1993. *The Fold: Leibniz and the Baroque.* Minneapolis: University of Minnesota Press.

Deleuze, Gilles, and Félix Guattari. 1987. *A Thousand Plateaus: Capitalism and Schizophrenia.* Translated by Brian Massumi. Minneapolis: University of Minnesota Press.

Delinger, Mary Ann, and Alexis D. Hart, eds. 2020. *ePortfolios@edu: What We Know, What We Don't Know, and Everything in Between.* Fort Collins, CO: WAC Clearinghouse. https://wac.colostate.edu/books/practice/portfolios/.

De Raad, Boele. 2000. *The Big Five Personality Factors: The Psycholexical Approach to Personality.* Seattle, WA: Hogrefe and Huber.

deWinter, Jennifer, and Stephanie Vie. 2015. "Sparklegate: Gamification, Academic Gravitas, and the Infantilization of Play." *Kairos* 20 (1). http://kairos.technorhetoric.net/20.1/topoi/dewinter-vie/index.html.

Dilger, Bradley. 2007. "Extreme Usability and Technical Communication." In *Critical Power Tools: Technical Communication and Cultural Studies,* edited by J. Blake Scott, Bernadette Longo, and Katherine V. Wills, 47–69. Albany: SUNY Press.

"Disney's Approach to Employee Engagement." n.d. Disney Institute. Accessed November 30, 2021. https://www.disneyinstitute.com/disneys-approach-employee-engagement/.

Dobrin, Sidney. 2015. *Writing Posthumanism, Posthuman Writing.* Anderson, SC: Parlor.

Drummond, Tom, and Kayla Shea Owens. 2020. "Making Learning Visible." https://tomdrummond.com/helping-other-adults/making-learning-visible/.

Duggan, Lisa. 2002. "The New Homonormativity: The Sexual Politics of Neoliberalism." In *Materializing Democracy: Toward a Revitalized Cultural Politics,* edited by Russ Castronovo and Dana D. Nelson, 175–94. Durham, NC: Duke University Press.

Duggan, Lisa. 2003. *The Twilight of Equality: Neoliberalism, Cultural Politics, and the Attack on Democracy.* Cambridge, MA: Harvard University Press.

Dunlap, Joanna, Devshikha Bose, Patrick R. Lowenthal, Cindy S. York, Michael Atkinson, and Jim Murtagh. 2016. "What Sunshine Is to Flowers: A Literature Review on the Use of Emoticons to Support Online Learning." In *Emotions, Technology, Design, and Learning,* edited by Sharon Y. Tettegah and Martin Gartmeier, 163–82. London: Academic Press.

"EAB Helps You Support and Graduate More Students." n.d. EAB. Accessed November 30, 2021. https://eab.com/colleges-and-universities/student-success/.

ECU. n.d. "University Writing Program: History." Accessed November 19, 2021. https://writing.ecu.edu/history/.

ECU. n.d. "Writing Across the Curriculum: ECU Writing Outcomes." Accessed November 19, 2021. https://writing.ecu.edu/wac/about-wac/ecu-writing-outcomes/.

Edelman, Lee. 2004. *No Future: Queer Theory and the Death Drive*. Durham, NC: Duke University Press.

Edgington, Anthony. 2005. " 'What Are You Thinking?': Understanding Teacher Reading and Response through a Protocol Analysis Study." *Journal of Writing Assessment* 2 (2): 125–47.

Ehrenreich, Barbara. 2009. *Bright-Sided: How Positive Thinking Is Undermining America*. New York: Metropolitan Books.

Eidman-Aadahl, Elyse, Kristine Blair, Dànielle Nicole DeVoss, Will Hochman, Lanette Jimerson, Chuck Jurich, Sandy Murphy, Becky Rupert, Carl Whithaus, and Joe Wood. 2013. "Developing Domains for Multimodal Writing Assessment: The Language of Evaluation, the Language of Instruction." In *Digital Writing Assessment and Evaluation*, edited by Heidi A. McKee and Dànielle Nicole DeVoss. Logan, UT: Computers and Composition Digital Press.

Elbow, Peter. 1993. "Ranking, Evaluating, Liking: Sorting Out Three Forms of Judgment." *College English* 55 (2): 187–206.

Elbow, Peter. 1997. "Taking Time Out from Grading and Evaluating While Working in a Conventional System." *Assessing Writing* 4 (1): 5–27.

Elbow, Peter. 2000. "Getting Along without Grades—and Getting Along with Them Too." In *Everyone Can Write: Essays Toward a Hopeful Theory of Writing and Teaching Writing*, 399–421. New York: Oxford University Press.

Elliot, Norbert. 2005. *On a Scale: A Social History of Writing Assessment in America*. New York: Peter Lang.

Elliot, Norbert. 2016. "A Theory of Ethics for Writing Assessment." *Journal of Writing Assessment* 9 (1). http://journalofwritingassessment.org/article.php?article=98.

Ericsson, Patricia Freitag, and Richard H. Haswell, eds. 2006. *Machine Scoring of Student Essays: Truth and Consequences*. Logan: Utah State University Press.

Eubanks, David. 2019. "Reassessing the Elephant Part 2." *Assessment Update* 31 (3): 6–7, 13.

Evans-Winters, Venus. 2019. *Black Feminism in Qualitative Inquiry: A Mosaic for Writing Our Daughter's Body*. New York: Routledge.

"Everyone's a Critic." 2020. *This American LIfe*, NPR. February 28.

Fallows, James. 2021. "Best Schools' Rankings Are Meaningless—and Harmful, Critic Says." By Michel Martin. *All Things Considered*, NPR. October 16. https://www.npr.org/2021/10/16/1046779479/best-schools-rankings-are-meaningless-and-harmful-critic-says.

Farkas, Kerrie, and Christina Haas. 2012. "A Grounded Theory Approach for Studying Writing and Literacy." In *Practicing Research in Writing Studies: Reflexive and Ethically Responsible Research*, edited by Kristina Powell and Pamela Takayoshi, 81–95. Cresskill, NJ: Hampton.

Fendler, Lynn, and Irfan Muzaffar. 2008. "The History of the Bell Curve: Sorting and the Idea of Normal." *Educational Theory* 58 (1): 63–82. http://doi.org/10.1111/j.1741-5446.2007.0276.x.

Fenwick, Tara, and Jim Parsons. 2000. *The Art of Evaluation: A Handbook for Educators and Trainers*. Toronto: Thompson Educational.

Fitzgerald, Lauren, and Melissa Ianetta. 2015. *The Oxford Guide for Writing Tutors: Practice and Research*. New York: Oxford University Press.

Flaherty, Colleen. 2019. "Grading for STEM Equity." *Inside Higher Ed*, December 18. https://www.insidehighered.com/news/2019/12/18/study-suggests-professors-should-standardize-their-grading-curves-boost-womens.

Florida State Senate. 2022. HB 1557: Parental Rights in Education. https://www.flsenate.gov/Session/Bill/2022/1557.

Function Point. n.d. "5 Steps to Define Your Company's True Core Values." Accessed November 24, 2020. https://functionpoint.com/blog/5-steps-to-define-your-companys-true-core-values/.

Gallagher, Chris. 2010. "Assess Locally, Validate Globally: Heuristics for Validating Local Writing Assessments." *WPA: Writing Program Administration* 34 (1): 10–32.

Gallagher, Chris. 2011. "Being There: (Re)Making the Assessment Scene." *College Composition and Communication* 62 (3): 450–76.

Gamson, William, and David S. Meyer. 1996. "Framing Political Opportunities." In *Comparative Perspectives on Social Movements: Political Opportunities, Mobilizing Structures, and Cultural Framings*, edited by Doug McAdam, John D. McCarthy, and Mayer N. Zald, 275–90. Cambridge, MA: Cambridge University Press.

Gay, Roxanne. 2013. "The Unbearable Whiteness of Emoji." In *Emoji: A Special Print Edition of Womanzine*, edited by Mercedes Kraus, Lindsey Weber, and Jenna Wortham. New York: Womanzine and Forced Meme Productions. https://issuu.com/lindseyweber5/docs/emoji_by_womanzine.

Gee, James Paul. 2008. "Video Games and Embodiment." *Games and Culture* 3 (3–4): 253–63.

Gee, James Paul. 2014. *An Introduction to Discourse Analysis Theory and Method*, 4th ed. New York: Routledge.

George, Diana, ed. 1999. *Kitchen Cooks, Plate Twirlers, and Troubadours: Writing Program Administrators Tell Their Stories*. Portsmouth, NH: Heinemann.

Gere, Anne Ruggles, Anne Curzan, J. W. Hammond, Sarah Hughes, Ruth Li, Andrew Moos, Kendon Smith, Kathryn Van Zanen, Kelly L. Wheeler, and Crystal J. Zanders. 2021. "Communal Justicing: Writing Assessment, Disciplinary Infrastructure, and the Case for Critical Language Awareness." *College Composition and Communication* 72 (3): 384–412.

Gilbert, Erik. 2018. "An Insider's Take on Assessment: It May Be Worse Than You Thought." *Chronicle of Higher Education*, January 12. https://www.chronicle.com/article/an-insiders-take-on-assessment-it-may-be-worse-than-you-thought/.

Gilbert, Jeremy. 2013. "What Kind of Thing Is 'Neoliberalism'?" *New Formations: A Journal of Culture/Theory/Politics* 80/81: 7–22.

Gillespie, Paula, and Neal Lerner. 2008. *The Longman Guide to Peer Tutoring*, 2nd ed. New York: Pearson.

Gold, Larry, Gary Rhoades, Mark Smith, and George Kuh. 2011. *What Faculty Unions Say About Student Learning Outcomes Assessment*. National Institute for Learning Outcomes Assessment. https://www.learningoutcomesassessment.org/wp-content/uploads/2019/02/OccasionalPaper9.pdf.

Goldberg, Suzanne B. 2021. "Education in a Pandemic: The Disparate Impacts of COVID-19 on America's Students." Washington, DC: US Department of Education, Office for Civil Rights. https://www2.ed.gov/about/offices/list/ocr/docs/20210608-impacts-of-covid19.pdf.

Gray, James. 2000. *Teachers at the Center: A Memoir of the Early Years of the National Writing Project*. Berkeley: National Writing Project.

Green, Neisha-Anne. 2018. "Moving beyond Alright: And the Emotional Toll of This, My Life Matters Too, in the Writing Center Work." *Writing Center Journal* 37 (1): 15–34.

Greenfield, Laura. 2019. *Radical Writing Center Praxis: A Paradigm for Ethical Political Engagement*. Logan: Utah State University Press.

Grieve, Rachel, Robyn L. Moffitt, and Christine R. Padgett. 2019. "Student Perceptions of Marker Personality and Intelligence: The Effect of Emoticons in Online Assignment Feedback." *Learning and Individual Differences* 69: 232–38.

Gross, Daniel M., and Jonathan Alexander. 2016. "Frameworks for Failure." *Pedagogy* 16 (2): 273–95.

Gutiérrez, Kris D., and Barbara Rogoff. 2003. "Cultural Ways of Learning: Individual Traits or Repertoires of Practice." *Educational Researcher* 32 (5): 19–25.

Halberstam, Jack. 2005. *In a Queer Time and Place: Transgender Bodies, Subcultural Lives.* New York: New York University Press.

Halberstam, Jack. 2011. *The Queer Art of Failure.* Durham, NC: Duke University Press.

Hanson, F. Allan. 1993. *Testing Testing: Social Consequences of the Examined Life.* Berkeley: University of California Press.

Haraway, Donna. 1997. *Modest Witness@Second_Millennium.FemaleMan©_ Meets_OncoMouse™: Feminism and Technoscience.* New York: Routledge.

Hart, Ray, Michael Casserly, Renata Uzzell, Moses Palacios, Amanda Corcoran, and Liz Spurgeon (Council of the Great City Schools). 2015. *Student Testing in America's Great City Schools: An Inventory and Preliminary Analysis.* https://www.cgcs.org/cms/lib/DC00 001581/Centricity/Domain/87/Testing%20Report.pdf.

Haswell, Richard, and Norbert Elliot. 2019. *Early Holistic Scoring of Writing: A Theory, a History, a Reflection.* Logan: Utah State University Press.

Haswell, Richard, and Susan Wyche-Smith. 1994. "Adventuring into Writing Assessment." *College Composition and Communication* 45 (2): 220–36.

Herrnstein, Richard J., and Charles Murray. 1994. *The Bell Curve: Intelligence and Class Structure in American Life.* New York: Free Press Paperbacks.

Hicks, Troy, ed. 2015. *Assessing Students' Digital Writing: Protocols for Looking Closely.* New York: Teachers College Press.

Hidalgo, Alexandra. 2021. "A Response to Cushman, Baca, and García's *College English* Introduction." *Constellations: A Cultural Rhetorics Publishing Space* (4): 1–14. https://constell8cr.com/wp-content/uploads/2021/10/Issue-4-A-Response-to-College-English-Hidalgo-PDF.pdf.

Hilgers, Thomas L., Edna L. Hussey, and Monica Stitt-Bergh. 2000. "The Case for Prompted Self-Assessment in the Writing Classroom." In *Student Self-Assessment and Development in Writing: A Collaborative Inquiry,* edited by Jane Bowman Smith and Kathleen Blake Yancey, 1–24. Cresskill, NJ: Hampton.

Hillocks, George. 2003. "How State Assessments Lead to Vacuous Thinking and Writing." *Journal of Writing Assessment* 1: 5–21.

Hindeman, Jane E. 2003. "Thoughts on Reading 'The Personal': Toward a Discursive Ethics of Professional Critical Literacy." *College English* 66 (1): 9–20.

Hochschild, Arlie R., and Anne Machung. 1989. *The Second Shift.* New York: Avon Books.

Hull, Brittany, Cecilia D. Shelton, and Temptaous McKoy. 2020. "Dressed but Not Tryin' to Impress: Black Women Deconstructing 'Professional' Dress." *Journal of Multimodal Rhetorics* 3 (2). http://journalofmultimodalrhetorics.com/3-2-hull-shelton-mckoy.

Huot, Brian. 2002. *(Re)Articulating Writing Assessment for Teaching and Learning.* Logan: Utah State University Press.

Huot, Brian, and Michael Neal. 2006. "Writing Assessment: A Techno-History." In *Handbook of Writing Research,* 2nd ed., edited by Charles A. MacArthur, Steve Graham, and Jill Fitzgerald, 417–32. New York: Guilford.

Huot, Brian, Peggy O'Neill, and Cindy Moore. 2010. "A Usable Past for Writing Assessment." *College English* 72 (5): 495–517.

Huws, Ursula. 2014. *Labor in the Global Digital Economy: The Cybertariat Comes of Age.* London: Monthly Review.

"Hyperbolic Space." n.d. Crochet Coral Reef. Accessed February 19, 2022. https://crochetcoralreef.org/artscience/hyperbolicspace/.

IMS Global Learning Consortium. 2020. "Open Badges." https://openbadges.org/about/history.

Inoue, Asao B. 2005. "Community-Based Assessment Pedagogy." *Assessing Writing* 9 (3): 208–38.

Inoue, Asao B. 2014. "Theorizing Failure in US Writing Assessments." *Research in the Teaching of English* 48 (3): 330–52.

Inoue, Asao B. 2015. *Antiracist Writing Assessment Ecologies: Teaching and Assessing Writing for a Socially Just Future.* Fort Collins, CO: WAC Clearinghouse.

Inoue, Asao B. 2019. *Labor-Based Grading Contracts: Building Equity and Inclusion in the Compassionate Writing Classroom.* Fort Collins, CO: WAC Clearinghouse.

Inoue, Asao B. 2020. "Stories about Grading Contracts, or How Do I Like Through the Violence I've Done?" *Journal of Writing Assessment* 13 (2). http://journalofwritingassessment .org/article.php?article=154.

Inoue, Asao B., and Mya Poe. 2012a. *Race and Writing Assessment.* New York: Peter Lang.

Inoue, Asao B., and Mya Poe. 2012b. "Racial Formations in Two Writing Assessments: Revisiting White and Thomas' Findings on the English Placement Test after 30 Years." In *Writing Assessment in the Twenty-First Century: Essays in Honor of Edward M. White,* edited by Norbert Elliot and Les Perelman, 343–61. Cresskill, NJ: Hampton.

Ito, Mizuko, Kris Gutiérrez, Sonia Livingstone, Bill Penuel, Jean Rhodes, Katie Salen, Juliet Schor, Julian Sefton-Green, and S. Craig Watkins. 2013. *Connected Learning: An Agenda for Research and Design.* Irvine, CA: Digital Media and Learning Research Hub.

Jacobs, Dale, and Laura Micciche. 2003. *A Way to Move: Rhetorics of Emotion and Composition Studies.* Portsmouth, NH: Heinemann.

Jaschik, Scott. 2021. " 'U.S. News' Announces New Rankings . . . of Elementary Schools." *Inside Higher Ed,* October 14. https://www.insidehighered.com/quicktakes /2021/10/14/%E2%80%98us-news%E2%80%99-announces-new-rankings%E2%80 %A6-elementary-schools.

Joe_Tutorials. n.d. "How to Fold an Origami Fortune Teller + How to Use." Accessed November 19, 2021. https://www.instructables.com/How-to-Fold-an-Origami-Fortune -Teller-How-to-Use/.

Johnson, Nan. 1991. *Nineteenth-Century Rhetoric in North America.* Carbondale: Southern Illinois University Press.

Johnson, Nan. 2002. *Gender and Rhetorical Space in American Life, 1866–1910.* Carbondale: Southern Illinois University Press.

Jones, Natasha N. 2017. "Rhetorical Narratives of Black Entrepreneurs: The Business of Race, Agency, and Cultural Empowerment." *Journal of Business and Technical Communication* 31 (3): 319–49. http://doi.org/10.1177/1050651917695540.

Juul, Jesper. 2013. *The Art of Failure: An Essay on the Pain of Playing Video Games.* Cambridge: MIT Press.

Kafer, Alison. 2013. *Feminist Queer Crip.* Bloomington: Indiana University Press.

Kane, Michael T. 2006. "Validation." In *Educational Measurement,* 4th ed., edited by Robert L. Brennon, 17–64. Westport: American Council on Education.

Kane, Michael T. 2010. "Validity and Fairness." *Language Testing* 27 (2): 177–82.

Kane, Michael T. 2011. "The Errors of Our Ways." *Journal of Educational Measurement* 48 (1): 12–30.

Kane, Michael T. 2015. "Explicating Validity." *Assessment in Education: Principles, Policy and Practice* 23 (2): 198–211.

Kelle, Udo. 2007. "The Development of Categories: Different Approaches in Grounded Theory." In *The SAGE Handbook of Grounded Theory,* edited by Anthony Bryant and Kathy Charmaz, 191–213. London: SAGE.

Kelly-Riley, Diane, and Norbert Elliot. 2014. "The WPA Outcomes Statement, Validation, and the Pursuit of Localism." *Assessing Writing* 21: 89–103.

Kelly-Riley, Diane, and Norbert Elliot, eds. 2020. *Improving Outcomes: Disciplinary Writing, Local Assessment, and the Aim of Fairness.* New York: MLA.

Kelly-Riley, Diane, Norbert Elliot, and Alex Rudniy. 2016. "An Empirical Framework for ePortfolio Assessment." *International Journal of ePortfolio* 6 (2): 95–116.

Kennedy, Gail, ed. 1955. *Education at Amherst: The New Program.* New York: Harper.

Kent, Thomas. 1993. *Paralogic Rhetoric: A Theory of Communicative Interaction.* Lewisburg, PA: Bucknell University Press.

Kent, Thomas, ed. 1999. *Post-Process Theory: Beyond the Writing-Process Paradigm.* Carbondale: Southern Illinois University Press.

Klobucar, Andrew, Paul Deane, Norbert Elliot, Chaitanya Raminie, Perry Deess, and Alex Rudniy. 2012. "Automated Essay Scoring and the Search for Valid Writing Assessment." In *International Advances in Writing Research: Cultures, Places, Measures,* edited by Charles Bazerman, Chris Dean, Jessica Early, Karen Lunsford, Suzie Null, Paul Rogers, and Amanda Stansell, 103–19. Fort Collins, CO: WAC Clearinghouse.

Kovach, Margaret. 2010. *Indigenous Methodologies: Characteristics, Conversations, and Contexts.* Toronto: University of Toronto Press.

Krohn, Franklin B. 2004. "A Generational Approach to Using Emoticons as Nonverbal Communication." *Journal of Technical Writing and Communication* 34 (4): 321–28.

Kynard, Carmen. 2018. "*This Bridge*: The BlackFeministCompositionist's Guide to the Colonial and Imperial Violence of Schooling Today." *Feminist Teacher* 26 (2–3): 126–41.

Ladson-Billings, Gloria. 1995. "Toward a Theory of Culturally Relevant Pedagogy." *American Educational Research Journal* 32 (3): 465–91.

Ladson-Billings, Gloria. 2021. *Culturally Relevant Pedagogy: Asking a Different Question.* New York: Teachers College Press.

Lam, Ricky. 2020. "Writing Portfolio Assessment in Practice: Individual, Institutional, and Systemic Issues." *Pedagogies: An International Journal* 15 (3): 169–82.

Law, John. 2004. *After Method: Mess in Social Science Research.* New York: Routledge.

Lederman, Josh, and Nicole Warwick. 2018. "The Violence of Assessment: Writing Assessment, Social (In)Justice, and the Role of Validation." In *Writing Assessment, Social Justice, and the Advancement of Opportunity,* edited by Mya Poe, Asao B. Inoue, and Norbert Elliot, 229–55. Fort Collins, CO: WAC Clearinghouse.

Lee, Carol D. 2007. *Culture, Literacy, and Learning: Taking Bloom in the Midst of the Whirlwind.* New York: Teachers College Press.

Lesesne, Teri. 2010. *Reading Ladders: Leading Students from Where They Are to Where We'd Like Them to Be.* Portsmouth, NH: Heinemann.

Lewis, Michael. 2019. *Against the Rules* (podcast). https://atrpodcast.com/.

Lindblom, Kenneth, William Banks, and Rise Quay. 2007. "Mid-Nineteenth-Century Writing Instruction at Illinois State Normal University: Credentials, Correctness and the Rise of a Teaching Class." In *Local Histories: Reading the Archives of Composition,* edited by Patricia Donahue and Gretchen Flesher Moon, 94–113. Pittsburgh: University of Pittsburgh Press.

López, Nancy, Christopher Erwin, Melissa Binder, and Mario Javier Chavez. 2018. "Making the Invisible Visible: Advancing Quantitative Methods in Higher Education Using Critical Race Theory and Intersectionality." *Race and Ethnicity Education* 21 (2): 180–207.

Lotier, Kristopher. 2021. *Postprocess Postmortem.* Fort Collins, CO: WAC Clearinghouse.

Love, Heather. 2009. *Feeling Backwards: Loss and the Politics of Queer History.* Cambridge, MA: Harvard University Press.

MacArthur, Charles A., and Zoi A. Philippakos. 2015. "Self-Regulated Strategy Instruction in College Developmental Writing." *Journal of Educational Psychology* 107 (3): 855–67. https://doi.org/10.1177/009155211348450.

Martinez, Aja Y. 2016. "A Plea for Critical Race Theory Counterstory: Stock Story vs. Counterstory Dialogues Concerning Alejandra's 'Fit' in the Academy." In *Performing Antiracist Pedagogy in Rhetoric, Writing, and Communication,* edited by Frankie Condon and Vershawn Ashanti Young, 65–85. Fort Collins, CO: WAC Clearinghouse.

Martinez, Aja Y. 2020. *Counterstory: The Rhetoric and Writing of Critical Race Theory.* Urbana, IL: NCTE.

Mastrangelo, Lisa. 2012. *Writing a Progressive Past: Women Teaching and Writing in the Progressive Era.* Anderson, SC: Parlor.

Mayor, Christine. 2018. "Whitewashing Trauma: Applying Neoliberalism, Governmentality, and Whiteness Theory to Trauma Training for Teachers." *Whiteness and Education* 3 (2): 198–216. http://doi.org/10.1080/23793406.2019.1573643.

Mays, Chris, Nathaniel A. Rivers, and Kellie Sharp-Hoskins, eds. 2017. *Kenneth Burke + the Posthuman*. State College: Pennsylvania State University Press.

McCall, Leslie. 2001. *Complex Inequality: Gender, Class, and Race in the New Economy*. New York: Routledge.

McConnell, Kate Drezek. 2018. "What Assessment Is Really About." *Inside Higher Ed*, March 1. https://www.insidehighered.com/views/2018/03/01/assessment-isnt-about-bureaucracy-about-teaching-and-learning-opinion.

Messick, Samuel. 1989. "Validity." In *Educational Measurement*, 3rd ed., edited by Robert L. Linn, 13–103. New York: American Council on Education.

Micciche, Laura. 2014. "Writing Material." *College English* 76 (2): 488–505.

Milu, Esther. 2021. "Diversity of Raciolinguistic Experiences in the Writing Classroom: An Argument for a Transnational Black Language Pedagogy." *College English* 83 (6): 415–41.

Mislevy, Robert J. 2016. "How Developments in Psychology and Technology Challenge Validity Argumentation." *Journal of Educational Measurement* 53 (3): 265–92.

Mislevy, Robert J. 2018. *Sociocognitive Foundations of Educational Measurement*. New York: Routledge.

Mislevy, Robert, Geneva Haertel, Britte H. Cheng, Liliana Ructtinger, Angela DeBarger, Elizabeth Murray, David Rose, Jenna Gravel, Alexis M. Colker, Daisy Rutstein, and Terry Vendlinski. 2013. "A 'Conditional' Sense of Fairness in Assessment." *Educational Research and Evaluation* 19 (2–3): 121–40.

Moffitt, Robyn, Christine Padgett, and Rachel Grieve. 2020. "Accessibility and Emotionality of Online Assessment Feedback: Using Emoticons to Enhance Student Perceptions of Marker Competence and Warmth." *Computers and Education* 143 (January). https://doi.org/10.1016/j.compedu.2019.103654.

Moll, Luis C., Cathy Amanti, Deborah Neff, and Norma Gonzalez. 1992. "Funds of Knowledge: Using a Qualitative Approach to Connect Homes and Classrooms." *Theory into Practice* 31 (2): 132–41.

Moore, Cindy, Peggy O'Neill, and Angela Crow. 2016. "Assessing for Learning in an Age of Comparability: Remembering the Importance of Context." *Reclaiming Accountability: Improving Writing Programs through Accreditation and Large-Scale Assessments*, edited by Wendy Sharer, Tracy Ann Morse, Michelle F. Eble, and William P. Banks. Logan: Utah State University Press.

Moore, Jesse L., and Randall Bass, eds. 2017. *Understanding Writing Transfer: Implications for Transformative Student Learning in Higher Education*. Sterling, VA: Stylus.

Morris, Monique W. 2018. *Pushout: The Criminalization of Black Girls in School*. New York: New Press.

Morrison, Margaret. 2015. " 'Some Things Are Better Left Unsaid': The 'Dignity of Queer Shame.' " *Mosaic: An Interdisciplinary Critical Journal* 48 (1): 17–32. http://www.jstor.org/stable/44030732.

Moss, Pamela A. 1994. "Can There Be Validity without Reliability?" *Educational Researcher* 23 (2): 5–12.

Moss, Pamela A., Diana C. Pullin, James Paul Gee, Edward H. Haertel, and Lauren Jones Young. 2008. *Assessment, Equity, and Opportunity to Learn*. Cambridge: Cambridge University Press.

Muhammad, Gholdy. 2020. *Cultivating Genius: An Equity Framework for Culturally and Historically Responsive Literacy*. New York: Scholastic Teaching Resources.

Muñoz, José Esteban. 1997. " 'The White to Be Angry': Vaginal Davis's Terrorist Drag." *Social Text* 52/53, 15 (3–4): 80–103.

Muñoz, José Esteban. 1999. *Disidentifications: Queers of Color and the Performance of Politics.* Ann Arbor: University of Michigan Press.

Muñoz, José Esteban. 2009. *Cruising Utopia: The Then and There of Queer Futurity.* New York: New York University Press.

Myers, Kelly. 2019. "Unspeakable Failures." *Composition Studies* 47 (2): 48–67.

Nakamura, Lisa. 2002. *Cybertypes: Race, Ethnicity, and Identity on the Internet.* New York: Routledge.

National Academies of Sciences, Engineering, and Medicine. 2018. *How People Learn II: Learners, Contexts, and Cultures.* Washington, DC: National Academies Press. https://doi.org/10.17226/24783.

National Commission on Excellence in Education. 1983. *A Nation at Risk: The Imperative for Educational Reform.* Washington D.C.: United States Department of Education.

National Research Council. 2012. *Education for Life and Work: Developing Transferable Knowledge and Skills in the Twenty-First Century.* Washington, DC: National Academies Press.

National Writing Project. n.d. "What Is Connected Learning?" Accessed November 1, 2021. https://lead.nwp.org/knowledgebase/what-is-connected-learning/.

Neely, Michelle. 2018. "Helping Faculty Self-Regulate Emotional Responses in Writing Assessment: Use of an Overall Response Rubric Category." *Journal of Writing Assessment* 11 (1). https://escholarship.org/uc/item/7ds38413.

Neff, Joyce Magnotto. 1998. "Grounded Theory: A Critical Research Methodology." In *Under Construction: Working at the Intersections of Composition Theory, Research, and Practice,* edited by Chris Anson and Christine Farris, 124–35. Logan: Utah State University Press.

Newkirk, Thomas. 2002. *Misreading Masculinity: Boys, Literacy, and Popular Culture.* Portsmouth, NH: Heinemann.

New Zealand Ministry of Education. 2007. *The Quality of Assessment in Early Childhood Education.* Wellington, NZ: Education Review Office. https://ero.govt.nz/our-research/the-quality-of-assessment-in-early-childhood-education.

Nilson, Linda B. 2015. *Specifications Grading: Restoring Rigor, Motivating Students, and Saving Faculty Time.* Sterling, VA: Stylus.

North, Stephen M. 1987. *The Making of Knowledge in Composition: Portrait of an Emerging Field.* Portsmouth, NH: Heinemann.

Nowacek, Rebecca S. 2011. *Agents of Integration: Understanding Transfer as a Rhetorical Act.* Carbondale: Southern Illinois University Press.

Osorio, Ruth. 2021. "Constellating with our Foremothers: Stories of Mothers Making Space in Rhetoric and Composition." *Constellations: A Cultural Rhetorics Publishing Space* (4). https://constell8cr.com/articles/mothers-making-space-rhet-comp/.

Pajares, Frank, and Gio Valiante. 2008. "Self-Efficacy Beliefs and Motivation in Writing Development." In *Handbook of Writing Research,* edited by Charles A. MacArthur, Steve Graham, and Jill Fitzgerald, 158–70. New York: Guilford.

Palmeri, Jason. 2012. *Remixing Composition: A History of Multimodal Writing Pedagogy.* Carbondale: Southern Illinois University Press.

Paris, Django, and H. Samy Alim. 2017. *Culturally Sustaining Pedagogies: Teaching and Learning for Justice in a Changing World.* New York: Teachers College Press.

Parks, Jay. 2007. "Reliability as Argument." *Educational Measurement: Issues and Practice* 26 (4): 2–10.

Patel, Leigh. 2016. *Decolonizing Educational Research: From Ownership to Answerability.* New York: Routledge.

Payne, Robert. 2014. *The Promiscuity of Network Culture: Queer Theory and Digital Media.* London: Routledge.

Perelman, Les. 2012. "Construct Validity, Length, Score, and Time in Holistically Graded Writing Assessments: The Case Against Automated Essay Scoring (AES)." In *International Advances in Writing Research: Cultures, Places, Measures,* edited by Charles Bazerman, Chris Dean, Jessica Early, Karen Lunsford, Suzie Null, Paul Rogers, and Amanda Stansell, 121–32. Fort Collins, CO: WAC Clearinghouse.

Perkins, Maureen. 2013. "Omissions and Presuppositions in Kei Tua o Te Pae: A Critical Discourse Analysis." *New Zealand Research in Early Childhood Education* 16: 71–82.

Perry, Jeff. 2014. "The Unfulfilled Promise of Portfolios." Paper presented at the annual meeting of the Conference on College Composition and Communication, Indianapolis, IN, March 19–22.

Perry, Jeffrey W. 2012. "Critical Validity Inquiry." In *Practicing Research in Writing Studies: Reflexive and Ethically Responsible Research*, edited by Katrina M. Powell and Pamela Takayoshi, 187–211. Cresskill, NJ: Hampton.

Poe, Mya. 2021a. "A Matter of Aim: Disciplinary Writing, Writing Assessment, and Fairness." In *Improving Outcomes: Disciplinary Writing, Local Assessment, and the Aim of Fairness*, edited by Diane Kelly-Riley and Norbert Elliot, 17–25. New York: MLA.

Poe, Mya. 2021b. "Working Toward Justice in Program Assessment: Naming a Future We Want to Know." Virtual presentation sponsored by the College of Arts and Sciences and the Office for the Advancement of Teaching and Learning, University of Rhode Island.

Poe, Mya, and Asao B. Inoue, eds. 2016. "Toward Writing Assessment as Social Justice." Special issue, *College English* 79 (2).

Poe, Mya, and Qianqian Zhang-Wu. 2020. "Super-Diversity as a Framework to Promote Justice: Designing Program Assessment for Multilingual Writing Outcomes." *Composition Forum* 44. http://compositionforum.com/issue/44/northeastern.php.

Poe, Mya, Asao B. Inoue, and Norbert Elliot, eds. 2018. *Writing Assessment, Social Justice, and the Advancement of Opportunity*. Fort Collins, CO: WAC Clearinghouse.

Poe, Mya, Jessica Nastal, and Norbert Elliot. 2019. "An Admitted Student Is a Qualified Student: A Roadmap for Writing Placement in the Two-year College." *Journal of Writing Assessment* 12 (1). http://journalofwritingassessment.org/article.php?article=140.

Porter, James E., Patricia Sullivan, Stewart Blythe, Jeffrey T. Grabill, and Libby Miles. 2000. "Institutional Critique: A Rhetorical Methodology for Change." *College Composition and Communication* 51 (4): 610–42. http://doi.org/10.2307/358914.

Potter, Michael K., and N. Baker. 2011. *A Primer on Authentic Assessment*. Windsor, ON: University of Windsor, Center for Teaching and Learning.

Powell, Malea, Daisy Levy, Andrea Riley-Mukavetz, Marilee Brooks-Gillies, Maria Novotny, and Jennifer Fisch-Ferguson. 2014. "Our Story Begins Here: Constellating Cultural Rhetorics." *Enculturation* 18. http://enculturation.net/our-story-begins-here.

Probyn, Elspeth. 2005. *Blush: Faces of Shame*. Minneapolis: University of Minnesota Press.

Proffitt, Dennis. 2006. "Embodied Perception and the Economy of Action." *Perspectives on Psychological Science* 1 (2): 110–22. http://doi.org/10.1111/j.1745-6916.2006.00008.x.

Rafoth, Ben. 2015. *Multilingual Writers and Writing Centers*. Logan: Utah State University Press.

Rand, Erin J. 2014. *Reclaiming Queer: Activist and Academic Rhetorics of Resistance*. Tuscaloosa: University of Alabama Press.

Randall, Jennifer. 2021. "'Color-Neutral' Is Not a Thing: Redefining Construct Definition and Representation through a Justice-Oriented Critical Antiracist Lens." *Educational Measurement: Issues and Practice* 40 (4): 82–90.

Randall, Jennifer, David Slomp, Mya Poe, and Maria Elena Oliveri. 2022. "Disrupting White Supremacy in Assessment: Toward a Justice-Oriented, Antiracist Validity Framework." *Educational Assessment* 27 (2): 170–78. https://doi.org/10.1080/10627197.2022.2042682.

Ratcliffe, Krista. 2005. *Rhetorical Listening: Identification, Gender, Whiteness*. Carbondale: Southern Illinois University Press.

Reid, Alex. 2022. *Rhetorics of the Digital Nonhuman*. Carbondale: Southern Illinois University Press.

Reigstad, Thomas J., and Donald A. McAndrew. 1984. *Training Tutors for Writing Conferences*. Urbana, IL: NCTE.

Reynolds, Nedra, and Elizabeth Davis. 2013. *Portfolio Keeping: A Guide for Students*, 3rd ed. Boston: Bedford/St. Martin's.

Rhee, Jeong-Eun. 2021. *Decolonial Feminist Research: Haunting, Rememory and Mothers*. New York: Routledge.

Rhodes, Jacqueline. 2004. "Homo Origo: The Queertext Manifesto." *Computers and Composition* 21 (3): 387–90.

Rhodes, Jacqueline. 2015. "The Failure of Queer Pedagogy." *Writing Instructor* (March). http://parlormultimedia.com/twitest/rhodes-2015-03.

Ritter, Kelly. 2009. *Before Shaughnessy: Basic Writing at Yale and Harvard, 1920–1960*. Carbondale: Southern Illinois University Press.

Rule, Hannah J. 2019. *Situating Writing Processes*. Fort Collins, CO: WAC Clearinghouse.

SACSCOC. n.d. "Quality Enhancement Plans: Lists and Summaries Since 2007." Accessed November 19, 2021. https://sacscoc.org/quality-enhancement-plans/.

Salamon, Gayle. 2010. *Assuming a Body: Transgender and Rhetorics of Materiality*. New York: Columbia University Press.

Salen, Katie, and Eric Zimmerman. 2003. *Rules of Play: Game Design Fundamentals*. Cambridge: MIT Press.

Samuels, Ellen. 2017. "Six Ways of Looking at Crip Time." *Disability Studies Quarterly* 37 (3). https://dsq-sds.org/article/view/5824/4684.

Schendel, Ellen, and William J. Macauley. 2012. *Building Writing Center Assessments That Matter*. Logan: Utah State University Press.

Scott, Tony. 2005. "Creating the Subject of Portfolios: Reflective Writing and the Conveyance of Institutional Prerogatives." *Written Communication* 22 (1): 3–35.

Selfe, Cynthia L., and Gail Hawisher. 2004. *Literate Lives in the Information Age: Narratives of Literacy from the United States*. New York: Routledge.

Sengupta, Sudeshna, and Shubhika Sachdeva. 2017. "From Double Burden of Women to a 'Double Boon': Balancing Unpaid Care Work and Paid Work." Policy Brief. New Delhi, India: Institute of Social Studies Trust. https://www.isstindia.org/publications /1503391477_pub_India_PB_v3_FINAL_(1).pdf.

Sharer, Wendy, Tracy Morse, Michelle F. Eble, and William P. Banks, eds. 2016. *Reclaiming Accountability: Improving Writing Programs through Accreditation and Large-Scale Assessments*. Logan: Utah State University Press.

Sharma, Manu. 2016. "Seeping Deficit Thinking Assumptions Maintain the Neoliberal Education Agenda: Exploring Three Conceptual Frameworks of Deficit Thinking in Inner-City Schools." *Education and Urban Society* 50 (2): 136–54. http://doi.org/10.1177 /0013124516682301.

Sheils, Merrill. 1975. "Why Johnny Can't Write." *Newsweek*, December 8.

Shelton, Cecilia. 2019. "Shifting Out of Neutral: Centering Difference, Bias, and Social Justice in a Business Writing Course." *Technical Communication Quarterly* 29 (1): 18–32.

Sheskin, David. 2011. *Handbook of Parametric and Nonparametric Statistical Procedures*, 5th ed. Boca Raton, FL: Chapman & Hall/CRC.

Shor, Ira. 1996. *When Students Have Power: Negotiating Authority in a Critical Pedagogy*. Chicago: University of Chicago Press.

Silliman, Stephen W. 2006. "Struggling with Labor, Working with Identities." In *Historical Archaeology*, edited by Martin Hall and Stephen W. Silliman, 147–66. Oxford: Blackwell.

Singer-Freeman, Karen, Christine Robinson, and Linda Bastone. 2020. "Balancing the Freedom to Teach with the Freedom to Learn: The Critical Role of Assessment Professionals in Ensuring Educational Equity." In *Teaching and Learning Practices for Academic Freedom* (*Innovations in Higher Education Teaching and Learning*, Vol. 34), edited by Enakshi Sengupta and Patrick Blessinger, 39–51. Bingley, UK: Emerald. https://doi .org/10.1108/S2055-364120200000034005.

References 249

Slomp, David. 2016. "An Integrated Design and Appraisal Framework for Ethical Writing Assessment." *Journal of Writing Assessment* 9 (1). http://journalofwritingassessment .org/article.php?article=91.

Slomp, David H., Julie A. Corrigan, and Tamiko Sugimoto. 2014. "A Framework for Using Consequential Validity Evidence in Evaluating Large-Scale Writing Assessments: A Canadian Study." *Research in the Teaching of English* 48 (3): 276–302.

Smekens, Kristina. 2020. "Six Traits of Writing: The Ultimate Guide." Smekens Education Solutions. https://www.smekenseducation.com/6-traits-of-writing/.

Smith, Linda Tuhiwai. 2012. *Decolonizing Methodologies: Research and Indigenous Peoples*, 2nd ed. London: Zed Books.

Spidell, Cathy, and William H. Thelin. 2006. "Not Ready to Let Go: A Study of Resistance to Grading Contracts." *Composition Studies* 24 (1): 35–68.

Sraffa, Piero. 1960. *The Production of Commodities by Means of Commodities: Prelude to a Critique of Economic Theory*. Cambridge: Cambridge University Press.

"Starfish by Hobsons Expanded Impact on Higher Education Student Success During a Turbulent Year." 2020. CISION, PRNewswire, December 15. https://www.prnewswire .com/news-releases/starfish-by-hobsons-expanded-impact-on-higher-education -student-success-during-a-turbulent-year-301192527.html.

Stewart, Kathleen. 2007. *Ordinary Affects*. Durham, NC: Duke University Press.

Stitt-Bergh, Monica, Catherine M. Wehlburg, Terrel Rhodes, and Natasha Jankowski. 2019. "Assessment for Student Learning and the Public Good." *Change: The Magazine of Higher Learning* 51 (2): 43–46. http://doi.org/10.1080/00091383.2019.1569972.

Stockton, Kathryn Bond. 2009. *The Queer Child, or Growing Sideways in the Twentieth Century*. Durham, NC: Duke University Press.

Street, Brian V. 1984. *Literacy in Theory and Practice*. Cambridge: Cambridge University Press.

Street, Brian V. 1995. *Social Literacies: Critical Approaches to Literacy in Development, Ethnography and Education*. London: Routledge.

Stuckey, J. Elspeth. 1991. *The Violence of Literacy*. Portsmouth, NH: Boynton/Cook.

Suskie, Linda. 2010. "Why Are We Assessing?" *Inside Higher Ed*, October 26. https://www .insidehighered.com/views/2010/10/26/why-are-we-assessing.

Swain, Sherry, and Paul G. LeMahieu. 2012. "Assessment in a Culture of Inquiry: The Story of the National Writing Project's Analytic Writing Continuum." In *Writing Assessment in the Twenty-First Century: Essays in Honor of Edward M. White*, edited by Norbert Elliot and Les Perelman, 45–66. New York: Hampton.

Sweeney, Miriam E., and Kelsea Whaley. 2019. "Technically White: Emoji Skin-Tone Modifiers as American Technoculture." *First Monday* 4 (7). https://journals.uic.edu/ojs/in dex.php/fm/article/download/10060/8048.

Taleb, Nassim Nicholas. 2007. *The Black Swan: The Impact of the Highly Improbable*. New York: Random House.

Taylor, Frederick Winslow. 1911. *The Principles of Scientific Management*. New York: Harper and Brothers.

Tchudi, Stephen, ed. 1997. *Alternatives to Grading Student Writing*. Urbana, IL: NCTE.

Teston, Christa. 2012. "Considering Confidentiality in Research Design: Developing Heuristics to Chart the Un-chartable." In *Practicing Research in Writing Studies: Reflective and Ethically Responsible Research*, edited by Katrina Powell and Pamela Takayoshi, 303–26. Cresskill, NJ: Hampton.

Torre, Emanuela. 2019. "Training University Teachers on the Use of the ePortfolio in Teaching and Assessment." *International Journal of ePortfolio* 9 (2): 97–110.

Turner, Jennifer D., and Autumn A. Griffin. 2020. "Brown Girls Dreaming: Adolescent Black Girls' Futuremaking through Multimodal Representations of Race, Gender, and Career Aspirations." *Research in the Teaching of English* 55 (2): 109–33.

Tyack, David B. 1974. *The One Best System: A History of American Urban Education.* Cambridge, MA: Harvard University Press.

University of Oregon Social Sciences Feminist Network Research Interest Group. 2017. "The Burden of Invisible Work in Academia: Social Inequalities and Time Use in Five Departments." *Humboldt Journal of Social Relations* 1 (39): 228–45.

University of Rhode Island. 2006. "Mission Statement." Accessed November 19, 2021. https://www.uri.edu/about/leadership/.

Varnum, Robin. 1986. "From Crisis to Crisis: The Evolution toward Higher Standards of Literacy in the United States." *Rhetoric Society Quarterly* 16 (3): 145–65.

Varnum, Robin. 1996. *Fencing with Words: A History of Writing Instruction at Amherst College during the Era of Theodore Baird, 1938–1966.* Urbana, IL: NCTE.

Waite, Stacy. 2017. *Teaching Queer: Radical Possibilities for Writing and Knowing.* Pittsburgh: University of Pittsburgh Press.

Waite, Stacy. 2019. "How (and Why) to Write Queer: A Failing, Impossible, Contradictory Instruction Manual for Scholars of Writing Studies." In *Re/Orienting Writing Studies: Queer Methods, Queer Projects,* edited by William P. Banks, Matthew B. Cox, and Caroline Dadas, 42–53. Logan: Utah State University Press.

Wang, Zhaozhe. 2021. "Too Green to Talk Disciplinarity." *Composition Studies* 49 (1): 160–63.

Wardle, Elizabeth. 2007. "Understanding 'Transfer' from FYC: Preliminary Results of a Longitudinal Study." *WPA: Writing Program Administration* 31 (1–2): 65–85.

Wardle, Elizabeth. 2012. "Creative Repurposing for Expansive Learning" *Composition Forum* 26. https://compositionforum.com/issue/26/creative-repurposing.php.

Wardle, Elizabeth. 2013. "Intractable Writing Program Problems, *Kairos*, and Writing about Writing: A Profile of the University of Central Florida's First-Year Composition Program." *Composition Forum* 27. http://compositionforum.org/issue/27/ucf.php.

Warner, Michael. 1999. *The Trouble with Normal: Sex, Politics, and the Ethics of Queer Life.* Cambridge, MA: Harvard University Press.

Warner, Michael. 2005. *Publics and Counterpublics.* New York: Zone Books.

Welch, Nancy. 2008. *Living Room: Teaching Public Writing in a Privatized World.* Portsmouth, NH: Boynton/Cook.

Welch, Nancy, and Tony Scott, eds. 2016. *Composition in the Age of Austerity.* Logan: Utah State University Press.

West-Puckett, Stephanie. 2016. "Making Classroom Writing Assessment More Visible, Equitable, and Portable through Digital Badging." *College English* 79 (2): 127–51.

West-Puckett, Stephanie J. 2017. "Materializing Makerspaces: Queerly Composing Space, Time, and (What) Matters." PhD diss., East Carolina University.

Wetherell, Margaret. 2012. *Affect and Emotion: A New Social Science Understanding.* Thousand Oaks, CA: SAGE.

White, Edward M. 1985. *Teaching and Assessing Writing: Understanding, Evaluating, and Improving Student Performance.* San Francisco: Jossey-Bass.

White, Edward M., Norbert Elliot, and Irvin Peckham. 2015. *Very Like a Whale: The Assessment of Writing Programs.* Logan: Utah State University Press.

"Why Johnny Can't Write—and What's Being Done." 1981. *U.S. News & World Report,* March 16, 47–48.

Williams, Bronwyn T. 2007. "Why Johnny Can Never, Ever Read: The Perpetual Literacy Crisis and Student Identity." *Journal of Adolescent and Adult Literacy* 51 (2): 178–82. http://doi.org/10.1598/JAAL.51.2.8.

Williams, Jessica, and Carol Severino. 2004. "The Writing Center and Second Language Writers." *Journal of Second Language Writing* 13 (3): 165–72.

Wilson, Christine Brown, Christine Slade, Misty M. Kirby, Terri Downer, Marie B. Fisher, and Shane Neussler. 2018. "Digital Ethics and the Use of ePortfolio: A Scoping Review of the Literature." *International Journal of ePortfolio* 8 (2): 115–25.

Wilson, Jenna. 2018. "Write Outside the Boxes: The Single Point Rubric in the Secondary ELA Classroom." *Journal of Writing Assessment* 11 (1). http://journalofwritingassessment.org/article.php?article=126.

Windelband, Wilhelm. 1980. "Rectorial Address, Strasburg, 1894." *History and Theory* 19 (2): 169–85. http://dx.doi.org/10.2307/2504798.

Wood, Tara. 2017. "Cripping Time in the College Composition Classroom." *College Composition and Communication* 69 (2): 260–86.

Yancey, Kathleen Blake. 1999. "Looking Back as We Look Forward: Historicizing Writing Assessment." *College Composition and Communication* 50 (3): 483–503.

Yancey, Kathleen Blake, Liane Robertson, and Kara Taczak. 2014. *Writing across Contexts: Transfer, Composition, and Sites of Writing*. Logan: Utah State University Press.

Yang, John. 2021. "College Students' Stress Levels Are 'Bubbling Over.' Here's Why, and How Schools Can Help." PBS News Hour, November 2. https://www.pbs.org/newshour/show/college-students-stress-levels-are-bubbling-over-heres-why-and-how-schools-can-help.

Yosso, Tara J. 2005. "Whose Culture Has Capital? A Critical Race Theory Discussion of Community Cultural Wealth." *Race Ethnicity and Education* 8 (1): 69–91. http://doi.org/10.1080/1361332052000341006.

Zhang, Qilong. 2016. "Do Learning Stories Tell the Whole Story of Children's Learning? A Phenomenographic Enquiry." *Early Years* 37 (3). http://doi.org/10.1080/09575146.2016.1151403.

Zuberi, Tukufu, and Eduardo Bonilla-Silva. 2008. *White Logic, White Methods: Racism and Methodology*. Lanham, MD: Rowman and Littlefield.

INDEX

Page numbers followed by *f* indicate figures. Page numbers followed by *t* indicate tables.

ABOUT THE AUTHORS

Stephanie West-Puckett (she/her/hers) is an assistant professor of writing and rhetoric and director of first-year writing at the University of Rhode Island. Her research focuses on equity, access, and diversity in writing curriculum and assessment, and she specializes in digital, queer, and maker-centered composition practices. Her scholarship has been published in *College English, Journal of Adolescent & Adult Literacy, Contemporary Issues in Technology and Teacher Education*, and *The Journal of Multimodal Rhetorics*, as well as in several edited collections.

Nicole I. Caswell (she/her/hers) is an associate professor of English and director of the University Writing Center at East Carolina University. Her research interests include writing centers, writing assessment, and emotional labor/work. Nicole's research has been published in the *Journal of Writing Assessment*, the *Journal of Response to Writing, Composition Forum*, and various book chapters. Her book *The Working Lives of New Writing Center Directors* (coauthored with Grutsch McKinney and Jackson) was awarded the 2017 International Writing Centers Association Outstanding Book Award.

William P. Banks (he/him/his) is a professor of rhetoric, writing, and professional communication at East Carolina University. In addition to directing the University Writing Program and the Tar River Writing Project, Will teaches courses in writing, research, pedagogy, and LGBTQ and young-adult literatures. His essays on digital rhetorics, queer rhetorics, writing assessment, pedagogy, and writing program administration have appeared in several recent books, as well as in *College Composition and Communication, College English*, and *Computers and Composition*. He has coedited five recent collections of scholarship, including *English Studies Online: Programs, Practices, Possibilities* (2021) and *Re/Orienting Writing Studies: Queer Methods, Queer Projects* (2019).